Thirty Plays

DATE DUE

Demco, Inc. 38-293

Thirty Plays
from
Favorite Stories

Royalty-free dramatizations of
myths, folktales, and legends
from around the world

Edited by

SYLVIA E. KAMERMAN

Publishers   Plays, Inc.   *Boston*

Library of Congress Cataloging in Publication Data

Thirty plays from favorite stories : royalty-free dramatizations of
   myths, folktales, and legends from around the world / edited by
   Sylvia E. Kamerman
      p.   cm
      Summary: A collection of one-act plays based on a variety of
   traditional stories including Rumpelstiltskin, Cinderella, Clever
   Peter, Pandora's Box, The Crowded House, The Tiger and the Brahman,
   and others.
      ISBN 0-8238-0306-6 (pbk.)
   1. Children's plays, American. 2. Mythology—Juvenile drama.
    3. Folklore—Juvenile drama. 4. Legends—Juvenile drama.
   [1. Fairy tales—Drama. 2. Folklore—Drama. 3. Mythology—Drama.
    4. Plays.] I. Kamerman, Sylvia E.
   PS625.5.T48   1997
   812'.041089282—dc21   97-1039
                                                             CIP
                                                             AC

Manufactured in Canada

Contents

Thirty Plays
from
Favorite Stories

The Princess and the Pea

by Helen Louise Miller

Characters

KING
QUEEN
PRINCE PETER
DELLA ⎫
ELLA ⎭ *maids-in-waiting*
ZARA
ZELDA
ZINNIA
PRINCESS PATACAKE

SETTING: *The throne room of the royal palace. Three thrones are center. Fireplace is right. Large screen is up center.*
AT RISE: KING *is reading names from a list so long it reaches to the floor.* QUEEN *is embroidering.* PRINCE PETER *is slumped down in his throne, looking very unhappy.* ELLA *and* DELLA *stand beside* QUEEN. DELLA *holds a pincushion,* ELLA *a pair of scissors.*
KING (*Reading from list*): Princess Amy, Princess Ann, Princess Audrey! Princess Barbara, Princess Betty, Princess Beth! Princess Candy, Princess Carrie, Princess Cathy! (*Puts down list*) All these names, and you (*To* PRINCE) can't find a princess you want to marry.
PRINCE PETER: But, Father, how can I be sure she is a *real* princess?
QUEEN: It *says* "Princess" right on the list.
KING (*Reading*): Princess Debby, Princess Dinah, Princess Dora! Princess Elsie, Princess Ethel, Princess Eva!
QUEEN: Every single one is a princess.

3

PRINCE PETER: How do we know the list is a true one? How do we know every girl is a true princess?

KING (*Putting list aside*): Prince Peter, you give me a headache! (*Removes crown*) This heavy crown is making it worse.

PRINCE PETER (*Trying on crown*): Let me try it. I want to know how it feels to wear a crown.

KING (*Taking crown from* PETER): You may not wear a crown until you find a wife.

QUEEN (*To* ELLA): Scissors, please, Ella. Snip the thread right here. (QUEEN *holds thread and* ELLA *cuts it with scissors.*) Now, Della, I will need a pink thread, please. (DELLA *takes a needle threaded with pink thread from the pincushion and hands it to* QUEEN. *The* QUEEN *goes on with her work.*)

PRINCE PETER: Then I will *never* wear a crown. I will never marry anyone but a *real* princess, and I don't know where to find one.

QUEEN: "M" is my lucky letter. Ask your father to read the names that begin with "M."

KING (*Wearily picking up the list*): Princess Mabel, Princess Mary, Princess Maude.

PRINCE: Princess Mabel and Princess Mary were very beautiful.

QUEEN: Then why didn't you choose one of them for your bride?

PRINCE PETER: Because they didn't have handkerchiefs. No *real* princess would ever be without a handkerchief, you know.

KING: What about Princess Maude?

PRINCE PETER: She cried when she stuck her finger with a needle. No *real* princess would ever cry.

QUEEN: I don't know about that.

PRINCE PETER: What are you making, Mother?

QUEEN: A lovely new shirt for your wedding.

PRINCE PETER: Take your time. I won't need it for a long, long while.

KING: You will need it next week. I have set your wedding date.

PRINCE PETER: How will I ever find a *real* princess by next week?

KING: There are three girls I want you to meet. They are from the "Z" list—Princess Zara, Princess Zelda and Princess Zinnia. Ella and Della will show them in. (ELLA *and* DELLA *collect a few pieces of the* QUEEN's *sewing and exit.*)

QUEEN: My son, this is your last chance.

PRINCE: Each one will pretend to be a *real* princess. How can I make sure?

QUEEN: Ask them some questions.

KING: Give them a test. (ELLA *and* DELLA *usher in* ZARA, ZELDA *and* ZINNIA, *who are dressed in fancy costumes. They advance to the thrones and curtsey.*) Welcome to our kingdom. (*Bowing to* QUEEN) This is my wife.

QUEEN: Delighted to see you, my dears.

KING (*Nodding to* PETER): And this is my son, Peter.

PRINCE PETER (*Rising*): I trust that one of you may turn out to be my *real* princess.

ZARA: I am a real princess. My father was a king.

ZELDA: My mother was a queen.

ZINNIA: My grandfather was an emperor.

PRINCE PETER: Every princess should be able to sing. Will you sing for me?

ZARA, ZELDA *and* ZINNIA (*With a curtsey*): We will be happy to sing for you, your Highness. (*Girls sing any appropriate song.*)

PRINCE PETER (*As* KING *and* QUEEN *applaud*): Fine! Fine! Very nice indeed, but I am not yet satisfied. Tell me, can you dance? Every princess should be able to dance.

ZARA, ZELDA *and* ZINNIA: If you will supply the music, sire, we will be glad to dance for you.

KING: I will signal the musicians to give us a tune. (*He waves his hand and music plays offstage. Girls do any simple folk dance.*)

QUEEN: I must say you are very graceful.

KING: Charming. Charming.

PRINCE PETER: Mother, have you any further test in mind?

QUEEN: Every princess should be able to do fine needlework. (*Hands embroidery to* ZARA) See what you can do with this. (*Each girl takes a few stitches, which are inspected by* KING, QUEEN *and* PRINCE.) Excellent. Excellent.

KING: The stitches are very small and dainty.

PRINCE PETER: Very nice. But there is something not quite right. I am still not sure.

KING: Don't be stupid.

QUEEN: Don't be silly. They have passed all the tests.

PRINCE PETER: But how do we know if they are the proper tests?

KING: They can sing and dance.

QUEEN: They can do fine needlework.

KING: And look at their beautiful dresses.

PRINCE PETER: Anyone can wear a beautiful dress who can pay for it.

QUEEN: But you can see these girls are of royal blood just by looking at them.

PRINCE PETER: They look like any other girls to me.

ZARA: I will not stay here to be insulted!

ZELDA (*Stamping her foot*): I *won't* look like any other girl! I won't! I won't! I won't!

ZINNIA (*Making a face*): I will tell my father what you said! And *my* father will make war on *your* father!

ALL THREE: We hope you *never* find a *real* princess! Never! Never! Never! (ZARA, ZELDA, *and* ZINNIA *flounce out in anger.*)

PRINCE PETER: You see, Father, I was right. No *real* princess would ever lose her temper in public! (*Offstage roar of thunder*)

QUEEN: I have lost all patience with you, Prince Peter! (*Another roar of thunder*)

ELLA (*With a curtsey*): I hear the sound of thunder, your Majesty.

DELLA (*With a curtsey*): Shall we close the palace windows?

QUEEN: Yes, yes! Close them at once. I do not want the new draperies to get wet. (ELLA *and* DELLA *exit. More thunder.*)

KING: This sounds like a bad storm.

PRINCE PETER: I pity anyone who is out on a night like this. (ELLA *and* DELLA *run in.*)

ELLA: Please, sire. There is someone at the gate!

DELLA: A beggar maid, sire. She is dripping wet.

QUEEN: Take her to the kitchen and get her some dry clothes.

KING: Tell the cook to give her some hot soup.

ELLA: But, sire, she will not go to the kitchen.

PRINCE PETER: Why not? Isn't she cold and hungry?

DELLA: Yes, she is so cold that her teeth are chattering.

ELLA: And she is weak from hunger.

DELLA: But she will not go to the kitchen.

ELLA: Because she says kitchens are for beggar maids.

DELLA *and* ELLA (*In unison*): And she says she is a princess.

KING, QUEEN *and* PRINCE: What?

ELLA: That's what she says.

DELLA: She swears she is a real princess.

KING: Then bring her here at once.

PRINCE PETER: I can't wait to see her. Maybe she will be the one. (ELLA *and* DELLA *exit and return with* PRINCESS PATACAKE, *who is barefooted and dressed in rags.*)

ELLA *and* DELLA: Here she is, your Majesty.

KING: You say you are a princess?

QUEEN: What is your name, child?

PRINCESS PATACAKE: I am the Princess Patacake.

QUEEN: You will forgive me, child. But you do not look like a princess.

PRINCESS PATACAKE: I am very tired and hungry. I have been lost for many days.

KING: And you do not dress like a princess. Your clothing is in rags.

PRINCESS PATACAKE: My dress is ruined from the storm. And my shoes were worn out long ago from walking the roads.

PRINCE PETER: Please, Mother, see that the princess gets some dry clothing and a hot supper. In the meantime, I will try to think of a way to find out if she is telling the truth.

QUEEN: Come along, my child. I will take you to my own room and see that you are cared for.

KING: And I will give orders to the cook to send up your supper. (KING, QUEEN *and* PRINCESS PATACAKE *exit.*)

PRINCE PETER (*Walking up and down*): If only I could tell for sure. She doesn't look like a princess. She doesn't dress like a princess, and yet, she seems different from all the others.

ELLA: Do you think she is a *real* princess, sire?

DELLA: Do you believe her story?

PRINCE PETER: I almost believe it. But I am not sure. If only there was a way to find out.

ELLA: I know of a way, sire.

PRINCE PETER: You do? What is it?

ELLA: It's a test my grandmother told me about when I was very small.

PRINCE PETER: Tell me.

ELLA: The princess is very tired. She will want to rest. So we will make up a bed for her here by the fire. Della can help me bring the mats and comforters.

DELLA: I'll be glad to help. But what is the test?

ELLA: Under the bottom mattress we will put a very small, dried pea.

DELLA: I can get one in the kitchen.

ELLA: On top of the pea, we will pile a great heap of quilts and pillows and comforters.

DELLA: It will be a bed of clouds.

ELLA: But if Princess Patacake is a *real* princess, she will not sleep a wink.

PRINCE PETER: Why not?

ELLA: Because of the pea. She will roll and toss all night.

PRINCE PETER: How can she feel anything through all those comforters?

ELLA: She will feel it only if she is a *real* princess. A *real* princess is so delicate she will feel the smallest bump.

PRINCE PETER: It is worth a try.

DELLA: I will get a dried pea from the kitchen. (*Exits*)

PRINCE PETER (*To* ELLA): And you must bring all the pillows and comforters you can find. (ELLA *exits and returns almost at once with quilts, mats, pillows, etc.*) This is the best spot for the bed. We can watch her from behind the screen.

DELLA (*Enters*): Here is the dried pea.

ELLA (*Arranging pads and pillows*): Let's pile them one on top of the other. (*They do so.* PRINCE PETER *tries bed every now and then to see if it is soft.*)

PRINCE PETER: Fine! Fine!

DELLA (*Spreading quilt on top*): Now, it is finished.

ELLA: The little princess should sleep soundly.

PRINCE PETER: Thank you. (*To* ELLA) Please tell my mother to bring the princess back to the throne room. (ELLA *exits.*) We will try the test as soon as possible.

KING (*Entering and seeing bed*): What is this? What is this bed in the throne room?

PRINCE PETER: It is for Princess Patacake. I thought she might like to rest by the fire. (ELLA *reenters.*)

KING (*As* PRINCESS *and* QUEEN *enter*): A very good idea, my son.

PRINCE PETER (*To* PRINCESS PATACAKE): You are looking better. Would you like to lie down and rest by the fire?

PRINCESS PATACAKE: Yes, thank you. I am very tired. (*Sits on pile of cushions*) This looks like a soft bed.

QUEEN: Make yourself comfortable, my dear. (*Covers her*)

KING: You will feel better after a good rest.

PRINCE PETER: Come, Father, let us leave the princess in peace and quiet. (KING *and* PRINCE *exit behind screen.*)

QUEEN: Della and Ella will be within call, if you need anything. Sweet dreams, little Princess. (*Also withdraws behind screen.* DELLA *and* ELLA *sit near the bed.*)

PRINCESS PATACAKE (*Sitting up and plumping her pillow*): Something is wrong with this bed.

DELLA: Is there anything I can do, Princess?

PRINCESS PATACAKE: No, thank you. I guess I am just tired and weary. (*Settles herself again*)

ELLA: Perhaps if we were to sing you a lullaby, you would fall asleep.

PRINCESS PATACAKE: That might help, but it feels as if I am lying on a great, sharp stone. (DELLA *and* ELLA *sing to the tune of "Sleep, Baby, Sleep."*)

DELLA and ELLA:
Sleep, Princess, sleep.
Thy father guards the sheep,
Thy mother is shaking the dreamland tree,
And down comes a beautiful dream for thee.
Sleep, Princess, sleep.

PRINCESS PATACAKE: It's no use. I feel stiff and sore all over.
I tell you there are rocks in this bed.

ELLA: Let me straighten your covers.

DELLA: I will fluff up your pillow.

PRINCESS PATACAKE (*Getting up*): I can't stand it another
minute. I will sit by the fire all night rather than sleep in
this bumpy bed. But please do not tell the good King and
Queen. I would not want to hurt their feelings. (KING,
QUEEN *and* PRINCE PETER *come out from behind screen.*)

PRINCE PETER: Dear Princess Patacake, you will not hurt our
feelings. You have proved beyond the shadow of a doubt that
you are a *real* princess.

PRINCESS PATACAKE: But what have I done?

QUEEN: Our son has explained to us that Ella put a dried pea
under the mattresses when she made up your bed.

KING: Only a true princess would be so delicate.

PRINCESS PATACAKE: I can scarcely believe that it was only
a dried pea. It felt like a rock.

PRINCE PETER: At last I have found my real princess.

KING: Princess Patacake, will you do us the honor of remaining
in our kingdom as the wife of our son, Prince Peter?

PRINCESS PATACAKE: I should like nothing better, your
Majesty!

QUEEN: You have made us very happy, my child.

KING: The wedding will take place in a week's time.

QUEEN: Oh, my goodness! Della! Ella! Bring me my embroidery! I must get to work at once on Prince Peter's wedding
shirt and a fine new dress for the princess.

KING (*As* PRINCE PETER *rummages through the bed clothing*): What on earth are you doing, Prince Peter?

PRINCE PETER: I am hunting for that wonderful dried pea.
(*Holding up the dried pea*) Here it is. I shall order it to be
placed in the state museum, where everyone can see the living
proof that my royal bride is a real, true princess. (*Curtain*)

THE END

Production Notes

THE PRINCESS AND THE PEA

Characters: 2 male; 7 female.
Playing Time: 15 minutes.
Costumes: All wear court costumes.
Properties: List of names, for King; sewing materials, for Queen; needle with pink thread, pin cushion, pea, for Della; scissors, for Ella; quilts, mats, pillows, etc.
Setting: The throne room of the royal palace. There are three thrones: one for the King, one for the Queen, and one, next to the King's, for Prince Peter. Large screen is up center. Fireplace is right. Flashlight may be used to simulate glow of fire.
Lighting: No special effects.
Sound: Music, thunder.

Rumpelstiltskin

by Rowena Bennett

Characters

KING
MESSENGER
TWO SERVANTS
MARION, *the miller's daughter*
RUMPELSTILTSKIN
COURTIERS, *extras*

SCENE 1

SETTING: A *room in a king's castle. Table and chair are center. Small closet is in up right corner.*
AT RISE: KING *is sitting at table counting out a very small pile of money. Great piles of unpaid bills are stacked around him. He thumbs through the top ones.*
KING (*To himself*):
Bills from the hatters, bills from the tailors,
Bills for outfitting my soldiers and sailors.
Bills from the bakeries, markets and mills—
Nothing but bills, no, *nothing but bills!* (*He sweeps them from the table in an angry gesture and they flutter everywhere.*)
MESSENGER (*Entering from right, running hastily forward and kneeling before* KING): Oh, your Majesty, I think I have found a way to pay the bills!
KING: What? Do you really mean it?
MESSENGER: I have found a miller's daughter who can spin straw into gold.
KING: What are you waiting for? Bring her in. Tell my courtiers to come in, too. I want them to know the good news.

12

MESSENGER (*Rising and hurrying out*): I go at once. (SERVANTS *enter left, carrying brooms, and sweep up the bills.*)

KING (*To* SERVANTS): Pile them up neatly this time. I'm going to pay them.

SERVANTS (*Amazed ad lib*): Pay them? What with? (*Etc.*)

KING: You'll see. Just fetch me the last three bales of straw from the stable and a spinning wheel from the attic.

SERVANTS: Yes, your Majesty. (*They bow and go out as* COURTIERS *enter, right. They are talking excitedly to each other about the girl who can spin straw to gold.*)

KING (*As they all bow to him*): Well, I see you have heard the news—(*He looks offstage, right.*) Here comes the magic maiden now. (MESSENGER *enters, right, with* MARION.)

COURTIERS (*Admiringly*): Oh-h-h!

KING (*As* MARION *bows before him*): I see you have spun your own hair to gold. Would you spin my straw for me—for the good of your country and mine? We must have gold or the land will be lost.

MARION (*Frantically*): Oh, your Majesty, I should like nothing better! But I cannot work such magic.

MESSENGER: Your father tells me you can.

MARION: But my father likes nothing better than to brag and boast about me. He thinks there is nothing I cannot do.

MESSENGER (*Aside to* KING): She is too modest.

KING: *That,* I can see.

COURTIERS (*As* SERVANTS *enter, carrying bales of straw and a spinning wheel and stool*): Ah-h-h!

KING (*As* SERVANTS *come forward*): Splendid! Put the bales in that closet over there, and the wheel in front of the door. (*He points toward the closet and* SERVANTS *obey.*)

MARION (*In panic*): Must I spin before all these people?

KING (*Kindly*): No, no. We shall leave the room. When the straw is spun to gold, we shall come back. (KING, COURTIERS *and* SERVANTS *exit, right. As the last one disappears,* MARION *bursts into tears. As she sobs,* RUMPELSTILTSKIN *enters from left, on tiptoe.*)

MARION (*Going to the closet and looking at straw*): Oh, dear, oh, dear! What shall I do? I can't possibly spin straw into gold. Who in the world can?

RUMPELSTILTSKIN (*Running up to her*): I can.

MARION (*Looking around, startled*): You? Who are you?

RUMPELSTILTSKIN: Someone whose name you could never guess.

MARION: Where did you come from?

RUMPELSTILTSKIN: From the end of the world, from the edge of nothing.

MARION: How did you get in here? The door is locked.

RUMPELSTILTSKIN: I can get into any room, locked or not. What's more, I can spin straw into gold.

MARION: I don't believe it.

RUMPELSTILTSKIN: Well, I can, and what's more, I will! What will you give me if I spin these three bales for you?

MARION: Anything! Anything!

RUMPELSTILTSKIN: I must have one thing for each bale.

MARION: Well, here is my necklace for one. (*She hands it to him.*)

RUMPELSTILTSKIN (*Taking it*): Very well. It will do.

MARION: Here is my ring for another.

RUMPELSTILTSKIN: Yes. That is better. (*He slips it onto his own finger.*)

MARION (*Distressed*): I can't think of anything else to give.

RUMPELSTILTSKIN: Why not give a promise.

MARION (*Puzzled*): A promise?

RUMPELSTILTSKIN: Yes, promise you will give me your first-born baby when you become queen.

MARION (*Laughing*): You funny little man. You're cheating yourself. A king would never marry a miller's daughter. I shall *never* be a queen.

RUMPELSTILTSKIN: I'll take a chance on it.

MARION: Very well. I promise. Only don't blame me if—

RUMPELSTILTSKIN (*Shutting closet door*): Ah, here goes, then! (*He seats himself at wheel and chants as he spins.*) Whirr, whirr, spin, spin, Gold is heavy and straw is thin Turn the wheel with a pixie-purr—

Spin, spin, whirr, whirr.

Oh, he who is versed in the Good Folks' law

Shall spin bright gold out of straw, straw, straw. (*The wheel stops and the closet door flies open, revealing three pails instead of three bales.*)

MARION (*Rushing over to closet and looking in*): Oh, it's done! (*She scoops up handfuls of gold from the pails and tosses the coins wildly into the air. They fall clinking to the floor.* RUMPELSTILTSKIN *tiptoes out, a sly look on his face.* MARION *dances about.*) Enough to save a kingdom. Gold! Gold! Gold!

KING (*Entering hurriedly from right*): What? Did you say, "Gold"? Is it spun already? (*He looks into pails.*) The magic is done! (COURTIERS *enter, running from all directions.*)

COURTIERS (*Ecstatically*): Ohh!

KING (*Turning toward* MARION): The most beautiful gold in all the world is the gold of this maiden's hair. Marion, the miller's daughter, shall be my queen.

COURTIERS (*Bowing*): Hail, to Marion, the miller's daughter!

MARION (*Amazed*): What? *I* shall be a queen? (*Curtain*)

* * * * *

SCENE 2

TIME: A *year later.*

SETTTNG: *Same. A baby's cradle is at center.*

AT RISE: QUEEN MARION *is seated by the cradle, rocking it.*

MARION: How can I be so lucky! To have a kind and gentle king for my husband and now to have you, little one. What fun we'll all have as you grow up. (*Hums as she rocks cradle*)

RUMPELSTILTSKIN (*Tiptoeing in left; with an evil laugh*): I'm not so sure about that.

MARION (*Frightened*): Oh, dear, it's you! I'd forgotten all about you.

RUMPELSTILTSKIN: Forgotten about your promise? I've come for your baby.

MARION (*Throwing her arms about the cradle*): No, no! I will give you anything else—gold, jewels, *my* half of the kingdom.

RUMPELSTILTSKIN: I have heard that none of these things is so precious as a baby.

MARION (*Sobbing*): You are asking me to pluck the moon out of the sky and live in shadow, to snatch away the sun and dwell in darkness. You are asking me to tear the heart out of my breast and—(*Her words dissolve into a moan.*)

RUMPELSTILTSKIN (*Stamping his foot and brushing a hand across his eyes*): Stop, stop! You'll have me crying, too, if you're not careful.

MARION (*Looking at him hopefully*): Oh, you do have mercy in your heart! You won't take my baby away?

RUMPELSTILTSKIN: I didn't say *that*. But I'll give you one more chance. (*He smiles slyly.*) If you guess my name by nightfall you may keep your baby.

MARION (*Delighted*): I shall start guessing at once.

MESSENGER (*Entering with a big book under his arm and bowing to* MARION): Your Majesty, I could not help hearing all that has been said. The King, when he rode off to the hunt today, bade me never to go far from your door.

MARION: It is well.

MESSENGER: I have brought you the great book of names— names collected from all over the kingdom. It may be of use to you now.

MARION: Good messenger, you shall be knighted for this. Come, we'll read off the names to the little man.

MESSENGER (*Opening book and beginning*): Tom or John?
Jake or Harry?
Bob or Rob?
Lonnie, Larry?—(*He pauses and looks at* RUMPELSTILT-SKIN, *who shakes his head* "No.")

MARION (*Coming over to* MESSENGER *and reading also from book*): James or John?
Jack or Jerry?
Mike or Ike?
Ted or Terry? (*She looks up expectantly.*)

RUMPELSTILTSKIN: No, no, no. Ho, ho, ho!
That's a book I happen to know.
You won't find it there. I'm telling you so!

MARION: It must be a very odd name, then, like Kataklump or Diddledop.

MESSENGER (*Closing book*): Or Bandyback.

RUMPELSTILTSKIN (*Laughing harder than ever*): No, no, you'll *never* guess it. I'll run out for afternoon tea and if you haven't guessed it by the time I get back—

MESSENGER: Very well, go along. It will give us a little time to look up more names.

MARION (*Looking doubtful*): We can at least try.

RUMPELSTILTSKIN (*Singing as he goes off*):
Today I'll brew,
tomorrow I'll bake
But now I'll go for tea and cake
And then the queen's child I shall take. (*He dances off.*)

MARION (*To MESSENGER in stage whisper*): Quick! Follow him. You may learn something.

MESSENGER (*Nodding*): It's our only chance. (*He goes out on the run.*)

MARION (*Hurrying back to cradle*): There, there! Don't cry and I'll sing to you. (*She sings lullaby with intermittent sighs and sobs. Suddenly MESSENGER reenters.*) What? Back so soon? I thought he lived at the edge of the earth.

MESSENGER: Perhaps he does, but he went only as far as the woods. He built a fire, for brewing tea, I suppose, or mischief. But he danced around it first, and sang.

MARION: That dreadful song about taking my child?

MESSENGER: Yes, but what do you think he added? (*He laughs.*)

MARION (*Hopefully*): Tell me. Oh, tell me quickly!

MESSENGER (*Singing and acting it out*):
Today I brew.
Tomorrow I bake
Tonight the queen's child I shall take—
She doesn't know, poor foolish dame,
That Rumpelstiltskin is my name.

MARION (*Clapping her hands in delight*): Rumpelstiltskin!

MESSENGER (*Looking offstage*): Shh! Here he comes. (RUMPELSTILTSKIN *enters left.*)

RUMPELSTILTSKIN (*Gleefully*): Do you know my name yet, my fair queen? I will give you three guesses.

MARION (*Hesitantly*): Well—could it be Woodleworm?

RUMPELSTILTSKIN (*Delighted*): No!

MARION: It's not Minimone, is it?

RUMPELSTILTSKIN (*Going near cradle and dancing about*): It is not! One more guess—and then the child is mine!

MARION (*Smiling a little*): Could your name be Rumpelstiltskin?

RUMPELSTILTSKIN (*Flying into a rage*): The fairies must have told you! The fairies must have told you. I have lost my chance forever! (*He runs from the room, screaming.*)

KING (*Rushing on, followed by* COURTIERS): What's happened? What was that noise?

MARION (*Going to cradle and rocking it*): The baby was frightened and cried a little. But everything is all right now. Yes, everything is all right. (KING *and* COURTIERS *surround the cradle as the curtain closes.*)

THE END

Production Notes

RUMPELSTILTSKIN

Characters: 3 male; 3 female; courtiers may be male and female.

Playing Time: 15 minutes.

Costumes: The King wears long purple robe and crown. Marion wears simple, long dress in Scene 1. In Scene 2 she wears long robe and crown. The servants wear long dark dresses with white aprons and caps. Rumpelstiltskin is dressed in brown, and has long, tight-fitting pants. He wears pointed slippers with bells attached to the toes, and pointed cap. The male Courtiers wear dark-colored knee-pants, and white shirts. The female Courtiers wear long dresses.

Properties: Play money, bills, two brooms, three bales of straw, spinning wheel, stool, necklace, ring, gold coins (paper or foil), pennies, three pails, large book. Note: The closet in which the straw is placed should have two openings: the door in front, visible to the audience, and a dark curtain at the back which may be lifted by a stagehand who exchanges the bales of straw for pails of gold while Rumpelstiltskin is spinning with the closet door shut. The pails may be nearly filled with paper padding which is covered on top with paper coins and pennies, so that the coins will make noise when they are tossed about.

Setting: A room in a castle. There are entrances at left and right. There is a small closet in one corner. The room may be furnished as elaborately as desired. A table and chair are the only necessary furnishings for Scene 1. In Scene 2, a cradle and a chair for the Queen should be added.

Lighting: No special effects.

Clever Peter

by Mary Thurman Pyle

Characters

CLEVER PETER, *a country bumpkin, about nineteen*
PETER'S MOTHER
LITTLE OLD MAN
TWO TALL MEN IN BLUE
PARLOR MAID
LADY-IN-WAITING
KING
PRINCESS
TWO TALL MEN IN BLACK
TWO BOYS
TWO GIRLS

SCENE 1

TIME: *A long time ago.*
SETTING: *A fork in the road leading to town. Tree stump is center.*
AT RISE: PETER *enters carrying a basket of eggs and whistling in a carefree manner. He goes to stump and sits, putting basket on ground beside him.* BOYS *and* GIRLS *enter, talking and laughing. They see* PETER *and stop and stare at him, nudging each other and giggling.*
1ST GIRL: Hello, Peter.
1ST BOY: You mean, *clever* Peter! Hello, clever Peter!
2ND BOY: His mother thinks him clever, anyway. (BOYS *laugh.*)
1ST BOY: I said, hello, clever Peter! Haven't you ears in your head?

PETER: Yes, and eyes, too, my little man.

2ND GIRL: Where have you been, Peter, this fine spring day?

PETER: I'm on my way to town, to do an errand for my mother.

2ND GIRL: Tell us what the errand is, Peter.

PETER: My mother gave me this basket of eggs and said, "My clever Peter, take these to town and sell them this day at the market."

1ST GIRL: It's near midday, Peter! Haven't you been to town yet?

PETER: Not yet, for I stopped by a stream to watch the little silver fish play among the golden pebbles; then I lay down on the sweet green grass, watched the clouds; and I listened to a little brown bird sitting in a tree, and calling "Cuckoo! Cuckoo!"

2ND BOY: He's an odd one!

1ST GIRL: Well, anyway, his mother loves him!

PETER: It isn't what's in your head that counts—it's what's in your heart. (BOYS *and* GIRLS *run off, laughing.* PETER *scratches his head, slides down from the stump and sits on the ground with his back against it. He starts to whistle, happily and lazily. Finally his eyes close, and he dozes. In a moment an odd-looking* LITTLE OLD MAN *enters, looks about cautiously, then comes close to* PETER. *After watching* PETER *a moment, he taps him on the head with his cane.*)

LITTLE OLD MAN: Tut, tut, tut! Are you such a sleepyhead, then? *That* didn't earn you the name of Clever Peter—for if your eyes are shut, how can you see the good things of life? (PETER *opens his eyes and stares at* OLD MAN.)

PETER (*Rising and taking off his cap respectfully*): Good day to you, sir.

OLD MAN: Good day, Peter. Will you strike a bargain with me for your eggs?

PETER: What will you give me for them?

OLD MAN (*Taking a small black bottle from his pocket*): I will give you this.

PETER (*Examining bottle*): It is a pretty little, good little, sweet little bottle, but it is not worth as much as my basket of eggs.

OLD MAN: Now you are not talking like the wise Peter. You

should never judge by the outside of things. What would you like to have?

PETER: A fine new suit of clothes for myself and a silk dress for my mother.

OLD MAN: Nothing easier. (*He rubs bottle.*) When the cork goes pop, pop, pop, two tall men will hop, hop, hop. (*He takes the cork out. At once* TWO TALL MEN IN BLUE *enter. They bow before* OLD MAN.)

1ST MAN: What do you wish, sir?

2ND MAN: Your orders, sir.

OLD MAN: Bring me a fine new suit for Peter and a silk dress for Peter's mother. (MEN IN BLUE *exit, then quickly reenter, one carrying a velvet suit and a hat with a plume for* PETER, *the other, a silk dress and a bonnet with ribbons and flowers.*) Put them down on the stump. (*They obey, as* PETER *stares in wonder.* OLD MAN *corks up the bottle, and* MEN IN BLUE *quickly exit.*)

PETER (*Eagerly*): Yes, I will give you my basket of eggs for the little black bottle.

OLD MAN (*Seriously*): Keep the bottle safe, for if it should get out of your possession, then all it has brought you will disappear.

PETER: I will keep it safe—never fear. (*They make the exchange, bow to each other, and then* OLD MAN *exits left.* PETER *examines the new clothes with satisfaction, removes cork from bottle.*) When the cork goes pop, pop, pop, two tall men will hop, hop, hop. (MEN IN BLUE *enter and bow to* PETER.)

MEN IN BLUE (*Together*): Your orders, sir!

PETER (*Entranced*): Something to take home for dinner. (MEN IN BLUE *exit and return, carrying baskets filled with bread, vegetables, fruit, cheese, etc. They set the baskets down by* PETER. PETER *recorks bottle, and* MEN IN BLUE *exit, as* PETER *pats bottle lovingly and puts it in his pocket.* PETER'S MOTHER *enters.*)

MOTHER: Wherever have you been, Peter, my boy? I've been waiting for you to come with the egg money, so I could buy the victuals we need. Did you sell the eggs? (PETER *has his back to the stump, and* MOTHER *does not notice the fine clothes.)*

PETER: Yes, Mother, I sold the eggs.

MOTHER: And how much did you get for them, my little duck?

PETER: I got this bottle, Mother. (*Holds bottle out for her to see*)

MOTHER: A bottle! Then truly I'm almost of the same mind as the village folk who call thee a dull block.

PETER: Never judge by the outside of things. Already the bottle has brought us two baskets of food and all these fine new clothes.

MOTHER: *What?* From a bottle? Whatever can you mean?

PETER: Let us go home, Mother, and I will show you what I mean. We shall have a grand new house, I promise you, and horses and carriages, and shall dress in silks and satins, and have our purses full of gold. There's nothing we cannot have, Mother, as long as I have this little black bottle. (*They gather up, with some difficulty, all the new clothes and the baskets of food and exit. Curtain*)

* * * * *

SCENE 2

SETTING: *The King's Parlor. Ornate table is upstage. Three gilt chairs are center. Outside door is up right.*

AT RISE: *Room is empty. After a moment there is a knock at the outside door.* PARLOR MAID *enters and opens door to* PETER *and* MOTHER, *who wear their grand new clothes.*

PETER (*Tipping hat; with quite an air*): Is the King at home, my dear?

MAID (*Curtseying*): Yes, the King is at home. Won't you come in and sit down? (PETER *and* MOTHER *enter.*)

MOTHER: I hope we won't disturb the King by coming unannounced.

MAID: The King is still in his dressing gown and slippers. But I'm sure he won't mind if you don't.

PETER (*Sagely*): Never judge by appearances, my dear.

MAID (*Very respectfully*): Oh, no, sir!

MOTHER: Be so good as to tell the King we are here.

MAID: Please, what name shall I say?

PETER: Peter Higgins and his mother. (MAID *curtsies and exits*. PETER *and* MOTHER *sit*.) I hope the King will take kindly to my request.

MOTHER: My Peter is as good as anybody; and surely you can offer as much as any prince or lord, now that you have the bottle.

PETER: That is true. Princess Marilyn *is* very pretty! I saw her but last week as she drove through the town in her golden carriage. (KING *enters*. PETER *and* MOTHER *rise and bow*.)

KING: Good morning. Sit down, pray, and make yourselves comfortable. (*They all sit*.) And what do you want, Lord Peter?

PETER (*Hesitating, then boldly*): I want to marry your daughter.

KING (*Taken aback*): Marry my daughter?

MOTHER: A right good lad my Peter is, and wise, too, your Majesty. The Princess could do worse.

PETER (*Quickly*): I can provide well for her—and I love her truly.

KING: No one can marry my daughter unless he can first bring her a basketful of diamonds, emeralds, rubies, and all manner of precious stones.

PETER: Is that all? Nothing is easier! I'll be right back. (PETER *exits*.)

MOTHER: By this request I see you think to be rid of my Peter. But wait and see.

KING (*Skeptically*): Where, pray, would your son acquire a basketful of precious stones—and at a moment's notice? (PETER *reenters, carrying a basket with a napkin over it*.)

PETER: Here, sir. (*Hands basket to* KING, *who takes the napkin off, revealing a glistening mass of jewels*)

KING (*Surprised*): Upon my word! Your mother was right. You must be a very wealthy prince.

PETER: Now, can I marry your daughter?

KING: I promised Princess Marilyn's mother that no man should marry her unless he could bring her a pair of slippers of pure gold, ornamented with flowers of rubies and sapphires.

PETER: Nothing easier. (PETER *exits*.)

KING (*Considering*): Truly, he cannot bring these at once, for such slippers would need to be made to order.

MOTHER: You don't know my Peter—or what magic thing he has in his possession.

KING: What's that you say? Magic, did you say? (PETER *returns and hands a pair of small gold slippers, ornamented with jewels, to* KING, *who is flabbergasted.*)

PETER: Now may I marry your daughter?

KING: Truly these gifts are rich and beautiful beyond compare. But can you furnish plain, everyday things as well?

PETER: What would you like to have?

KING: Our supply of towels is running low. Can you furnish the Palace with new towels? Only the best, mind you!

PETER: Nothing easier! (PETER *exits.*)

KING: Marry, if he can bring towels, I can think of no other test or excuse.

MOTHER: Peter can get anything he asks for! Why, a week ago we were just plain poor folk, going to market with our eggs in order to keep a roof over our heads and buy victuals enough to keep life within us.

KING (*Very curious*): And then what happened?

MOTHER (*Garrulous*): Then Peter met the Little Man, who gave him the magic—(*She stops suddenly and claps her hand over her mouth.*)

KING: Yes, yes! Gave him the magic—*what?*

MOTHER: Never mind what! (PETER *reenters, carrying an armful of neatly folded towels, which he puts on table.*)

PETER: There are more outside on the doorsill.

KING (*Ringing small bell for* MAID): Truly, this is marvelous! (MAID *enters and curtsies.*) Go outside with Lord Peter and fetch in our new towels.

MAID (*Ecstatically*): Towels? New towels, did you say?

PETER: Come with me. (*He and* MAID *exit and soon return, carrying more towels, which they place on table.*) And now, I should like to marry your daughter, if you please.

KING: Yes, you may marry the Princess. (*To* MAID) Go summon Princess Marilyn; then tell Cook to prepare lunch for

two extra persons. (MAID *curtsies and exits.*) You will lunch
with us, of course?

MOTHER: Yes, and thank you.

PETER: Aye, that we will.

MOTHER: To think! My Peter to marry a Princess! Who would
have thought, a fortnight ago, such a thing could happen?
That was a lucky day, Peter, when you traded the basket of
eggs.

KING: Pray, what did you get for your basket of eggs? (PRIN-
CESS *enters right, accompanied by* LADY-IN-WAITING, *who
curtsies to* KING, *then steps aside, upstage.* PRINCESS *bows
her head slightly to* KING.)

PRINCESS: You called for me, Father?—Oh, we have guests!

KING: Marilyn, my dear, this is Peter Higgins, and Dame Higgins, his mother. (PETER *and* MOTHER *bow.*)

PRINCESS (*Graciously*): I am pleased to meet you.

PETER: May I kiss your hand, my affianced bride?

PRINCESS (*Shocked*): Your—*what?*

KING (*Quickly*): My dear, I have given Lord Peter permission
to marry you.

PRINCESS (*Protesting*): But, Father, I thought to marry a—a—
someone more—more—

KING: Yes, I understand, my dear. (*Significantly*) But Lord Peter has great wealth and remarkable powers! See, he has
brought you this basket of jewels.

PRINCESS (*Pleased*): Oh!

KING: And these gold slippers—just the right size.

PRINCESS (*Delighted*): *Oh!*

KING: And a supply of new towels.

PRINCESS (*Ecstatic*): Oh, oh, oh!

PETER: Now will you marry me? You are the prettiest girl I've
ever seen. (PRINCESS *looks down coyly, but holds out her
hand to* PETER, *who kisses it with a flourish.*)

KING (*To* PETER): And now, perhaps, you will tell us what
magic power you own, to procure all these things at a moment's notice.

PETER: A secret must be kept, else it is no longer a secret.

KING: But the Princess cannot bear secrets, can you, Marilyn?

PRINCESS: Oh, no! (*Prettily*) Tell me your secret, Peter, please do.

PETER: That I cannot, my dear.

PRINCESS (*Pouting*): Not even to *me*—your bride-to-be?

PETER (*Flustered*): How can I refuse? What say you, Mother?

PRINCESS (*Stamping her foot*): I won't marry a man who has to ask his mother everything. Nor one who keeps secrets from me.

MOTHER: Better give in, Peter. I'm sure they will never tell a soul.

PETER: Very well, then. (*He takes the bottle from his pocket and shows it to* PRINCESS *and* KING, *who inspect it with interest.*) This is no ordinary bottle, I'll have you know. (MAID *reenters.*)

MAID: Luncheon is served.

KING: But we're just about to hear a *very* interesting story.

PETER (*Putting bottle away*): I'll tell it while we eat.

KING: Good! Good! (*To* MAID) Tell the Mistress of the Bedchamber to prepare two guest rooms for tonight. Peter and his mother must not journey home before tomorrow. (MAID *curtsies and exits.*)

PRINCESS: Come, Father—and (*Bashfully*) Peter. Let us go to lunch. (PETER *offers his arm to the* PRINCESS, *and the* KING *gallantly offers his to* MOTHER.)

KING: Will you come into the dining room, Dame? (*Winks broadly*) Shall we precede the young couple? Mayhap they have a few tender nothings to say to each other.

MOTHER (*Taking* KING's *arm*): 'Twill not be a nothing if my Peter says it, for he is very wise as well as being a handsome lad.

KING: And my Marilyn is witty as well as beautiful. (KING *and* MOTHER *exit. As they pass* LADY-IN-WAITING, KING *motions her to follow. She does so. When they are off,* PETER *tries clumsily to kiss* PRINCESS, *but she evades him.*)

PRINCESS: Now about the bottle—you were saying—

PETER: I was saying that I was on my way to the market to sell a basket of eggs, and I fell asleep in the warm sunshine, and suddenly someone tapped me with a cane, and it was a strange little old man.

PRINCESS (*Eagerly*): And then?

PETER: I shall tell the story over the lunch table, my dear. (*He again offers his arm. She takes it, and they go out, the* PRINCESS *smiling, and* PETER *looking triumphant. Curtain*)

* * * * *

SCENE 3

SETTING: *The fork in the road, next day.*

AT RISE: PETER *and* MOTHER *enter, walking dejectedly and wearing their old clothes.* MOTHER *sighs and sits on stump, putting a basket she is carrying down beside her.* PETER *sits on ground near her, looking up at the trees and the sky.*

MOTHER (*Upset*): Whatever are we to do now, Peter?

PETER: Do as the little birds do and trust the sunshine.

MOTHER: If only you hadn't *told* them about the bottle.

PETER (*Shaking his head sadly*): Then they would never have stolen it from me.

MOTHER: And all our fine things wouldn't have disappeared.

PETER: At least the King can't use the magic bottle himself, for he doesn't know the rhyme. I didn't tell them that. The Two Men in Blue will never come to do his bidding, as they came to me.

MOTHER (*Sighing*): That's some comfort.

PETER: Yes—but now we are right back where we started. Oh, well! Take the good with the bad, I say. 'Tis a fair, fine day, I'll be bound, riches or no riches.

MOTHER (*Picking up basket*): Here, Peter, is another basket of eggs from our hen house. Take them to market and sell them, for we have not a penny to buy food.

PETER: Very well, Mother.

MOTHER: And I'll go put our former humble home to rights. (MOTHER *exits.* PETER *takes basket and starts off left, but is met by the* OLD MAN.)

OLD MAN: Will you strike a bargain for your basket of eggs?

PETER (*Overjoyed*): Yes, I will, and gladly. (OLD MAN *takes out a black bottle, like the other one.*)

OLD MAN: Two men are in this bottle. When they have done all you want them to do, say, "No, no, no! Back you go! Work well done, rest has won." (*They solemnly make the exchange, shake hands, and bow to each other. OLD MAN exits.*)

PETER: First of all, I'll get another suit of fine clothes. (*He rubs the bottle. At once,* TWO TALL MEN IN BLACK *enter carrying sticks and begin chasing* PETER, *waving sticks menacingly. Loudly*) No, no, no! Back you go! Work well done, rest has won. (MEN IN BLACK *at once exit.* PETER *sits down on stump, trying to catch his breath. He studies bottle a moment. Then suddenly he jumps up.*) Mother, Mother! Get ready! We are going to pay another visit to the King! (*He runs off, murmuring the new rhyme as he goes. Curtain*)

* * * * *

SCENE 4

SETTING: *The King's Parlor. Same as Scene 2.*

AT RISE: MAID *is dusting room and singing merrily.* PRINCESS *and* LADY-IN-WAITING *enter, each carrying embroidery.* MAID *curtsies, continues to hum to herself.*

PRINCESS: Pray go somewhere else with your dusting—*and* your singing!

MAID (*Cheerfully*): Certainly, Your Highness. (*She exits.* PRINCESS *and* LADY-IN-WAITING *sit and begin working on embroidery.*)

PRINCESS: You know, Gretta, Peter Higgins had a right pretty wit, when you come to think of it. And do you not think he wore his fine attire with quite an air?

LADY-IN-WAITING: Aye, with quite an air. (*Giggling*) But he certainly cut a sorry figure next morning when he appeared in the clothes of a country bumpkin. Was it a joke, Marilyn, to make you laugh?

PRINCESS: Not such a laughing matter, when all the fine presents he gave me disappeared—even the towels. (KING *enters, carrying bottle.*)

KING (*Muttering to himself*): Peter said all he did was rub this bottle. (*Rubs bottle, holds it up, inspecting it*)

PRINCESS: There's no use trying any more, Father.

KING (*Startled*): Why, upon my soul! I didn't know anyone was in here. Why don't you stay in your part of the house, Marilyn, and not be scaring me out of my wits? (LADY-IN-WAITING *hides a smile behind her embroidery frame.*)

PRINCESS: Because I choose to sit in this room—(*Dramatically*) for 'twas in here I met Lord Peter. Such a fine figure of a man! And *so* gallant! And *so* wise and clever!

KING: I thought him very plain, if you must know.

PRINCESS: Never judge by the outside of things—that's what he said. You told me I should marry him—and I let myself get to like him very, very much.

KING: Because of the presents, my dear?

PRINCESS (*Sniffling*): At first because of the gifts, then for his own dear, wise, sweet self. And now I'll never see him again. If you had only let well enough alone, Father! (*She begins to cry into her embroidery;* LADY-IN-WAITING *comforts her.*)

KING: Oh, come now—no tears, I pray. I don't want you to get married. (*Loud knock is heard.*)

LADY-IN-WAITING: I wonder who that can be, this time of morning? (MAID *hurries in and opens door to* PETER *and* MOTHER. PETER *holds the new black bottle.*)

PETER (*Cheerfully*): A very good morning to you. (PRINCESS *perks up and rearranges her hair.*)

KING (*Gruffly*): What? Are you back again?

PETER: Yes, I am back again.

KING: What do you want this time?

PETER: I want to marry the Princess.

KING: And have you brought anything this time?

PETER: I have brought another bottle.

KING (*Rubbing his hands with pleasure*): Come right in! Come in, good dame! (*To* PRINCESS) Did you hear that, my dear? Lord Peter has brought another bottle with him. (PETER *and* MOTHER *enter.*)

PETER: Good morning, Princess Marilyn.

PRINCESS: Good morning, Peter.

KING: About this bottle you have brought. Will you let me see it? (PETER *holds up bottle for him to see.*) Ah-ha!

PETER: Perhaps you would like to take the cork out?

KING: Indeed, yes! Truly, it is a pretty little bottle. What do I do, Peter?

PETER (*Handing the* KING *the bottle*): Rub it on both sides, take the cork out, and you will get a surprise. (KING *does as told. At once* TWO TALL MEN IN BLACK *rush in and begin to chase* KING *around room, waving their sticks.* KING's *crown falls off, and he loses one of his slippers.* PETER *and* MOTHER *look on with satisfaction.*)

KING: Peter! Peter! Cork up your men again!

PETER: Will you give me back the bottle you took from me?

KING: Yes, yes! (KING *manages to hand both bottles back to* PETER.)

PETER (*Calling out loudly*): No, no, no! Back you go! Work well done, rest has won. (MEN IN BLACK *run out at once.* KING *flops in chair exhausted.*)

PRINCESS (*Looking at* PETER *with new admiration*): Oh, Peter, you saved my father!

PETER: Will you marry me?

PRINCESS: Of course I will, Peter.

PETER (*To* MAID, *authoritatively*): Go fetch the minister at once.

KING (*Out of breath*): Yes, yes, at once. We want Peter in the family.

PRINCESS (*Coyly*): Oh, Peter! At once?

MOTHER (*To* MAID): You might as well tell the Cook to prepare a wedding feast. (MAID *curtsies to one, then to another, in a dither.*)

MAID: Yes, Your Highness! Yes, Lord Peter! Yes, Peter's mother! (MAID *exits.*)

PETER (*Rubbing bottle*): When the cork goes pop, pop, pop, Two Tall Men will hop, hop, hop. (*He removes cork and* TWO TALL MEN IN BLUE *instantly enter.*)

MEN IN BLUE: Your orders, sir?

PETER: The finest wedding dress in all the realm for my bride! (*To* LADY-IN-WAITING) Go with them, and take the dress to the Princess' room. (*To* MEN) And see that proper apparel is made ready for me and my mother. And one thing more. I'd like those gold slippers back again, and the basket of jewels.

PRINCESS (*Excitedly*): And, Peter, the towels, too? The Palace is awfully short on towels.

PETER: And the towels! Deliver those at the rear entrance.

KING (*Resigned*): They might as well take the clothes for you and your mother to the guest rooms. No use your going all the way home before the wedding. (MEN IN BLUE *exit with* LADY-IN-WAITING. PETER *goes to the* PRINCESS *and takes her hand.* MOTHER *picks up the* KING's *crown from the floor and takes it to him.*)

MOTHER: Here's your crown, Your Highness. (*He puts it on, but can't get it straight.* MOTHER *straightens it for him.*)

KING: Thank you kindly, Dame.

MOTHER (*Flirtatiously*): 'Tis plain to be seen that you need someone to look after you—now that the Princess will have a husband to look after.

KING (*Smiling*): Mayhap! Mayhap!

PRINCESS: Peter, you are *so* sweet to me. How happy we are going to be.

PETER: Of course we shall. (MAID *reenters, carrying gold slippers, basket of jewels, and as many towels as she can hold.*)

MAID: Here are the presents, just as before. (LADY-IN-WAITING *reenters.*)

LADY-IN-WAITING (*Gleefully*): The wedding dress is ready, Princess Marilyn.

PRINCESS: I must have one *old* thing for my wedding costume. (MOTHER *takes a handkerchief from her pocket and hands it to* PRINCESS.)

MOTHER: A handkerchief with fine embroidery, my dear, made by Peter's grandmother many years ago.

PRINCESS: Thank you kindly, good Mother.

LADY-IN-WAITING (*Taking off a pin and giving it to* PRINCESS): Here is a pin you may borrow.

PRINCESS: Thank you, Gretta. "Something old, something new, something borrowed, something blue"—but I haven't anything blue. (PETER *takes from his pocket a few half-wilted forget-me-nots and hands them to* PRINCESS.)

PETER: Here, my love, are some forget-me-nots I picked from our garden for you as I left this morning. Not nearly so blue as your eyes.

MOTHER: Now *that's* the sort of thing women like to hear! You always were my wise and clever Peter.

PETER: The head is wise only when the heart speaks, Mother. (*Curtain*)

THE END

Production Notes

CLEVER PETER

Characters: 9 male; 6 female.

Playing Time: 20 minutes.

Costumes: Scene 1: Peter wears modest country clothes. Peter's Mother wears a full dark skirt, white blouse and bonnet. In Scene 2, Peter and his mother are dressed in clothes they received in first scene—a velvet suit and a hat with a plume for Peter, and a silk dress and a bonnet with ribbons and flowers for mother. Little Old Man has long gray beard and wears fine black velvet suit with cape and a black velvet hat with a plume. Two Blue Men wear bright blue clothes and pointed blue caps with little bells on them. Parlor Maid wears maid's uniform. King wears a dressing gown, slippers, and a crown. Princess wears long white dress, pearl necklace and satin cap, on top of which is a gold crown. Lady-in-Waiting wears a long, dark dress. The Two Men in Black wear black suits and caps and carry stout sticks.

Properties: Basket of eggs; silver-headed cane; two small bottles with corks; velvet suit and hat with a plume; silk dress, bonnet with ribbons and flowers; baskets filled with bread, vegetables, fruit; basket of jewelry, covered with a napkin; pair of small gold slippers; towels of various kinds and sizes; stout sticks; embroidery; small white handkerchief; jeweled pin; a few wilted flowers.

Setting: Scenes 1 and 3: May be played before the curtain. Tree stump large enough to sit on is center. Scenes 2 and 4: The King's Parlor. Several gilt chairs with red cushions are placed about the room. A small table or two are also used. Door outside is up right.

Lighting: No special effects.

A Baker's Dozen

by *Elsi Rowland*

Characters

THREE WOMEN, *villagers*
DAME POTHERBY
DAME GREENSMITH
MILLER HODGE
SIMEON HALFPENNY, *apprentice*
FOUR MEN, *villagers*
COURT CLERK
JUDGE
COURT ATTENDANT
JOHN CHUBB, *a baker*
SQUIRE HUMPHREY ⎫
THOMAS HOOD   ⎬ *assistants*
WILLIAM DAWSON ⎪
DAVID COBB   ⎭
SPECTATORS, *extras*

TIME: *Late sixteenth century.*
SETTING: *Courtroom in English village. Judge's raised bench, with gavel and stool, is back center. Clerk's table is down center, with prisoner's table on one side, witness stand at the other. On either side of the stage are benches for spectators.*
AT RISE: THREE WOMEN *are seated on benches, talking animatedly.*
1ST WOMAN: For years he has been cheating us.
2ND WOMAN: But now we have brought him to justice.
3RD WOMAN: The Courts of Law are a great thing. They can decide what's right and what's wrong and no more arguing about it.

1ST WOMAN: It's plenty of arguing I have done with John Chubb about his short weight.

2ND WOMAN: Yes, and much good it has done. (DAME POTHERBY *and* DAME GREENSMITH *enter and walk toward them.*)

GREENSMITH: Good morning, neighbors.

1ST WOMAN: Are you going to testify, Dame Greensmith?

GREENSMITH: Indeed I am! As shall Dame Potherby.

POTHERBY (*Patting her pocket*): I have brought some buns with me as evidence. (THREE WOMEN *nod in approval.*) I shall tell the judge—(*They continue conversation, ad lib, in low tones, as* FOUR MEN *enter, talking animatedly as they walk to benches and sit.* SPECTATORS *enter in twos and threes during the following exchange, seating themselves at benches.*)

1ST MAN: I wonder what John Chubb will have to say for himself.

2ND MAN: I doubt if he ever baked a loaf of bread in his life that was full weight.

3RD MAN: His money chests are not short weight, though. I believe he is the richest man in town. (MILLER HODGE *and* SIMEON HALFPENNY *enter and walk to benches.*)

1ST MAN: There's no doubt about that.

3RD WOMAN (*Vehemently*): Shame on him to rob honest people and to starve their children!

MILLER: Aye to that! And I'll see that he is shamed!

SIMEON (*Quietly*): I'll be happy to see that myself, Miller Hodge.

4TH MAN (*Patting* SIMEON *on his shoulder*): Well, the case will have a full hearing this day and it may be that John Chubb's money chests will not be filled so quickly after this. (*Sound of trumpet is heard offstage.* COURT CLERK, SQUIRE HUMPHREY, THOMAS HOOD, WILLIAM DAWSON, *and* DAVID COBB *enter, followed by* JUDGE. *All rise.* JUDGE *sits at his bench,* SQUIRE HUMPHREY *and* THOMAS HOOD *stand to right of bench, and* WILLIAM DAWSON *and* DAVID COBB *stand to left of bench.* COURT CLERK, *picking up document from desk, addresses the court.*)

CLERK (*Reading from paper*): Hear ye! Hear ye! Attend the opening of this Court of Law where the judge is authorized to administer impartial and even justice and to uphold the laws of the kingdom in the name of his royal Highness, the King of England. (SPECTATORS *sit*.) The first case is that of John Chubb against the people of this town.

JUDGE: Let the prisoner be brought to the bar. (SPECTATORS *whisper as* COURT ATTENDANT *enters with* JOHN CHUBB, *who wears chains on his wrists*.) What is the charge against him?

CLERK: Your Honor, the defendant John Chubb is a baker by trade. He is charged with selling his products short in weight.

JUDGE: Who are the witnesses for the prosecution?

CLERK: Dame Greensmith, Dame Potherby, Miller Hodge, and Simeon Halfpenny. Dame Greensmith will be first to testify. (CLERK *sits*. DAME GREENSMITH *goes to stand*.)

JUDGE: Dame Greensmith, what do you know of Baker Chubb's products?

GREENSMITH: Your Honor, John Chubb has sold bread to me for the past two years. During that time, my children have become thin and pale. Night after night they go to bed crying with hunger. John Chubb's buns can be gobbled up in two bites. Unless your Honor can make him give us full weight, I do not know what will become of us. We are the poor people of the town who own no wheat fields.

JUDGE: Have you ever charged the defendant with giving you short weight?

GREENSMITH: Many a time. But he has become angry and told me that if my children were still hungry, they could go out in the fields and eat grass.

JUDGE: Thank you, Dame Greensmith. You may step down. (*She takes her seat*.)

CLERK (*Rising*): Next witness, Dame Potherby. (CLERK *sits*. POTHERBY *comes forward*.)

JUDGE: What is your testimony?

POTHERBY: Your Honor, it is a burning shame! Will you look at this? (*Produces a bun from her pocket*) This is what John

Chubb calls a bun. This is what he sells to the town for six-pence. (JUDGE *takes bun and examines it.*)

JUDGE: Is this the regular-sized bun?

POTHERBY: It is, your Honor.

JUDGE (*Licking his lips*): I think that there might be three bites in this bun instead of two. However, the proof of the pudding, as they say—(*He begins to eat the bun.*)

POTHERBY (*Wagging his finger*): Any decent bun, your Honor, should have eight bites in it.

JUDGE: I am inclined to agree with you. (*Chews*) Yes, it can be done in two bites, but three would be more genteel. Have you any further testimony, Dame Potherby?

POTHERBY: I have, your Honor. What John Chubb's buns are made of, only he knows, but I'll wager it's nothing good. I strongly suspect that his flour is mixed with chaff.

JUDGE: In Courts of Law, suspicions cannot be accepted as evidence. Suspicions are not facts.

POTHERBY (*Firmly*): Well, his buns taste as though they were made of straw, your Honor, and that's no suspicion—it's a fact.

JUDGE (*Thoughtfully*): Yes, that can be accepted as evidence. I have just eaten a bun.

POTHERBY: You might eat a dozen, your Honor, and still be hungry.

JUDGE (*Quickly*): I will take your word for that, Dame Potherby. Thank you. That is all. (*She takes her seat.*)

CLERK (*Rising*): Next witness, Miller Hodge. (CLERK *sits.* MILLER *takes the stand.*)

JUDGE: Miller Hodge, have you done business with the defendant, John Chubb?

MILLER: I have, your Honor.

JUDGE: And have your relations with him been satisfactory?

MILLER (*Emphatically*): John Chubb is a difficult customer, your Honor.

JUDGE: Why do you say that?

MILLER (*Bitterly*): He will not buy my flour, your Honor. He says it is too dear. He is a great one for a bargain, is John Chubb.

JUDGE: Then how do you do business with him?

MILLER: Well, you see, your Honor, he brings me his wheat to grind.

JUDGE: That is not an unusual practice on the part of the townspeople who raise wheat, is it?

MILLER: No, your Honor. I do a lot of milling besides my own. The difference is that John Chubb's wheat is ground up, chaff and all. His full flour sacks don't weigh six stone. Mine weigh a full eight.

JUDGE: Thank you, Miller Hodge. That will do. (MILLER *returns to his seat.*)

CLERK (*Rising*): Simeon Halfpenny, will you take the stand? (CLERK *sits.* SIMEON *nervously walks to stand.*)

JUDGE (*Kindly*): Don't be afraid, my boy. Simply answer my questions truthfully, and all will be well.

SIMEON (*Meekly*): I shall do my best, your Honor.

JUDGE: You are the apprentice to Baker Chubb, are you not? (SIMEON *nods.*) What do you do in his shop?

SIMEON: At four o'clock in the morning, I open the shop and start the fires going. Then I bring in the sacks of flour. Then I set out the pans. Then the master comes in and he mixes the buns. I stand by and sweep up the flour he spills on the floor and put it back in the sacks.

JUDGE: Go on.

SIMEON: Then I watch the buns while they bake. After the buns are done, I take them out in the little cart to sell. Sometimes I don't sell all the buns and Master gives them to me. He says that I can start paying him for them when I finish my apprenticeship. I am not good at figures but Master keeps it all in his big books. He says that I owe him forty pounds already. (SPECTATORS *gasp and shake their heads in disapproval.* JOHN CHUBB *squirms in his seat.* SIMEON *continues.*) After the buns are sold, I wash the pans, rake over the fires, close the shutters, and then go home. Master stays behind to count the money.

JUDGE: Thank you, Simeon. You may step down.

CLERK (*Rising*): The Court has heard the evidence of the prosecution. It will now hear the case of the defendant.

JUDGE: Who are the witnesses for the defense?

CLERK: John Chubb has no witnesses, your Honor. He will plead his own cause.

JUDGE: Very well. John Chubb, will you take the stand? (*He does so.*) Baker Chubb, you have heard the evidence of the prosecution. Have you anything to say?

CHUBB (*Emphatically*): It's all lies, your Honor. My flour is as good as any in this town, and my buns are all full weight. (SPECTATORS *gasp and murmur loudly.* JUDGE *pounds gavel for silence.*)

JUDGE: You saw the bun which Dame Potherby gave to me. Was it one of your buns, Baker Chubb?

CHUBB: It was, your Honor.

JUDGE: How much does one of your buns weigh?

CHUBB (*Stubbornly*): A full pound, your Honor. Not an ounce less.

JUDGE: You testify that the buns all weigh a pound and that they are made of the best flour?

CHUBB: I do, your Honor.

JUDGE: Is Simeon Halfpenny your only apprentice?

CHUBB: Yes, your Honor. I have a fatherly interest in the boy. (*Greedily*) His name appeals to me. (SPECTATORS *titter.*)

JUDGE: Do you make a fair profit in your business, Baker Chubb?

CHUBB: Little or nothing, your Honor. (*Sweetly*) I am so kind-hearted that I cannot bear to see any one lack for bread. Last year I must have given away a dozen buns.

JUDGE (*Dryly*): Your generosity is very commendable. (*Pause*) How much do you weigh, Baker Chubb?

CHUBB (*Taken aback*): Why, your Honor, 'twas only this morning I stepped on my scales. I tipped the balance at one hundred and fifty pounds. But why does your Honor want to know?

JUDGE: That will be evident in due time, sir. You may be seated. (*He resumes his place in the prisoner's dock.*) The Court has heard the evidence of the plaintiffs and that of the defendant. This evidence will be weighed carefully. Squire Humphrey, will you go to Baker Chubb's shop next door with Thomas Hood and put one hundred and fifty of his buns into a sack and bring it to the Court?

SQUIRE HUMPHREY: Yes, your Honor. (*He and* THOMAS HOOD *exit.*)

JUDGE: William Dawson and David Cobb, will you go to the anteroom and fetch to the Court the plank and trestle which you will find there? (WILLIAM DAWSON *and* DAVID COBB *nod and exit.* SPECTATORS *murmur for a moment or two.* DAWSON *and* COBB *reenter carrying plank and trestle and place them before Judge's bench.*)

DAWSON: Now what, your Honor?

JUDGE: Balance the plank upon the trestle so that both ends are equally distant from the floor. (*They do so.*)

COBB: That's done, your Honor.

JUDGE: That is all, gentlemen. Thank you. (*They resume positions. To* SPECTATORS) What you see before you is a crude form of scales of justice. From time immemorial, justice has been represented by a blind-folded goddess, holding scales in her outstretched hand. The question to be decided is whether Baker Chubb's buns are short in weight, and with the help of our plank and trestle the case can be settled. (SQUIRE HUMPHREY *and* THOMAS HOOD *enter, each carrying one end of a large, full, burlap sack, tied off with a piece of rope.*)

HUMPHREY: Here are the buns, your Honor.

JUDGE: Now, gentlemen, will you bind the sack containing the one hundred and fifty one-pound buns to one end of the plank? (*They tie sack to plank, using rope ends from sack.*)

HOOD: There you are, your Honor.

JUDGE: Baker Chubb, will you mount the other end of the plank? (SPECTATORS *titter.* CHUBB *steps forward, sputtering angrily.*) If the one hundred and fifty pounds of your person balances with the one hundred and fifty buns, each supposedly weighing one pound, which are in the sack, your honesty will be proved. If, on the other hand, you are found to outweigh the buns, the charge against you will be upheld.

CHUBB (*Stammering*): Of all the blathering nonsense—

JUDGE (*Sternly*): Such expressions may be termed contempt of court, Baker Chubb. You will refrain from giving voice to them.

CHUBB: I beg your pardon, your Honor, but I might break my neck if I tried to get up there.

JUDGE (*Reassuringly*): There is little danger of that. (*To assistants*) Gentlemen, assist Baker Chubb to his position. (DAWSON *and* COBB *seize* CHUBB, *hoist him onto plank.*)

DAWSON: Up with you, Johnny!

COBB: All aboard! (CHUBB's *side of the plank comes down with a thud.*)

CHUBB: Ugh! (SPECTATORS *howl with laughter.*)

SPECTATORS (*Ad lib*): That settles it! I knew the judge would figure it out! (*Etc.* DAWSON *and* COBB *help* CHUBB *to his feet.*)

JUDGE (*Rapping gavel for silence*): Order in the court. (SPECTATORS *quiet down.*)

CHUBB (*Simpering*): All right, your Honor, I confess. I do make my buns short weight and there is chaff in my flour. But it will never happen again if your Honor will be easy with me.

JUDGE: I am glad that you have confessed your dishonesty, John Chubb. But such wrongdoing cannot go unpunished. You have robbed the people of this town and have grown rich at their expense. To make amends, you much change your bad practices. Not only must your bread be full weight and of the first quality, but from now on you must put an extra bun into every dozen that you sell. In this town, thirteen will be known as a baker's dozen.

ALL (*Cheering, ad lib*): Hooray! A baker's dozen! Three cheers for the judge! (*Etc. Curtain*)

THE END

Production Notes

A BAKER'S DOZEN

Characters: 14 male; 5 female; as many male or female extras as desired for Spectators.

Playing Time: 15 minutes.

Costumes: Everyday English dress of the late 1500s: Judge wears black robe. John Chubb is in shirt sleeves and wears a baker's apron and cap.

Properties: Small bun; long plank with trestle; filled sack weighing less than actor playing John Chubb.

Setting: English courtroom of the late 16th century. All furniture is plain and well-worn: High judge's bench stands back center; stool is behind bench, and gavel sits on top of bench. Clerk's table stands down center, on which are document, feather pen, and ink well. Prisoner's dock stands to one side of clerk's table, and witness stand on other side. On either side of stage are benches for spectators.

Lighting: No special effects.

Sound: Trumpet blare, as noted in text.

Scheherazade

by May Lynch

Characters

SCHEHERAZADE
SULTAN SCHAHRIAH
NUTMEG ⎫
POPPYSEED ⎬ *maids*
LOTUS PETAL ⎭
DINAZADE, *Scheherazade's sister*
ROYAL COOK
PAGE
EXECUTIONER
SEAMSTRESS
ATTENDANTS

SCENE 1

TIME: *Long, long ago.*
SETTING: *The throne room of the palace of the Sultan.*
AT RISE: NUTMEG *and* POPPYSEED *are dusting throne.*
LOTUS PETAL (*Offstage*): Nutmeg! Poppyseed! Nutmeg! Poppyseed! (*Enters*) Oh, there you are. I hope your work is all finished. Are you ready to greet the new queen?
POPPYSEED: Yes, Lotus Petal, we are trying to pronounce her name.
NUTMEG: I have it down in my mind now. Scheherazade. (*Slowly*) Sche-he-ra-zade.
POPPYSEED: I'll never learn it, Lotus Petal. Sche-heard-a—*what?*
NUTMEG: No, no. Listen. Sche-he-ra-zade—*zod*—*zod*. As in, "I am a zod when Lotus Petal catches me napping instead of dusting."

43

POPPYSEED: Well, I am a zod. Every day I must learn a new name. Each day the name is harder.

NUTMEG: Queens, queens, queens! Every day there is a new one on the throne. Let me see—I think today makes 435 queens.

POPPYSEED (*To herself*): Sche-he-ra-zade. Sche-herazade. Poor thing. She will die just as the others have died. Chop, chop, chop, and off rolls her pretty little head.

NUTMEG: The royal executioner has already worn out several hatchets. They say he really has an axe to grind.

POPPYSEED: Lotus Petal, you have been around here so long. Don't you think our grand and supreme ruler, commander-in-chief of twenty-one kingdoms, (*Pauses*) is a bit—well—*strange?*

LOTUS PETAL (*Jumping*): Shhhh! Careful, Poppyseed. The walls have ears and the keyholes have eyes.

POPPYSEED (*Whispering*): If you don't agree, Lotus Petal, I shall think *I* am the one who is crazy.

LOTUS PETAL (*Whispers*): One might say (*Pauses and looks around*), one might say (*Pause*) he is eccentric.

NUTMEG (*Laughing*): Eccentric!

LOTUS PETAL: Shhh!

NUTMEG (*In mocking tone*): Eccentric! Off with her head! Eccentric! (SEAMSTRESS *enters, wearing tape measure around her neck and carrying scissors and pin cushion.*)

SEAMSTRESS: Needles and pins, needles and pins, when the Sultan marries, the trouble begins.

LOTUS PETAL: What's the trouble, Royal Seamstress?

SEAMSTRESS: Trouble? Trouble? How would you like to make a wedding dress every day for 435 days? I can't see straight. (*She exits.*)

NUTMEG: Our Sultan is a bad old man.

POPPYSEED (*Nodding in agreement*): He's a wicked, mean old man.

LOTUS PETAL (*Closing door and looking secretive*): When you are as old as I, Poppyseed and Nutmeg, you will find there are reasons for everything.

POPPYSEED: What reason could explain his theory of decapitation?

NUTMEG (*To* LOTUS PETAL): That means chopping off somebody's head.

LOTUS PETAL: I know, I know.

POPPYSEED: Tell us more about the Sultan, Lotus Petal.

LOTUS PETAL: Well, his Majesty, the grand and supreme ruler and commander-in-chief of twenty-one kingdoms, was once a happy, young prince. However, he married a wicked young woman who treated him very badly. She deceived him and ran off with a palace guard. Because of this harsh treatment, the Sultan *hates women!*

NUTMEG: Really? All women? (*She holds her neck.*)

LOTUS PETAL: "All women are evil," declared the unhappy, once-happy prince, and he decided that no woman would ever be able to make him unhappy again. So he thought of this plan.

POPPYSEED: What plan?

LOTUS PETAL: Every day wedding bells would ring out, to be heard far and wide in the kingdom.

NUTMEG: How romantic.

LOTUS PETAL: But every day he would choose a different bride. Then the day after the wedding, the bride would have to appear before the Royal Court Advisor.

NUTMEG: What for?

LOTUS PETAL: To be beheaded *royally,* of course. All the brides are daughters of nobles.

POPPYSEED: But (*Slowly*) Sche-he-ra-zade is the daughter of the Court Advisor!

LOTUS PETAL: Alas, all the nobles' daughters have been used up.

NUTMEG (*Holding neck*): How many women are there in the kingdom?

LOTUS PETAL: If the Court Advisor fails to have the queen beheaded, he himself will be beheaded. (COOK *enters.*)

COOK: Lotus Petal, you must come help me. Please come help me. I'm having trouble with the cake bakers. They're all going on strike because they are sick of making wedding cakes. Can't you lend me some of your maids to mix the icing?

NUTMEG: Let us help, Lotus Petal. We love to lick the bowls.

LOTUS PETAL: Very well, if you are sure the dusting is done.

COOK (*In loud whisper*): Have you heard the news? The new queen is the daughter of the Court Advisor—and the second cook's brother knows the page who heard that she *volunteered* to marry the Sultan!

POPPYSEED: She must be a sorceress! How exciting! Only a witch would dare to marry our (*Whispers*) eccentric Sultan.

NUTMEG: The Court Advisor has yet another daughter—and that would make 436. (*Holds neck*) Who will be next? (*All exit as gong sounds. Curtain*)

* * * * *

SCENE 2

TIME: *Later the same day.*

SETTING: *Same as in Scene 1.*

AT RISE: PAGE *enters.*

PAGE: Make way for his Majesty, Schahriah, supreme ruler and commander-in-chief of twenty-one kingdoms. (SULTAN *enters, bows to audience, ascends throne.*) Make way for her Majesty, Scheherazade, royal bride of his Majesty, grand and supreme ruler of twenty-one kingdoms. (SCHEHERAZADE *enters, bows to audience, then ascends throne. ATTENDANTS enter. They bow before the royal pair, take places around throne.*)

ATTENDANTS: Hail to the Sultan! Hail to his beautiful bride!

SULTAN (*Turning to* SCHEHERAZADE): Ah, my dear, you are by far the most beautiful woman I have ever seen. No wonder our royal subjects stare at you so. They have never seen such a fair queen.

SCHEHERAZADE (*Humbly*): Surely, my husband exaggerates.

SULTAN (*Aside*): And modest, too! How sad that she must leave this world. (*Turning to* SCHEHERAZADE) Some trinkets for my bride. (*He gives her a box of jewelry.*)

SCHEHERAZADE: How lovely! (*She holds up gems.*) I've heard of such wonderful gems, but I've never seen any like these! (*She begins to weep.*)

SULTAN (*Concerned*): Why do you weep, my precious one? These are for you to wear. Pray do not weep tears that are bigger than these diamonds.

SCHEHERAZADE: I weep, dear husband, because I am homesick for my dear little sister, Dinazade. We have never been separated before.

SULTAN (*Clapping twice*): Page! Page! Dispatch a royal messenger and bring back the second daughter of the Court Advisor. (PAGE *exits.*) My bride must be happy (*He sighs. Aside*), at least for a little while. (COOK *enters.*)

COOK (*Bowing before* SULTAN): The royal wedding cake is prepared, your Highness, but I fear that there will be none tomorrow. The royal kitchen is on strike.

SULTAN (*Furiously*): On strike? How dare they!

COOK (*In resignation*): They are tired of making wedding cakes, your Highness. Today was the four-hundred-and-thirty-fifth. They want to make doughnuts or pies or tarts—*anything* but wedding cakes.

SCHEHERAZADE (*Clapping her hands*): Tarts! Tarts! I'd love some tarts! Let's have tarts tomorrow and doughnuts the next day and pie the day after that! (SULTAN *furrows his brow in contemplation.* COURT *begins to whisper and shake heads sadly.*)

SULTAN (*Gruffly*): Very well—er—tarts! Make tarts! (COURT *sighs in relief.* COOK *exits as* PAGE *enters.*)

PAGE: The daughter of the Royal Court Advisor and sister to the royal bride—Dinazade. (DINAZADE *enters, runs to* SCHEHERAZADE. *They embrace.*)

SCHEHERAZADE: Dear little sister, I was beginning to think we would never see each other.

DINAZADE: I thought we'd never put our heads together again.

SCHEHERAZADE (*To* SULTAN): Dear husband, before we depart for our marriage supper, may I take some moments of your time? I'd like to tell my little sister a story. I usually do before bedtime.

SULTAN (*Nodding*): Of course, of course, but isn't she big for bedtime stories?

SCHEHERAZADE: None are too old and none are too young. Come, little one, sit at my feet. (DINAZADE *sits and* SCHEHERAZADE *begins to tell story.*)

Once upon a time there was a fisherman who was too poor to get food for his wife and sons. The waters would yield no fish, and because he did not want the gods to think him greedy, he would cast his net only four times a day. However, one day when he was about ready to go home with nothing to show for his efforts, there appeared in his net a copper vessel. On it was the seal of Solomon. He opened it quickly with his knife and out came a genie. The great genie spoke: "You may be granted one favor before you die." "Well," said the fisherman, "I want you to answer one question." "Anything," said the genie. "Did you really come out of this vessel?" asked the man. "Of course," said the genie, with considerable indignation. "I don't believe it. How could such a enormous genie fit into such a little vessel? You must get back inside to prove it to me." So, of course, the genie—" (DINAZADE *is asleep.*)

Dinazade! Oh, my precious little sister, you are already asleep. I'll have to finish the tale another time. (*She yawns, stretches.*) I'm tired and sleepy, myself. (*She falls asleep.*)

SULTAN (*Wringing his hands*): Oh, dear, just when the story was getting interesting. You don't suppose the genie got back into the vessel, do you? Scheherazade! Wake up! (*He shakes her, but she sleeps on.*) Oh, dear, I'll have to wait until tomorrow to hear how the fisherman makes out.

PAGE: But, sir, you are committed to leave early in the morning for the twelfth kingdom inspection.

SULTON: So? I'll hear the end of the story tomorrow night.

PAGE: Is not the royal queen to be beheaded in the morning?

SULTAN: Summon the Court Advisor and Royal Executioner. Scheherazade's death must be postponed. (*Gong sounds as curtain closes.*)

* * * * *

SCENE 3

TIME: *One thousand and one nights later.*
SETTING: *Same.*
AT RISE: SCHEHERAZADE *is talking to* SULTAN.
SCHEHERAZADE: And so, Aladdin married the princess and
    took her to live in the palace the genie of the lamp had given
    him. (PAGE *enters and bows before* SULTAN.)
SULTAN: Haven't I told you never to interrupt me when I am
    listening to the stories of Scheherazade? You have done so for
    the past one thousand and one nights.
PAGE: Sir, there is trouble in the nineteenth and twentieth
    kingdoms. They have sent for you.
SULTAN: Tell them to settle their own troubles. My place is at
    the side of my wife. (COOK *enters.*)
COOK: Your Royal Highness—
SULTAN: Be off! How shall I find out what happened to
    Aladdin?
COOK: Your Highness, the kitchen help is on strike again.
SULTAN: Again? Why?
COOK: They claim that everyone in the palace is allowed to
    listen to the stories of the queen except them. They are always
    cooking and they never hear about Ali Baba or the Enchanted
    Horse or—or—
SULTAN (*Suspiciously*): Hm—how do you know about these
    tales? Who has been telling tales? (*He looks around the court.*)
COOK: Your Highness, I listened at the keyhole. My specialty
    was always wedding cakes, but lately, I have had nothing to
    do. (NUTMEG *and* POPPYSEED *enter and bow before the*
    SULTAN.)
NUTMEG: It's partly our fault, your Royal Highness. Since the
    arrival of our worthy and lovely queen, we have lost our will
    to dust. We've been sitting here with the rest of the court
    listening to these marvelous stories.
POPPYSEED: She must know a thousand and one of them, your
    Royal Highness. We love to hear them, and we knew how
    much everyone would enjoy them—

NUTMEG: So we told the royal cook to listen at the royal keyhole.

POPPYSEED: We didn't think you'd mind. You have become so kind and such a wonderful ruler. Everyone in the whole kingdom loves you now. (EXECUTIONER *enters, carrying flower.*)

EXECUTIONER (*Bowing and presenting flower to* SCHEHER- AZADE): I am no longer the Royal Executioner, your High- ness. I've thrown away my royal hatchet and have grown a beautiful garden where the queens used to be beheaded. Any- body in the kingdom will help me dig and plant and carry sod because they are so happy about the change in policy here. (SEAMSTRESS *enters, carrying two robes.*)

SEAMSTRESS (*Bowing; to* SCHEHERAZADE): The Royal Seamstresses wish to thank you, your Highness. Since you began telling stories, we've been able to get all the palace mending done. That hasn't happened in years because we were always stitching wedding dresses. To express our grati- tude, we've fashioned new robes for the Sultan and his queen. (*Presents robes to each*)

SCHEHERAZADE: I am most honored to receive all of your thanks. (DINAZADE *enters.*)

DINAZADE: Come, come, sister. Tell us the rest of the story or we shall never get on to the next one.

SULTAN: First, I must make a proclamation. I hereby make my promise and give my sacred word that there shall be no more beheadings anywhere in the twenty-one kingdoms. We shall live always in peace and happiness as we have been since Scheherazade has come to the throne. She is wise and good and has melted a wicked old heart.

COURT (*Rises*): Hail to the great Sultan, Schahriah! Hail to the clever Scheherazade! (*Curtain*)

THE END

Production Notes

SCHEHERAZADE

Characters: 4 male; 6 female; male and female extras.

Playing Time: 20 minutes.

Costumes: Royal Arabian dress: plain robes for Nutmeg, Poppyseed, Lotus Petal, Page, Attendants; ornate robe, turban for Sultan; billowing chiffon dress, veil for Scheherazade; robe, veil for Dinazade; harem pants, vest for Executioner; apron for Cook.

Properties: Feather dusters, tape measure, pin cushion, scissors, flower, two robes.

Setting: The throne room of the palace. There are two chairs at center of stage.

Sound: Gong sound, as indicated in text.

Pandora's Box

by Karin Asbrand

Characters

PANDORA
HELENA
PAULA
NYDIA
ANNA
NESTOR   } *her playmates*
LAERTES
CADMUS
HECTOR
SIX EVIL SPIRITS
HOPE

SETTING: *A garden. Box, large enough for Evil Spirits to hide in, is center.*

AT RISE: PANDORA *stands beside box.* EVIL SPIRITS *hammer on sides of box from inside.*

EVIL SPIRITS (*Screaming*): Let us out! Let us out!

PANDORA (*Sternly*): Be still or, by the gods of Olympus, you shall be severely punished. Epimetheus does not know that you are here, and if you are still, I shall not tell him.

EVIL SPIRITS (*Groaning loudly*): We don't like it in here! We want to be free.

PANDORA: The world would not like you out here. (*Taps gently on side of box*) So be quiet. I must go now. I will think about what to do with you, and when I know I will return and tell you. (PANDORA *exits left as* PLAYMATES *dance in right.*)

HELENA (*Looks with awe at box*): This is Pandora's box. I wonder what is in it.

LAERTES: Curiosity once killed a cat. It might kill you, too.

NESTOR: I think it is full of gold. That's what I think.

CADMUS (*Thoughtfully*): It might be at that. That much gold would make us all rich.

NYDIA: I think it is full of presents for everybody.

HECTOR: I think it would be better for you not to think about it at all.

ANNA: I think so, too. My father says that Pandora is a witch.

NESTOR: Then she is a very beautiful witch.

PAULA: My father says to keep away from her; that she will bring only vexation upon this earth.

LAERTES: How can anyone so beautiful bring anything but good?

PAULA (*Doubtfully*): I don't know. But I think we had better listen to our fathers. So let's go play somewhere else.

HELENA (*Shakes her head*): I like it here. The box can't do us any harm. It's only a box.

PAULA: My father says that anything that has to do with Pandora can do harm.

NYDIA: How can your father know so much about Pandora?

PAULA: My father knows a great many things. After all, he is a friend of Epimetheus, and he knows that Zeus sent Pandora to Epimetheus as a gift, and he was warned by Prometheus to take no gifts from Zeus.

CADMUS (*Tosses a ball at the box and catches it as it bounces back*): Perhaps there is a bad man in the box.

FIRST EVIL SPIRIT (*Yells*): Let me out of here!

PAULA (*Shivering, as* PLAYMATES *crouch together, frightened*): There is a bad man in the box.

SECOND EVIL SPIRIT: I am not a bad man. I am good. I will give you much gold, if you only let me out.

THIRD EVIL SPIRIT: I am only a little child. I will die in here, if you don't let me out!

NYDIA (*Aghast*): It's a child! A little child. Pandora must be a bad woman to close up a little child in a box.

FIRST EVIL SPIRIT: You shall have jewels, as many as you can wear, if you will open the box.

FOURTH EVIL SPIRIT: We will give you precious stones, if you will only let us out.

NESTOR: How many of you are in there?

FIFTH EVIL SPIRIT (*Wheedles*): You will see. Just open the box, and you will see.

ANNA: How do we know that you will not harm us?

SIXTH EVIL SPIRIT: We promise. (*Whines*) There is no air in here.

HELENA: Oh, the poor little things. (*Starts toward box*) I will open the box for you.

PAULA (*Seizes her arm*): Helena! Keep away from the box. It is dangerous. My father says . . .

HELENA (*Pulls her arm away impatiently*): I am sick of hearing what your father says all the time. I want to see who is in that box.

THIRD EVIL SPIRIT: You are a smart little girl. There is plenty of gold in this box for you.

CADMUS: Don't you believe it, Helena. I think Paula is right.

NESTOR: I'd like to see what is in the box, too.

LAERTES: I am afraid we will be punished, Nestor, if we open the box.

CADMUS: I think so, too. It isn't our box.

FIRST EVIL SPIRIT (*Pleads*): Please let us out. We are only little children, just like you.

SECOND EVIL SPIRIT: We would like to come out and play.

THIRD EVIL SPIRIT: We can teach you some new games.

HECTOR (*Doubtfully*): Well, maybe it wouldn't do any harm just to open the box a little crack, and peek.

LAERTES: I'm with you. Come on, I'll help you lift the cover. (LAERTES *and* HECTOR *go to box and try to lift the cover.*)

HECTOR (*Pants*): It's heavy. (*The* EVIL SPIRITS *push open the cover the rest of the way, and hop out. They run around wildly, pinching* PLAYMATES, *pulling their hair, and tearing flowers and greens apart.*)

NESTOR (*Sternly*): Stop it! Stop it, or we will put you back in the box.

FIRST EVIL SPIRIT (*Grins at him*): That you cannot do. We are out now.

NYDIA: Where is the gold you promised us?

HELENA: Where are the jewels? The precious stones?

SECOND EVIL SPIRIT: Gold? Jewels? Precious stones? (*Laughs heartily*) Whatever is the child talking about?

THIRD EVIL SPIRIT: We know nothing about any gold, or jewels, or precious stones. (*Pinches* ANNA's *arm.*)

ANNA (*Rubs her arm*): Ouch! What kind of beings are you that you only want to hurt people?

CADMUS: And you don't keep your word.

FOURTH EVIL SPIRIT (*Laughs*): We forget very easily.

PAULA: Who are you, anyway? We never saw anybody like you before.

FIFTH EVIL SPIRIT: Well, you're going to see a lot of us.

SIXTH EVIL SPIRIT: Who are we, she wants to know. Why don't we answer her?

FIRST EVIL SPIRIT: We are evil spirits, my little friend. (*Bows low*) And now that you have let us out of our box, we are going to inhabit the earth from corner to corner. I am Sickness. (*Bows low again*) I shall breathe disease into all parts of the earth.

SECOND EVIL SPIRIT (*Bows low*): I am Poverty. I shall go into castle and cottage. Believe me, I will have fun now, and plenty of it.

THIRD EVIL SPIRIT (*Bows low*): I am Crime. The world will get to know me well.

ANNA (*Groans*): Please, please, please, go back into the box. Hector and Laertes, you let them out. Please get them back.

FOURTH EVIL SPIRIT (*Jauntily*): That they cannot do. They are not strong enough.

FIFTH EVIL SPIRIT: We are the ones who are strong, now that we are out. (*Pinches* PAULA)

PAULA (*Rubs her arm, and stamps her foot*): Go away! You are bad, bad, bad, all of you.

SIXTH EVIL SPIRIT: We know that. We like to be bad. As my name is Jealousy, I think being bad is lots of fun. I was sent here by the green-eyed god.

ANNA: Is there no way to get rid of you?

CADMUS: I will find a way. (*Grabs* FIRST EVIL SPIRIT *by the arm, but* SPIRIT *gets hold of his ears, and hangs on*)

FIRST EVIL SPIRIT (*Hops up and down first on one foot then on the other, holding on to* CADMUS' *ears*): No way! No way! No way!

CADMUS (*Screams*): Help! Help!

FIRST EVIL SPIRIT (*Drops his hold of* CADMUS' *ears*): There! You see! (PANDORA *enters right. She stops short on seeing the* SPIRITS.)

PANDORA: So you managed to get out of your box. I was afraid of this.

SECOND EVIL SPIRIT (*Scoffs*): Afraid, mistress? You wanted it as much as we did.

THIRD EVIL SPIRIT: Yes, you wanted it, but you didn't want to open the box yourself, and let us out.

FOURTH EVIL SPIRIT: But you are glad that somebody else did.

HELENA (*Goes to* PANDORA): Dear, beautiful Pandora, what can we do now?

PANDORA (*Sighs*): Nothing, child. The harm is already done, and now the world will be full of evil. As long as these evil spirits were closed up tightly in their box, they could do no harm. But now—(*Shakes her head, sadly*) there is nothing anyone can do. (HOPE *enters, left*)

HOPE: Ah, yes, there is. Have you forgotten me? (*The* SPIRITS *cringe and crouch together in a corner, right.*)

PANDORA (*Angrily*): What are you doing here? This is not your territory.

HOPE: Any territory is mine, wherever I am needed. Go, Pandora. You have done enough harm for one day. (PANDORA *covers her face with both hands, and exits left.*)

NYDIA: And who, pray, are you?

HOPE: I am Hope, the only thing that is left when the spirits of evil inhabit the earth. I will stay by you, and if you will only believe in me, all will be well with you. (*To the* EVIL SPIRITS *as she raises her right arm and points toward left*) Begone, spirits of evil! You, too, have done enough harm for one day. (*The* EVIL SPIRITS *slink out, left.*)

PAULA (*With a sigh*): I am certainly glad to see them go.

ANNA (*Rubs her arm where she was pinched*): I am, too. They hurt me.

HELENA (*Eagerly*): Have they gone for good?

HOPE (*Shakes her head*): I am afraid not, my child. You have not seen the last of any of them. You will meet most of them, time and time again. But when you do, call upon me, and I will stand by you, for I am Hope. I can conquer any of them anywhere, any time, whether it be Poverty, Sickness, Crime, or Sorrow.

HECTOR (*Hopefully*): Can you lock them all up in the box again?

HOPE (*Sadly*): That I cannot do. (*Holds* HECTOR's *and* HELENA's *hands*) But if the evil spirits move in on you, I will move in, too, if you'll only have faith in me. That I promise you.

HELENA (*Confidently*): Then I am not afraid.

HECTOR: Then nobody needs to be afraid, as long as Hope is there, for I am sure that Hope is stronger than any evil spirit.

HOPE: You are right. Hope is strong enough to conquer anything.

THE END

Production Notes

PANDORA'S BOX

Characters: 4 male; 6 female; 6–8 male and female extras.

Playing Time: 10 minutes.

Costumes: Girl playmates wear short pastel-colored tunics with ribbons going over the shoulders crosswise across the chest and crossing again in back to a sash tied in front with long streamers. They may wear flowers or ribbon bandeaux in hair. Boy playmates wear short cotton tunics with figured gold or silver borders, and bands of silver or gold around head. Evil spirits wear costumes of brown with yellow or black horns, ears, and tails, or black with bright yellow or red horns, ears, and tails. Pandora wears a long Greek gown and a jeweled crown. Hope wears long white Greek gown and white flowers in hair. All wear sandals, preferably painted silver or gold.

Properties: Ball, flowers, greens.

Setting: A garden. The stage may be decorated with flowers and greens, small trees, etc. Center is Pandora's box, a large chest, big enough for the Spirits to hide in. It may have an open back and stand against center wall, giving children more room. Exits are at right and left.

Lighting: No special effects.

The Dreadful Dragon of Utrecht

by Barbara Winther

Characters

CHIMNEY SWEEP
ELDER
SAGE
MIDWIFE
MERCHANT
TOWN CRIER
MAYOR
THE DREADFUL DRAGON
CHILDREN
CITIZENS

SCENE 1

SETTING: *Medieval Dutch city of Utrecht. Wooden bench is center.*

AT RISE: *Flute accompanies pantomime action:* CHILDREN *play catch;* ELDER, *with cane, watches from bench;* CHIMNEY SWEEP *enters carrying stepladder with rag, broom, and mirror attached, and marches about;* CHILDREN *fall in behind, imitating his step;* SWEEP *removes* ELDER's *hat and dusts off head to* CHILDREN's *amusement and* ELDER's *disgust;* SAGE *enters, reading book;* MERCHANT *rushes on with pocket watch and money bag;* MIDWIFE *bustles in, wearing apron;* SWEEP *tips hat, then exits with* CHILDREN; SAGE, MERCHANT, and MIDWIFE *sit on bench. Music stops.*

TOWN CRIER (*Entering, ringing bell and shouting*): Hear ye,

59

hear ye! The Committee for Good in the fair city of Utrecht now meets in the town square. (*Exits, calling*) Hear ye, hear ye!

MIDWIFE: Well, get on with it. I am soon to deliver the VonWagonbergs' child into this world, and I have little time to sit around and talk.

MERCHANT: Nor have I. I must return to my spice shop before customers flock elsewhere.

SAGE: Yes, yes, be quick about it. I do not like to waste my valuable intellect.

ELDER (*Importantly*): Our beloved mayor formed this committee—

SAGE (*Impatiently*): Our mayor has set up twenty-six committees in the past two weeks, and each one sillier than the last. Yesterday morning it was a Committee for Clean Canals; at noon, the Committee for Creaky Windmills; at sunset, the Committee to Stop the Clopping of Wooden Shoes; and in the evening, the Committee to Ban Baggy Pants.

ELDER: Sir, be assured, this is no silly committee. We are instructed to—(*Searches pockets, finds piece of paper, puts on spectacles, and reads*) "to make sure no evil enters our beautiful city." Is there approaching disaster?

MERCHANT: Of course not. It would be bad for business.

ELDER: All is safe, then?

MIDWIFE: No! (*Others are startled.*) In my visits to homes, I have noticed unswept corners, cobwebs on rafters, and animals left outside at odd hours. (*Whispers*) Furthermore, rubbish heaps are growing.

MERCHANT (*Adamantly*): Not in my spice shop.

SAGE: The schools and churches are scrubbed every day at noon.

MIDWIFE: Yes, but evil hides, perhaps in an attic or a cellar or chimney. There could be—mind you, I only say "could be"—hidden evil so awful it might turn into a (*Pause*) dragon.

OTHERS (*Ad libbing*): Ridiculous! She is crazy. Midwives always spout nonsense. I refuse to listen to her. (*Etc.*)

MIDWIFE (*Rising, hushing them*): Why only last week, Mrs. Kook told me she heard of a giant creature roaming around

England. It has the hideous head of a lizard and eyes of fire. One look and sizzle, poof—nothing left of you but a heap of ashes.

SAGE: Complete, utter foolishness! Dragons exist only in fairy tales.

ELDER (*Rising; to* MIDWIFE): You must not repeat that story, Midwife. You could cause a panic with your foolishness.

MIDWIFE (*Folding arms*): Believe what you wish, but I know for a fact if you don't keep an eye on the roosters, evil can enter.

OTHERS (*Ad libbing*): Roosters? *Now* what is she talking about? Silly woman! (*Etc.*)

MIDWIFE (*Mysteriously*): Yes. A rooster slips out, lays an egg—

SAGE (*Laughing*): Roosters don't lay eggs; hens lay eggs.

MIDWIFE: An *enchanted* rooster can lay an egg. Then along comes a silver-backed mud turtle—

SAGE: A silver-backed mud turtle? What gibberish is this?

MIDWIFE (*Louder*): The turtle sits on the egg to keep it warm until one day it bursts open. Out crawls a lovely, pink baby dragon. While nobody is looking, it slithers into a dark, dirty place and grows green, ugly, and evil until it devours all the beauty for miles around. (*Shocked moment of silence*)

ELDER (*Backing up*): Hm-m-m, well, this is not what the Mayor expected from the Committee for Good. This session is hereby adjourned. In fact, the committee is dissolved. (*Hobbles away*)

MERCHANT (*Rising to check pocket watch and money bag*): I am certain to have customers waiting, for I have cut my ginger in half—the price, that is. (*Starts to exit;* SAGE *continues to read.* CITIZEN *enters running and screaming, and jumps onto bench.*)

OTHER CITIZENS, CHILDREN, *and* MAYOR (*Rushing in; ad libbing*): What is wrong? Why the yelling? An emergency? (*Etc.*)

CITIZEN (*Groaning*): Oh, my heart! It thumps faster than a windmill's arms can turn. (*Others buzz to each other in alarm.*)

MAYOR (*Climbing on bench*): Now, everybody calm down. (*To* CITIZEN) Do you need medical aid? Perhaps a committee could help—

CITIZEN (*Wailing*): No! Listen to me, oh citizens of fair Utrecht. I have discovered we are about to be destroyed! (*Stunned silence, then following exchange begins softly and slowing, growing gradually louder and faster.*) I went to the cellar for a bottle of wine.

OTHERS: She went to the cellar for a bottle of wine.

CITIZEN: Instead of cold, I met hot air.

OTHERS: Instead of cold, she met hot air.

CITIZEN: There came a heavy breathing sound.

OTHERS: She heard a heavy breathing sound.

CITIZEN: I saw red lights strike the wall.

OTHERS: She saw red lights strike the wall.

CITIZEN: Then all at once, a spiny tail—

OTHERS: A spiny tail?

CITIZEN: Flailed the barrels of salted cod.

OTHERS: Oh, my God! The salted cod.

CITIZEN: I flew from the cellar, bolted the door, and then I heard the ghastly roar.

OTHERS: The ghastly roar? Tell us no more, or we will sink right through the floor!

MAYOR (*Raising arms*): Stop this at once! Believe me, the woman tells an impossible tale. Why, I've kept a close watch on that section of town, and I can assure you there is nothing there that can—(*Sound of roar is heard. Lights blink. CITIZENS and CHILDREN scream and scatter to hide. SAGE and MAYOR scurry under bench. After a moment of silence, SWEEP enters left whistling, sees cringing crowd, shrugs, tips hat in greeting, then exits right. Curtain*)

* * * * *

SCENE 2

BEFORE RISE: TOWN CRIER, *ringing bell, enters before curtain.*

TOWN CRIER (*Shouting*): Hear ye, hear ye! The Committee for Getting Rid of the Dreadful Dragon recommends the following course of action: First, the Mayor will attempt to bribe the dragon with all the gold in the city treasury. If that is unsuccessful, citizens must arm themselves with weapons and attempt to destroy the dragon; and if that fails, as a last resort, we all must leap into the North Sea. (*Exits; curtain opens*)

* * *

AT RISE: DRAGON *sleeps, draped about the bench, and snoring in a wheezy fashion. Bags labelled* GOLD *surround him.* CITIZENS *sneak on from all angles, armed with brooms, mops, shovels, and carrying picket signs reading*: DOWN WITH THE DRAGON, TAKE A DRAGON TO LUNCH AND IT WILL EAT YOU, *and* THE ONLY GOOD DRAGON IS A DEAD ONE. *They are about to charge* DRAGON *when he sneezes, scattering them into hiding.*

DRAGON (*Roaring*): Aha! I am the handsomest dragon in Holland. Of course, presently, I am the only dragon in Holland, but soon I shall tempt forth a flock of gorgeous dragons for company. (*Notes* CITIZENS) Well, well, what have we here? (*Bursts into roaring laughter, frightening* CITIZENS *even more*) Citizens of Utrecht, you are under my mighty power. One aggressive move, and my magnificent, flaming eyes will vaporize you. Then, I will burn down all trees and wither every single tulip. (CHIMNEY SWEEP *enters whistling as before, sees* DRAGON, *tips hat, investigates* DRAGON's *tail, sweeps it clean, then shakes head.* DRAGON *roars, not fazing the* SWEEP.) Insignificant little chimney sweep, go away before I, the most beautiful dragon in the world, burn you to a crisp. (SWEEP *shrugs, sets up ladder before* DRAGON's *head, polishes mirror with rag, climbs ladder, and holds mirror so* DRAGON *can see face.* DRAGON *shrinks back.*) What is that hideously ugly creature you have captured in there? (SWEEP *gestures to* DRAGON.) Me? Impossible! (*Looks at self again then bursts into tears with much hissing of steam*) Oh, horrors! Indeed, that is me. From a lovely, pink baby dragon, I have turned into an enormous, scaly, ugly monster. Why, I cannot even stand the sight of myself. (*Looks around fearfully*) This place is far too beautiful for me. (*Starts to crawl away*) I shall search for the land where my ugly relatives live. For only among my own kind will I not be shunned and feared. (*Exits, roaring and hissing.* CITIZENS *rush forward with ad lib congratulations to* SWEEP.)

MERCHANT: He got rid of the dragon without giving him all our money!

MIDWIFE: He did it without a battle!

SAGE: He did it without a committee!

ELDER: I nominate the chimney sweep as the next mayor of Utrecht! (*General cheering*)

MAYOR (*Leaping on bench*): I hereby appoint a committee to investigate the nomination. (*Jumps down*)

MERCHANT (*Leaping on bench*): To the chimney sweep, I donate a lifetime supply of parsley, sage, rosemary, and thyme. (*Jumps down; all cheer.*)

MIDWIFE (*Yelling*): From now on, let's keep our eyes on the roosters. (*More cheers.* TOWN CRIER *enters.*)

TOWN CRIER (*Ringing bell, shouting*): Hear ye, hear ye! This week is proclaimed National Soot Week! (*More cheers;* SWEEP *raises arms for quiet. He climbs down ladder and holds mirror, moving so all* CITIZENS *see their reflections, each moaning at the sight.*)

MIDWIFE (*Wailing*): Alas, we, too, have grown ugly.

MAYOR: I am too atrocious to be mayor. I second the nomination of the sweep.

ELDER: I never imagined this could happen. What can we do to change?

SAGE (*Raising arms*): I, for one, plan to follow the way of the chimney sweep. Although he says little, he does much to make a cleaner world. (SWEEP *folds ladder, attaches mirror, broom, rag, and gives a whistle.* CHILDREN *enter, fall in step after* SWEEP, *march around stage.* SAGE *and* CITIZENS *fall in step after them whistling; all exit. Curtain*)

THE END

Production Notes

THE DREADFUL DRAGON OF UTRECHT

Characters: 8 male or female; 1 female (Midwife); as many children and citizens as desired.

Playing Time: 15 minutes

Costumes: Dutch. The Chimney Sweep wears a tall, black hat and has splotches of soot on his face. The Dragon's head is made of papier-mâché, and his long body is covered with green cloth, a ridge of cardboard spines along back. Midwife wears an apron. Elder wears a hat and glasses.

Properties: Stepladder; broom; rags; mirror; bell; pocket watch; money bag; instruction note; bags labelled GOLD; brooms, mops, and shovels; protest signs.

Setting: Backdrop painting of medieval Dutch city of Utrecht. Wooden bench that seats four.

Sound: Flute music, dragon roar, steam hissing.

Lighting: Lights blink when Dragon roars.

The Soup Stone

by Mary Nygaard Peterson

Characters

TRAVELER
TILDY
JOHN, *her husband*
ELMER ⎫
TOBY ⎬ *their children*
SUSY ⎭
1ST HOUSEWIFE
2ND HOUSEWIFE

SCENE 1

SETTING: *A street in a small village. A fence with three gates runs across back of stage. Three houses may be painted on backdrop.*

AT RISE: TRAVELER *walks slowly along street, holding a cane in one hand and carrying a stick with knapsack tied to one end over his shoulder. He pauses and looks around.*

TRAVELER: I've come a long way today. (*He looks at the sky.*) By the looks of the sun, it must be about noon—dinnertime. (*He sniffs the air.*) I haven't smelled anything cooking the whole length of the street—yet people must eat. (*He stops before a gate, thumps vigorously with his cane and calls loudly.*) Halloo! Halloo there! (*He listens, then thumps and calls again.*) Halloo! Halloo! Anybody home here? (*He peers over the fence.*)

1ST HOUSEWIFE (*From offstage*): I'm coming. I'm coming. (*She enters, stands behind her gate, looking very cross.*) What's the matter here? Why all the commotion? What do you want?

TRAVELER (*Bowing low*): Good day, ma'am. A beautiful day, isn't it?

1ST HOUSEWIFE (*Coldly*): What is it you want?

TRAVELER (*Bowing again*): Kind lady, I would appreciate a bite of something to eat—anything at all that you can spare. I have had nothing to eat yet today.

IST HOUSEWIFE: Humph! That is no concern of mine. I have little enough for myself, and certainly nothing to spare. Good day. (*She exits.*)

TRAVELER (*Turning away from the gate and scratching his head thoughtfully*): Hmm. Yes, indeed. Yes, indeed. (*He pats his stomach tenderly.*) Well, we didn't get much there, did we? We'll just have to try again. Perhaps next time we'll have better luck. (*He walks to second gate, begins thumping and calling.*) Halloo! Halloo there! (A *dog barks backstage.* TRAVELER *listens, then thumps and calls again, peering over gate.*) Halloo! Anybody home?

2ND HOUSEWIFE (*From offstage; crossly*): Coming. Coming. (*She appears, looking more dreadful than the* 1ST HOUSEWIFE. *She scolds the unseen dog at her feet, pointing to the house as she does so.*) Be quiet, Major. Go lie down. Go on. Go lie down. (*The dog growls a time or two. To* TRAVELER) Well, what do you want?

TRAVELER (*Bowing*): It's a fine day.

2ND HOUSEWIFE (*Tartly*): Whatever you're selling, I don't want any.

TRAVELER (*Hastily*): I have nothing to sell, lady. Nothing at all. I just thought you might share a little something to eat with a poor, hungry traveler—just a bite of something?

2ND HOUSEWIFE (*Angrily*): No one gives *me* anything. I certainly can't afford to feed every beggar that comes along. Begone with you before I call my dog. (*She exits.*)

TRAVELER (*Turning slowly from the gate, scratching his head thoughtfully*): This isn't getting us very far, is it? (*He pats his stomach tenderly.*) We shall have to think of something. (*He looks about, picks up stone from the ground, rubs it thoughtfully on his trouser leg, then holds it in the palm of his hand, looking at it and thinking.*) Hmm. Yes, indeed. Yes, indeed. I think we shall try this. (*He walks to the third gate and begins thumping and calling.*) Halloo! Yoo-hoo. Halloo, in there. (*Two dogs begin to bark.*) *Two* dogs! (*He speaks to them, coaxingly, over the fence.*) Nice doggies. (*The dogs become quiet. TRAVELER reaches over the fence as if patting a dog.*) Nice doggie!

TILDY (*Appearing suddenly at the gate and speaking furiously*): What are you doing with my dogs? What do you want?

TRAVELER (*Bowing low*): Good day, kind lady. Do you happen to have a large kettle?

TILDY: Yes, I do, but what is that to you?

TRAVELER (*Showing her stone*): I have here a soup stone. If I can find someone who will let me have a large kettle of water, I will make a kettle full of soup. I'm rather hungry. (*He pats his stomach*).

TILDY: A soup stone? (*She reaches out to take it.*)

TRAVELER (*Withdrawing it quickly*): Careful now.

TILDY (*Leaning forward to look into his hand*): Looks just like an ordinary stone to me. You mean you can actually make soup out of that?

TRAVELER: I should like to try, if you can spare me a large kettle of water.

TILDY: *That,* I should like to see. Well, a kettle of water is cheap enough. Come in. (*She opens the gate.*) This better not be a trick of any kind, or you'll be sorry. (TRAVELER *goes through the gate and they exit. Curtain*)

* * * * *

SCENE 2

SETTING: *Inside Tildy's house. Upstage center is hearth with shelves and cupboards on either side. Chairs, stools, and table are placed about.*

AT RISE: TRAVELER *and* TILDY *are hanging a kettle of water over the fire.* JOHN, TOBY, *and* SUSY *watch.*

TRAVELER: There. Now I will drop in my soup stone. (*He does so.*) Soon we will have soup. (*He takes a stool and looks about at the family.*) Naturally, we will have to wait a little while. (*All watch the fireplace.*)

SUSY: I'm hungry. I wish the soup would soon be ready. Mother said we wouldn't have any dinner because there was nothing in the house to eat.

TOBY: I'm hungry, too. I'm sure glad you came along with your soup stone, mister.

TRAVELER (*To* TILDY): I think I should have asked you for a little salt. I hate to bother you, but soup always tastes a bit flat without it, don't you think so?

JOHN: Why, that's no bother. We have plenty of salt. No use eating flat soup when we don't have to. (TILDY *hands crock of salt to* TRAVELER. *He adds some salt to the water.*)

TRAVELER: Thank you. (*He returns to his seat.*) Nothing to do now but wait. (*As they all sit silently, the* TRAVELER *looks about, craning his neck to see under shelves, over cupboards, etc.*) You know, it's wonderful what a couple of carrots will do for a kettle of soup. (*Adding hastily*) Of course, with the soup stone, the soup is always delicious—with or without carrots. But the carrots do add a pretty color.

JOHN: Surely we have some carrots, haven't we, Tildy?

TILDY (*Indifferently*): Oh, yes, there are always a few carrots lying about some place. (*She finds the carrots, hands them to* TRAVELER)

TRAVELER (*Removing the carrot tops and cutting the carrots into the kettle*): There. Now we'll wait just a little longer. The soup will soon be done.

TOBY: How does it look? (*He tries to look into the kettle but the* TRAVELER *hastily replaces the lid.*) I'm getting awfully hungry.

TRAVELER (*Sitting again and speaking kindly*): So are we all. I can remember so well the delicious soup my mother used to make when I was a child. (*He rolls his eyes and licks his lips appreciatively.*) That was real soup. (*After a pause*) As I remember it, she always put a small cabbage in it. Ummm. Delicious. It must be twenty years or more since I last tasted cabbage.

JOHN: Imagine that. We have it all the time. (*To* TOBY) Toby, why don't you run out into the garden and bring in a cabbage? We have lots of them. Let the stranger have some in his soup.

TOBY: Why, sure, Papa. (*He exits hastily and reenters, breathless, with a cabbage, which he hands to the* TRAVELER.)

TRAVELER (*Admiring the cabbage*): Isn't this a beautiful head? So sound and firm. (*He begins slicing it and pops a bite into his mouth.*) So crisp and tender. (*He takes another bite.*) So tart, and yet so sweet. (*He takes another bite. Then he notices the family watching him intently, so he hastily adds the rest of the cabbage to the soup.*) I hope you'll forgive me for tasting the cabbage. But, you know, after twenty years—it was delicious. (*He sits again.*)

JOHN: A man can understand that. After all, a mother's cooking is not to be had every day. (TILDY *glares at him.*)

TRAVELER: No, siree, it certainly isn't.

SUSY (*Sniffing*): The soup is beginning to smell good. I'll bet it's almost done.

TRAVELER (*Inhaling appreciatively*): It does smell good. But wait—something is missing. (*He sniffs the air. Others watch him anxiously.*) The onions, of course. (*To* TILDY) You wouldn't have a wee bit of onion about, I don't suppose?

TILDY (*Haughtily*): Oh, wouldn't I? How do you think I could cook without onions? (*She finds one and tosses it to him.*)

TRAVELER (*Catching the onion*): Thank you, ma'am. I'm sure you are right. A good cook always has onions. (*He peels it, cuts it into pieces, and adds it to the soup. The door opens and* ELMER *enters, carrying a rabbit.*)

SUSY (*Running to meet* ELMER): Oh, Elmer, you're back.

ELMER: Yep. I've been hunting.

TOBY: Did you get anything?

ELMER: Yep, I sure did. (*He holds up the rabbit.*) Isn't he a beauty?

TRAVELER: Rabbit! How it takes me back to my youth. There's nothing that adds so much flavor to soup as a little meat.

JOHN: Why not toss it in the pot, my friend? That soup of yours is beginning to smell powerful good.

TRAVELER: I think you're right, sir. Let's put it in the pot. (*He takes the rabbit, hastily prepares it and puts it in the pot.*)

ELMER: What's going on?

SUSY: This man has a *magic* soup stone. He's making soup for all of us.

ELMER: A magic soup stone? Never heard of such a thing.

TILDY: Neither had we, but it actually works. Can't you smell what delicious soup it makes?

ELMER: It smells good, sure enough.

TRAVELER (*Looking into the pot*): I believe we can try it. Of course, soup improves with the cooking, but since we are hungry, what do you say we taste it?

ALL (*Ad lib*): Yes, let's. Let's taste it. (*Etc.*)

TILDY: I'll get the bowls. (*She does so.* TRAVELER *and* TILDY *dish up the soup. All eat.*)

JOHN: This is *real* soup.

TRAVELER: Just like the kind my mother used to make.

SUSY: The soup stone makes wonderful soup, doesn't it, Mother?

TILDY (*Critically*): It *is* good. In fact, I must admit, I've never eaten better.

JOHN: How could one go about getting a stone like that?

TRAVELER (*Eating greedily*): Well, now, let me think. (*He thinks and eats, while they all watch him.*) It's rather difficult to find a good soup stone. (*They all look disappointed.*) But, I'll tell you what I'll do—I'll let you have mine.

JOHN (*Protesting*): Oh, come now. We appreciate your kindness, but we wouldn't think of depriving you of—

TRAVELER (*Interrupting*): Not at all. Not at all. You keep the soup stone. I'm sure you'll find it satisfactory. In my travels I'll just keep my eyes open and will probably soon find another.

TILDY: Don't argue with him. I'll be glad to have the soup stone—it's something none of my friends have. But tell me, is there any secret about how to use it?

TRAVELER: No, ma'am, none at all. It's very simple—just use the stone as we did today. Start with your big kettle of water, of course—and salt—don't forget the salt. Then add whatever you please—a carrot or two, some potatoes, an onion, a cabbage, some meat—you know, a little of this and a little of that. The soup stone always works. You will have good soup every time.

TOBY: Boy, that's what I call wonderful.

TRAVELER (*To* TOBY): It is wonderful. After this, when you get hungry, you just get the kettle of water, put in the stone, and start the soup yourself. (*He rises and prepares to leave.*) And now I must be on my way. (*He goes to the door, turns, and speaks again.*) I've enjoyed supping with you. (*Then, to* TILDY) I hope from now on, your kettle will always be full of soup, and your children never hungry.

TILDY: Thanks to you and your soup stone, I'm sure they'll never be hungry again. (*They all bow in farewell. The* TRAVELER *departs. Curtain*)

THE END

Production Notes

THE SOUP STONE

Characters: 4 male; 4 female; 3 offstage voices for dogs.

Playing Time: 15 minutes.

Costumes: Peasant clothes for all characters.

Properties: Cane, stick with knapsack tied to one end, stone, kettle of water with lid, crock of salt, carrots, pocket knife, onion, 6 soup bowls and spoons, for Tildy; cabbage, rabbit.

Setting: Scene 1: A street in a small village. A fence with three gates runs across back of stage; only the last gate needs to open. A painted backdrop of houses may be used, if desired. Scene 2: The interior of Tildy's house. Upstage center is the hearth, with a kettle hanging over the fire. There are shelves and cupboards on either side. Chairs, small tables, etc., placed around the stage. There is an exit at right.

Lighting: No special effects.

Sound: Barking and growling of dogs.

The Clever Judge

by Virginia A. Artist

Characters

AMIRA, *the narrator*
OBASU, *a healer*
SESI, *his wife*
MAAKAFI, *their daughter*
JUDGE
BAUNDI, *goldsmith*
TOTHI, *an apprentice to Baundi*
OTHER APPRENTICES, *at least four extras*
TOWNSPEOPLE, *extras*

TIME: *Long, long ago.*
SETTING: *An open area near the city wall in the imaginary African city of Dzharka.*
AT RISE: *Sound of African music is heard.* TOWNSPEOPLE *sit or stand in small groups around stage.* AMIRA *enters carrying basket. She sets down basket and moves to greet audience.*
AMIRA: Good day! My name is Amira. Amira means "Teller of Tales." Today I am going to tell you the story of the Clever Judge. Now, in ancient times the judge did not hold court in just one place. He traveled from city to city hearing cases and upholding the King's laws. One day in the ancient city of Dzharka, Obasu, the healer, his wife, Sesi, and their daughter Maakafi appeared before the judge. (AMIRA *picks up basket and exits.*)
JUDGE: I will now hear the case of Obasu versus Sesi and Maakafi.
OBASU: It is a very simple case, my lord Judge. My daughter

73

wants to do something I am opposed to. She wants to go to school.

JUDGE (*Horrified*): To school! A girl! Whoever heard of such a thing?

OBASU: That is exactly what I said, my lord Judge. In the history of Dzharka no girl has ever gone to school. Now my daughter wants to overturn three hundred years of tradition. And to make a bad matter worse, her mother supports her.

SESI (*Matter-of-factly*): Many fine families in other cities are now sending their daughters to school. Maakafi is so clever, she deserves to go to school.

JUDGE (*Sternly*): Speak when your turn comes, woman! (*Kindly*) Now, Obasu—poor man—how did your daughter get such an outlandish idea in her head?

OBASU (*Shaking his head*): I only wish I knew, my lord Judge.

JUDGE: Is she willful and disobedient?

SESI: Maakafi is a good girl and, after me, she is the best cook and housekeeper in the city.

JUDGE (*Sharply*): Your turn has not come. Tell me, Obasu, has your daughter had any unusual privileges for a young girl?

OBASU (*Hesitantly*): Well . . .

JUDGE: The court is your friend, Obasu. You may speak frankly.

OBASU: Well, I did teach her to be a healer like me, but only because none of my sons has the wit or the will to learn. A man must pass his skills on to someone.

JUDGE: Aha! I begin to see where the trouble lies!

TOWNSPEOPLE (*Ad lib*): He sees the trouble. He's going to get to the bottom of it. (*Etc.*)

SESI: My lord Judge, may I speak?

JUDGE: Not yet! Obasu, how often does a woman become a healer?

OBASU: Only once every hundred years or so does a woman become a healer.

JUDGE: Ah-ha! Maakafi *has* been unusually privileged for a girl. You have been too good to her! Now, Sesi, it is your turn to speak. Tell this court how your daughter has abused this poor man because he has been too kind a father to her!

SESI: Maakafi has not abused anyone. Every one of our sons has gone to school. I am sure Maakafi could do as well as they did. She is very clever.

JUDGE: Maakafi, have you anything to say?

MAAKAFI: My lord Judge, I am a good healer. I could be a better healer if I could read medicine books as my father does. If you let me go to school, I will study night and day to bring honor to my father's house.

OBASU: You see how it is, my lord Judge. When ideas like these come into a young girl's head, peace flies out the window. Already other young girls are asking their families why they can't go to school. If I send my daughter to school, where will this business of educating women end?

JUDGE (*Gravely*): Obasu, you were right to bring this case to me. This is a matter without precedent in our time and one that could have serious repercussions.

TOWNSPEOPLE (*Ad lib*): Serious repercussions. Did you hear those big words. A wise judge! A clever judge! (*Etc.*)

JUDGE: It is written that three things are most dangerous to a man: a beast that walks upright, a friend who becomes an enemy, and a woman with a little learning.

MAAKAFI (*Skeptically*): Where is that written? I will not believe it until I read it myself.

SESI: Well said, my daughter!

JUDGE: If Maakafi is allowed to go to school, other girls will demand the same privilege. Soon the whole order of nature will be overturned. Do you think men will want to marry learned women?

MAAKAFI: They will if there is no other kind for them to marry.

SESI: Well said, my daughter!

JUDGE: It is a great and terrible mistake to be too indulgent to our daughters, for some women are quick to get too high an opinion of themselves.

OBASU: True, true.

JUDGE: So, Maakafi, stop healing. Stay home and help your mother until you are married—if a husband can be found for you, which I seriously doubt, for no man wants a trouble-some woman.

MAAKAFI (*Upset*): I can't go to school?

JUDGE: No, you must stay home and tend your yam patch.

SESI *and* MAAKAFI (*In unison*): Oh, no!

JUDGE: Oh, yes.

OBASU (*Pleased*): They said you were a clever judge, and you are surely that! Come, wife. Come, daughter. Let us go home—and no more talk of school for our Maakafi. (OBASU, SESI *and* MAAKAFI *begin to move slowly away. Suddenly an angry voice, slapping noises, and yelps are heard off.*)

TOWNSPEOPLE (*Ad lib*): What's that noise? That howling! It's Baundi the goldsmith! (*Etc.* TOTHI *and* OTHER APPRENTICES *run on, pursued by* BAUNDI, *who has stick raised above his head threateningly. He sees* JUDGE *and lowers stick.*)

BAUNDI: Thank goodness the court is still sitting! Are you the Clever Judge?

JUDGE: I am. Who are you?

BAUNDI: I am Baundi the Goldsmith, as was my father before me and his father before him and—

JUDGE: Enough! It is obvious to me that you inherited a going concern. What is your problem?

BAUNDI: My lord judge, three months ago the King himself—may his name be praised—

ALL: May his name be praised!

BAUNDI: The King himself sent me a large pearl, as large as the ball of my thumb and like the very moon for beauty.

TOWNSPEOPLE (*Ad lib*): The King himself! What an honor! Such a beautiful stone! (*Etc.*)

BAUNDI: The pearl was to be set in a gold bracelet. The bracelet was to be a gift from the Crown Prince to his bride-to-be. (TOWNSPEOPLE *gasp in admiration.*)

JUDGE: Go on, Baundi.

BAUNDI (*Proudly*): My lord Judge, I am the only goldsmith in the city, in the kingdom, who could have set that pearl without harming it. The bracelet I made was a masterpiece, if I do say so myself. (*Angrily*) Now pearl and bracelet are gone!

Stolen! (TOWNSPEOPLE *gasp.*) And what makes a bad matter worse is that the thief had to be one of my own apprentices!

TOWNSPEOPLE (*Ad lib*): Who would do such a thing? What a disgrace! A hanging crime! (*Etc.*)

JUDGE (*Holding up hands to quiet* TOWNSPEOPLE): What do you want this court to do?

BAUNDI: I want you to find the thief.

JUDGE: Has anyone confessed?

BAUNDI: I have begged them on my knees to confess. I have given them my word that the thief will not be punished. I have beaten them until my arm is ready to fall off. All any of them will say is, "I am innocent."

TOTHI *and* APPRENTICES (*In unison*): I am!

BAUNDI (*Shaking stick at them angrily*): Thieves! Ingrates! (*To* JUDGE, *pleadingly*) Unless the real thief is revealed, I will be hanged as a thief and a traitor. My workshop will be burned to the ground. My family will be disgraced forever!

JUDGE (*Unconcerned*): Since no one has confessed, I can do nothing.

BAUNDI (*Shocked*): But you are known as the Clever Judge.

JUDGE: So I am. I am clever enough to stay out of the King's affairs. (*With a sweeping gesture*) Remove yourself and your apprentices from my court at once.

BAUNDI (*Desperately*): Oh! My poor wife! My poor children! They will starve to death and I will be hanged.

MAAKAFI: One moment, please. I think I can identify the thief.

OBASU (*Sternly*): Daughter, this is none of our business.

MAAKAFI: Father, yes it is. Think what will happen to all the businesses in Dzharka if the King says, "I sent a pearl to Dzharka and I, the King, was robbed"?

TOWNSPEOPLE (*Ad lib*): She has a point! The whole city would fall under the King's displeasure. Maakafi speaks the truth! (*Etc.*)

OBASU: By heavens, you think like a man. That is something I had not considered. People will say this whole city is a den of thieves. Commerce will come to a standstill. We will all suffer if the King's pearl isn't found.

BAUNDI: Find the thief for me, Maakafi, and I will dress you in jewels fit for a queen.

JUDGE: But she is only a girl!

BAUNDI: I don't care if she's a girl or a goat. I am a dead man unless the King's pearl is found!

JUDGE (*With resignation*): What do you suggest we do, Maakafi?

MAAKAFI: Someone must run to my house and get my work basket.

SESI: I will go, daughter. I know just where it is. (*She runs off.*)

OBASU: Find the King's pearl, my daughter, and you shall go to school—even to the university.

MAAKAFI: My father, you know my only wish is to bring honor to your house. (SESI *returns carrying basket; plants stick out of it.*)

SESI: Here is your work basket.

MAAKAFI: Thank you, Mother. (*To the others*) Now you all know that I am a healer.

TOWNSPEOPLE (*Ad lib enthusiastically*): That is so. Maakafi is a great healer. (*Etc.*)

MAAKAFI: I know the secret virtues of plants and minerals and animal organs.

TOWNSPEOPLE (*Ad lib agreement*): She knows these things. She is very wise. (*Etc.*)

MAAKAFI: So I know that this plant will help us find the thief. (*Pulls plant from basket*)

SESI: Daughter, that plant is—

MAAKAFI (*Interrupting her quickly*): A plant that will let us know who the thief is. (TOWNSPEOPLE *gasp.*) Master Goldsmith, have your apprentices squeeze this plant.

BAUNDI: Squeeze this plant, ingrates!

JUDGE (*Sternly*): You heard Baundi! Squeeze the plant. (*One by one,* TOTHI *and* APPRENTICES *squeeze plant.*)

MAAKAFI: Now, Master Goldsmith, look at their hands. Do you see anything strange?

BAUNDI (*Surprised*): Why, their hands are stained dark red!

MAAKAFI: Are all their hands stained?

BAUNDI: No. Tothi's are nearly clean.

MAAKAFI (*Matter-of-factly*): Then Tothi is your thief.

TOTHI: What!

MAAKAFI (*To* TOTHI): You are the thief. Give Baundi the King's pearl at once, or we will turn you over to the King.

TOTHI (*Terrified*): No. No. I stole the pearl, it is true. (*Drops to his knees*) Have mercy. I will tell you where it is hidden.

BAUNDI (*Hotly*): Thief! Ingrate! Where is the King's pearl?

TOTHI: Under a yellow brick on the floor of my room.

JUDGE: Seize him and hold him until we have the pearl. (TWO APPRENTICES *seize* TOTHI *and hustle him off.*) What magic is this you practice, Maakafi?

MAAKAFI: No magic, my lord judge, only something my mother taught me. This plant is used for making soap—red soap. The others knew they hadn't stolen the King's pearl, so they squeezed the plant as hard as they could to prove their innocence. The oil from the bark stained their hands and fingers dark red, as you all saw. Tothi knew he was guilty so he only *pretended* to squeeze the plant. That is why his palms were clean.

JUDGE: Maakafi, you are indeed a clever young woman.

OBASU: I have always said that Maakafi is as good as a son to me—every bit. She gets her clever wits from me, you know.

SESI *and* MAAKAFI: *We* know.

BAUNDI (*Gratefully*): Maakafi, my word is my bond. I will give you the finest jewelry any woman ever wore.

MAAKAFI: Father is sending me to school. That is reward enough for me.

BAUNDI: If you won't take the jewels as a reward, then take them as a gift. (*To crowd*) Call the drummers! Call the pipers! Let there be music and song and dancing! I will give a feast for the whole city. The King's pearl is safe and so is my life! (*Drums and pipes are heard. All dance. AMIRA enters.*)

AMIRA: So it came about that Maakafi was allowed to go to school. She was even allowed to go to the university, and there she was so very clever that she soon married a learned professor. When the people of Dzharka heard *that,* they all sent their daughters to school. Now that city of Dzharka is as famous for its beautiful, learned women as it is for its beautiful jewelry

and artwork. Some say this state of affairs is all due to the
Clever Judge. But I ask you—*who* was the Clever Judge?
(AMIRA *joins others in dance as curtains close.*)
THE END

Production Notes

THE CLEVER JUDGE

Characters: 4 male; 3 female; male and female extras.
Playing Time: 15 minutes.
Costumes: African clothing. Since Dzharka is a major trade center, the cloth-
ing may represent diverse ethnic groups. Judge carries a cow tail switch or
long gourd rattle to call court to order and as a symbol of his authority.
Properties: Two baskets, one with a plant in it; a large stick.
Setting: Simple set. Backdrop may be painted to represent a large stone wall
with grass growing at its base and palm trees painted here and there. Potted
palms or other tall foliage may be placed on stage.
Sound: Recordings of African music, as indicated.
Lighting: No special effects.

Persephone

by Claire Boiko

Characters

TWO NARRATORS
DEMETER
PERSEPHONE
MOTH FROM UNDERWORLD
SHEPHERD BOY
HADES
TWO BAT ATTENDANTS
ZEUS
HERMES
CHORUS, *extras*

SCENE 1

TIME: *Long ago.*
SETTING: *Ancient Greece.*
BEFORE RISE: *Greek music is heard, as* 1ST NARRATOR *enters down right, in front of curtain.*
1ST NARRATOR: Spring, fall, summer, winter. How did the seasons come to be? The Greeks had an explanation for it. Eons and eons ago, before your great-grandfather's great-grandfather was born, gods and goddesses lived on earth. (*Curtain opens.*)
AT RISE: *Demeter's garden. Backdrop of snowcapped mountains and blazing sun. At center is Demeter's temple. At right, pillars with a bench in front, on which* CHORUS, *in blue and white tunics and floral wreaths, sits, facing audience. Down left is grape arbor. All hold positions as* 1ST NARRATOR *speaks.*

1ST NARRATOR (*Looking around, then continuing*): In this very garden lived the goddess of summer and harvest, Demeter. (DEMETER *enters right, dressed in flowing green robe, sandals, and wearing a diadem of silver wheat stalks. She carries a cornucopia of fruit on a tray, which she places in front of* CHORUS. *Music fades out.*)

DEMETER: Children of the earth, I bring you rosy apples, plump figs, ripe olives and purple grapes. A horn of plenty!

CHORUS: Thank you, Demeter. You are most generous. (*All hold pose as* 2ND NARRATOR *enters.*)

2ND NARRATOR: And so it went, eon after eon. It was always summer in the land of legend, and there was always more than enough food and drink. But alas . . .

CHORUS (*Sighing*): Alas . . .

2ND NARRATOR: Demeter had a lovely daughter—Princess Persephone, the goddess of spring and flowers. (PERSE-PHONE *enters left, scattering flower petals from a basket. She crosses to* DEMETER, *who embraces her.*) Persephone was as unpredictable as spring. She was beautiful but willful, fickle, and just a little bit naughty.

1ST NARRATOR: Demeter loved Persephone—not wisely, but too well. (MOTH FROM UNDERWORLD *enters down left, hides in grape arbor, listening intently.*)

DEMETER (*To* CHORUS, *proudly*): Look, children of the earth. Feast your eyes on my beautiful Princess Persephone!

CHORUS (*Shaking heads*): Careful, Demeter—

DEMETER (*Pointing out* PERSEPHONE's *features*): Look at these sparkling eyes. That silken hair.

CHORUS: Speak no more, Demeter.

DEMETER (*Delighted*): She is more beautiful than Aphrodite.

CHORUS (*Alarmed*): Stop. Please stop!

DEMETER: Wiser than Athena.

CHORUS (*Urgently*): Danger! Danger!

DEMETER (*Excitedly*): She is a princess fit for a god! (CHORUS *gasps.*)

PERSEPHONE (*With false modesty*): Oh, Mother.

2ND NARRATOR (*Pointing to* MOTH, *who crosses down left to apron*): Do you see that gray moth? He is a messenger for Hades, the god of the underworld.

MOTH (*With evil laugh*): A princess fit for a god, to be sure, and I know which god ... Hades! I will lead this beautiful girl to him. And then (*Rubs hands together gleefully*)—ha! ha! How he will reward me! (*Returns to hiding place in grape arbor*)

DEMETER (*Warmly*): Have you eaten yet this morning, my beloved daughter? What would you like?

PERSEPHONE (*In a bored tone*): I would really like a pomegranate, Mother.

DEMETER: Persephone, dearest, you ate all the pomegranates yesterday.

PERSEPHONE (*Sighing*): You never grow enough pomegranates!

DEMETER: I'll grow more, just for you. (*Trumpet blares offstage.*) Oh, that is the trumpet of Zeus, calling us to Mount Olympus. I must go. (*Shakes her finger at* PERSEPHONE) While I am gone, promise me you will not leave this garden.

PERSEPHONE: But, Mother, I'm old enough to explore the world for myself. (*Thunder is heard off.*)

DEMETER (*Alarmed*): Thunder! I'd better hurry. (*Sternly*) Persephone, you must promise me not to leave.

PERSEPHONE: Oh, if I must, I must. (*Reluctantly*) I promise not to leave the garden.

DEMETER (*Relieved*): Good. Now, I can go in peace. (*Exits quickly.* MOTH *flutters on and circles* PERSEPHONE.)

PERSEPHONE (*Trying to shoo* MOTH *away; irritated*): Go away, Moth. You are a creature of the night. What are you doing here in the sunshine?

MOTH (*Slyly*): Persephone, aren't you hungry?

PERSEPHONE: Hungry? Hm-m. Well, yes.

MOTH: I've heard you're very fond of pomegranates. Rich, red, juicy pomegranates.

PERSEPHONE (*Clapping her hands*): Oh, yes, I adore pomegranates! But they're all gone.

MOTH: I know where there are some delicious pomegranates. (MOTH *beckons her.*) Come with me. It's not far. (PERSE-

PHONE *hesitates*.) You'll be back before your mother misses you.

PERSEPHONE (*Wavering*): Not far, you say?

MOTH (*Moving to exit left*): Only twenty steps. Follow me. (*She follows; they exit. Thunder is heard, as curtain closes*.)

* * * * *

SCENE 2

BEFORE RISE: SHEPHERD BOY *enters, carrying crook; a water flask hangs at his waist. He sits on edge of stage, puts down crook, and begins to play plaintive melody on flute, as* CHORUS *moves backdrop depicting rugged, bare mountains onto stage in front of curtain. There is a cleft in the mountains, center, where the curtain's opening is.*

SHEPHERD (*Looking around, uncomfortably*): This place seems strange to me. (*Shudders*) As soon as I find my lost lamb, I will go home. (*He rises and calls sheep*.) Ba-a-a. Ba-a! Where are you, little lamb? (MOTH *flutters on left, followed by* PER-SEPHONE. SHEPHERD *bows to* PERSEPHONE, *who nods her head at him, haughtily.* MOTH *flutters to center.* SHEP-HERD *addresses audience in an aside*.) By all the gods on Olympus! That is Princess Persephone. But why is she here, in this barren desert? (*Bows again to* PERSEPHONE) Good day, Princess. May I help you in some way?

PERSEPHONE (*Grandly*): How very nice of you. Perhaps you can tell me where the pomegranate tree is? I can't seem to find it, and I'm exceedingly hungry and thirsty.

SHEPHERD (*Astonished*): A pomegranate tree? Here? Why, not even a blade of grass could grow here. (*Holds water flask out to* PERSEPHONE) But if you are thirsty, please take some of my water.

PERSEPHONE (*Crossing to* SHEPHERD): Oh, thank you. (*He hands her flask and she drinks. While they are occupied with their backs to center stage,* MOTH *calls into opening between mountains*.)

MOTH (*Urgently*): Lord Hades! Come quickly. I have brought

you a princess! (HADES *enters through opening, followed by* BATS.) Look there, my Lord! (MOTH *points excitedly at* PERSEPHONE. *Thunder rolls loudly, as lights flash.*)

HADES (*Staring at* PERSEPHONE; *overwhelmed*): She is more beautiful than Aphrodite. (*To* MOTH) Well done, my small servant!

MOTH (*Crossing to* PERSEPHONE; *eagerly*): Pretty Persephone, come this way. I have a surprise for you. (SHEPHERD *sees* HADES, *gasps.*)

PERSEPHONE (*Excitedly*): A surprise? I love surprises! (*As she turns,* SHEPHERD *grabs her hand.*)

SHEPHERD (*Fearfully*): It's Hades, lord of the underworld. You must not go! I won't let him take you. (HADES *runs to* PERSEPHONE *and takes her other hand. She screams as they pull her in opposite directions. Thunder rolls.* HADES *waves to* BATS, *who surround* SHEPHERD, *flapping wings. He drops* PERSEPHONE'*s hand as he tries to fight them off.* HADES *laughs evilly and pulls* PERSEPHONE *through center opening.* BATS *and* MOTH *follow them off.* SHEPHERD *picks up crook, runs offstage left. After a moment,* CHORUS *enters and removes backdrop.*)

*   *   *   *   *

AT RISE: *Demeter's garden.* CHORUS *members have removed wreaths, now wear gray robes and sit somberly with heads bowed.* DEMETER, *also wearing long gray robe, paces upstage.* MOTH *flutters on right and hides.*

DEMETER (*Wringing her hands; distraught*): Where can my beloved Persephone be? Where has she gone? She promised not to leave the garden.

CHORUS (*Whispering eerily*): Persephone. Persephone. Persephone.

DEMETER: She could be anywhere. Lost. Frightened. Alone. (SHEPHERD *runs on left, throws himself at* DEMETER'*s feet.*)

SHEPHERD: Mighty Demeter! I have seen the Princess Persephone.

DEMETER (*Urgently*): Where is she, shepherd boy? Tell me!

SHEPHERD: Lord Hades has taken her to the underworld.

DEMETER (*Upset*): No! It can't be! (*Crosses down center shouting, shaking her fists*) Hades, hear me! Until Persephone returns to me, the sun will not shine in the heavens. (*Lights dim.*) No tree will bear leaves or fruit. No flower will bloom. Not a single blade of grass will grow upon the earth. (CHORUS *makes the sound of wind.*) And it will be winter— winter—winter! Forever! (DEMETER *moves left, sits on ground and weeps.*)

CHORUS: Winter . . . winter . . . winter. Forever. (1ST NARRATOR *enters right.*)

1ST NARRATOR: Demeter wept. So bitterly cold it was that her tears froze to drops of ice. And all the people in the hills and valleys of Greece wept with her, for they were cold and hungry. (SHEPHERD *rises, rubbing his arms and shivering. He exits right.*)

CHORUS (*Hands outstretched, pleading*): Mother Demeter, feed us. We are hungry. Send the sun to warm us. We are cold. Cold. Cold. (*They shiver.*)

1ST NARRATOR: At last Demeter could stand it no more. For the children of earth belonged to her, too. She called out to the greatest god of them all—Zeus. (*Exits*)

DEMETER (*Rising and stretching her arms out to heaven*): Father Zeus, hear me. Bring back my daughter! Bring back Persephone! (*Trumpet is heard off. Lights flash. ZEUS, followed by HERMES, enters left.*)

ZEUS: I hear you, Demeter. (DEMETER *runs to ZEUS.*) If I bring Persephone back, will the sun shine once again?

DEMETER (*Nodding*): Yes.

ZEUS: Will there be olives and grapes and roses for the children of earth?

DEMETER (*Eagerly*): Yes. Oh, yes!

ZEUS: Then, I will bring her back. But hear me! Persephone must not have eaten one meal in the underworld. If any food passes her lips, she must stay with Lord Hades forever.

DEMETER: I'm sure she will not eat. She is most particular

about her food. Oh, please bring her to me swiftly, Father Zeus!

ZEUS (*To* HERMES): Hermes, fly to the underworld. Tell Lord Hades I order him to release Princess Persephone. Then bring her back here to Demeter's garden.

DEMETER: Oh, thank you!

MOTH (*Crossing downstage; aside*): Oh, no! I must warn Lord Hades! (*Exits left*)

HERMES: Yes, Zeus. I am on my way. (*He mimes flying off right.*)

ZEUS: A bit of advice, Demeter: Don't boast about your child again. And try to keep her close to you.

DEMETER: I'll promise never to boast, though she is the most beautiful, the cleverest—

ZEUS (*Frowning*): Demeter!

DEMETER (*Lamely*): I mean, Persephone is nice enough—if you like princesses.

ZEUS: That's better. (*Curtain closes.*)

* * * * *

SCENE 3

SETTING: *Hades' palace, a cavern in shades of black and gray, with stalactites hanging from ceiling. Down center are two stalagmites cut into rough thrones.* HADES *is seated on one throne, watching* PERSEPHONE, *who sits on other, wailing loudly.* BATS *hover near her.* 1ST BAT *offers her a huge hand-kerchief.* 2ND BAT *has tray of food.*

1ST BAT (*Pleadingly*): Dry your tears, Princess Persephone.

2ND BAT: And you must eat. You haven't touched any food since Lord Hades brought you here.

PERSEPHONE (*Waving them away*): I don't want any food. I hope to starve. (*To* HADES) Then you'll be sorry. Aren't you tired of hearing me cry? Don't you want to send me home? (2ND BAT *puts tray down behind throne.*)

HADES (*Smiling*): Never. You will stay with me forever. Your tears are like a refreshing spring shower.

PERSEPHONE (*Aside; frustrated*): The worse I behave, the better Hades seems to like me! (*To* HADES, *meanly*) I am not charming. Look. (*She makes a face at him.* HADES *laughs heartily.*)

2ND BAT (*To* 1ST BAT; *shocked*): Look! Lord Hades is laughing.

1ST BAT: He never even smiled before. Things are certainly upside down in the underworld.

PERSEPHONE: I can be even uglier. (*She grimaces at him.* HADES *doubles up with laughter.*) Now, will you send me home?

HADES: Never, never, never. You make me laugh. Nobody ever made me laugh before.

PERSEPHONE: I will become a statue. Nobody laughs at statues. (*She folds her arms, closes her eyes, and freezes.* BATS, *alarmed, fan her vigorously.*)

2ND BAT: Lord Hades, what shall we do? She won't move.

HADES (*Rising; speaking dramatically*): Oh, Princess Persephone. You are lost to me forever. (HADES *motions to* BATS, *who cross down center with him.*) Don't worry. I know how to deal with my proud princess. Whatever I ask her to do—she will do the opposite. Watch. (BATS *follow* HADES, *who crosses behind* PERSEPHONE.) Persephone, you may remain a statue as long as you like. (*Sternly*) But whatever you do, don't sing. I repeat: Do not sing one of those sickly sweet songs your mother taught you. (HADES *smiles slyly and returns to his throne.* PERSEPHONE *rises haughtily and crosses downstage.*)

PERSEPHONE: You don't like sweet songs, Lord Hades? Then I shall sing the sweetest song I know. (*Music begins, and she sings song about spring, as* HADES *blissfully conducts an imaginary orchestra. After song,* PERSEPHONE *sits.*) There. I hope you hated that.

HADES (*Beaming*): Oh, yes. I hated that. It was dreadful.

PERSEPHONE (*Hopefully*): Was it dreadful enough to send me home?

HADES: From what I hear you weren't very nice to your mother. You disobeyed her.

PERSEPHONE (*Plaintively*): I was wrong to disobey her. If you let me go, I'll apologize to her. Please.

HADES: No, Persephone.

PERSEPHONE: Let me go, or I'll hold my breath until I expire! (*She inhales, blowing out her cheeks.*)

HADES (*Turning to her with great interest*): Will you? How fascinating. I've never seen anyone expire. (*As he stares at her, she exhales and wrinkles her nose in disgust.*)

PERSEPHONE: You don't amuse me.

HADES: I know. But you amuse me. That is why I will never let you go. (MOTH *flutters onstage, followed by* CHORUS.) Ah-h, here is my messenger and the shadows from the upper world. Welcome, my friends. This is Persephone. (*Indicating her*) Have you ever seen such a beautiful girl? (*She makes a face at him.*)

CHORUS (*Sighing sadly*): Ah-h, Persephone. Poor Persephone.

MOTH (*Pulling urgently at HADES' sleeve*): Lord Hades, I have something of great importance to tell you. (*Pulls him down right*)

HADES: Well, what is it?

MOTH: Zeus is sending Hermes to take Persephone back to the earth. He'll be here any minute.

HADES: No! (*Folding arms stubbornly*) I won't give her back.

MOTH: You will have to. Zeus is stronger than you are.

HADES: True. True. But—there must be a way to keep her here.

MOTH: There is. Has Persephone eaten anything?

HADES: Not a bite.

MOTH: Zeus says that if she eats anything in the underworld, she must stay here with you forever.

HADES (*Eagerly*): Then, bring me something for Princess Persephone to eat. Something she cannot resist!

MOTH (*Excitedly*): I know the very thing! (MOTH *flutters quickly off left and returns with pomegranate on tray. Pomegranate can be opened to disclose large red seeds.* MOTH *presents tray to* HADES, *who crosses to* PERSEPHONE, *thrusting tray under her nose.* PERSEPHONE *closes her eyes, turns away.*)

HADES (*Kindly*): Please, princess. Have a morsel of food.

PERSEPHONE: No. (CHORUS *gathers around her throne, anxiously*.)

CHORUS (*Sotto voce*): Do not eat, Persephone. Do not eat anything.

HADES (*Opening pomegranate, inhaling its fragrance*): M-m-m. There is no aroma as sweet as a fresh, juicy pomegranate. (PERSEPHONE *sniffs, smiles*.)

PERSEPHONE (*Pushing it away*): No, I will eat nothing here.

HADES (*With cunning*): Very well. Then there will be more for me. (*Pretending to eat*) M-m-m. Sweet, juicy seeds. (*As PERSEPHONE reaches for pomegranate, HADES snatches it away*.) Now, now. You had your chance.

PERSEPHONE (*Pulling pomegranate toward her*): It isn't polite to offer a person something and then take it away. Besides, I'm *so* hungry.

CHORUS (*Louder*): No, Persephone, no!

HADES, BATS *and* MOTH (*Sweetly*): Eat, Persephone, eat!

PERSEPHONE (*Pulling out three seeds*): Just three little seeds. One ... (*Thunder rolls after she eats each seed*.) Two ... Three ...

CHORUS: Woe. Oh, woe. What have you done, Persephone? What have you done? (*Trumpet sounds. HERMES runs on, carrying scroll. He crosses center, unrolls scroll*.)

HERMES (*Reading*): Hear the command of Zeus, Lord Hades. The Princess Persephone is to return to her mother, Demeter, immediately. (*Rerolls scroll*)

PERSEPHONE (*Running to HERMES*): I'm going home? (*To CHORUS, jubilantly*) Did you hear? I'm going home! (*To HADES, airily*) Goodbye, Lord Hades. (HADES *takes PERSEPHONE's hand and leads her back to throne*.)

HADES: Sit down, Persephone. You are not leaving me—ever!

HERMES (*Sternly, wagging a finger*): Zeus will be angry. You dare not disobey Zeus!

HADES (*Unconcerned*): I would not dream of disobeying Zeus. But is there not another line in that proclamation? Something about Persephone's eating?

HERMES (*Alarmed, to PERSEPHONE*): Persephone—answer

me truthfully. Did you eat while you were here in the under-world?

PERSEPHONE: Well, I ate only three little pomegranate seeds. (HADES *smiles broadly.*)

HERMES: This is most serious. You should not have eaten any-thing. Now, I must leave you here. (PERSEPHONE *wails and runs to* HERMES, *clinging to his arm.*)

PERSEPHONE (*Panicky*): No, no! Take me home. Take me to my mother!

HERMES: Quiet! Let me think. (*To* HADES) Lord Hades, I must take up this matter with Zeus.

HADES (*Smugly*): Do so, of course. (HERMES *starts off right.* PERSEPHONE *clings tightly to his arm.*)

PERSEPHONE (*Pleading*): You can't go without me. You must take me home.

HADES (*Relenting*): Very well. Let's all go to Demeter's garden and straighten out this whole matter. (HADES *takes* PER-SEPHONE's *free arm.*) Zeus will hear both sides of the ques-tion, and naturally I will win. Princess Persephone will be mine forever!

PERSEPHONE (*Whimpering*): Forever is much too long! (*Cur-tain closes.*)

* * * * *

SCENE 4

SETTING: *Demeter's garden, dimly lit.*

AT RISE: DEMETER *stands down left, still wearing gray robe.* CHORUS, *also in gray, is down right, huddled on benches, shivering. They make sounds of a desolate wind. Floral wreaths for each member of* CHORUS *are hidden under bench.*

DEMETER (*Calling out, mournfully*): Persephone . . .

CHORUS (*Echoing*): Persephone . . . (*They make more wind sounds until trumpet blares off. Lights flash and stage bright-ens.* ZEUS *enters.*)

ZEUS: Mother Demeter—

DEMETER: Father Zeus! (*Rushes to him, eagerly*) But where is Persephone? You promised me Persephone!

ZEUS (*Clearing his throat*): Ah, yes, Persephone. We must discuss the matter of Persephone. (*Trumpet sounds again. HERMES enters, with PERSEPHONE clutching his arm. HADES follows, holding her other hand. PERSEPHONE breaks away from them, runs to DEMETER, and embraces her.*)

PERSEPHONE: Mother! Oh, I am so sorry. I will never disobey you again! Will you ever forgive me?

DEMETER (*Joyfully*): My dear, dear child. Of course, I forgive you. Welcome home. (*As she spies HADES, he bows mockingly to her.*) Lord Hades, why are you here? (*She stands in front of PERSEPHONE, guarding her.*)

ZEUS: It seems, Demeter, there is a misunderstanding. Persephone was to be returned to you only if she had not eaten in the underworld. However, it seems that while she was with Lord Hades, she ate—

PERSEPHONE (*Interrupting*): Only three tiny pomegranate seeds.

DEMETER: Three pomegranate seeds. That's very little.

HADES (*Nonchalantly*): But the fact is—she did eat something. So, she belongs to me. (*He starts toward DEMETER, who holds her hand out warningly.*)

DEMETER: Take one step toward my daughter, and I will blow you back to the underworld. (*As she gestures, CHORUS howls like a strong wind.*)

PERSEPHONE: I was tricked. I didn't know I wasn't to eat anything.

ZEUS: This is truly a quandary. Quiet, everyone, while I think. (*He puts hands to head, closes eyes. All are quiet until ZEUS opens his eyes and smiles.*) I have the solution. Persephone will remain with Demeter for nine months of the year. But, for each pomegranate seed she ate, she must spend one month with Hades.

HADES (*Philosophically*): It's not what I hoped for. But, three months with Persephone are better than no months with Persephone.

DEMETER (*Coldly*): I promise you, Hades, every one of those months she spends with you will be winter, cold and gloomy.

ZEUS: So be it! (*Turns to DEMETER*) Now, Demeter. Will you

please do as you promised and bring back the sun, the fruit, and the flowers?

DEMETER (*Beaming*): I promise. (DEMETER *and* CHORUS *remove robes.* CHORUS *puts on wreaths.* DEMETER *puts on diadem. She waves her hand.*) Bring on the sunshine. (*Lights come up full.*) Enter blossoms, flowers, and fruit.

HADES (*Waving, airily*): Farewell, Persephone. I shall expect you in nine months. (*He exits.*)

DEMETER (*To* CHORUS): Come, children of earth. Spring has returned! (*To audience*) Come, everyone. Eat, drink, sing, dance! Let the music begin! (*Music is heard. All on stage may sing and dance as curtain closes.*)

THE END

Production Notes

PERSEPHONE

Characters: 4 male; 2 female; 5 male or female for Narrators, Moth, Bats. At least 6 male or female for chorus.

Playing Time: 20 minutes.

Costumes: All wear sandals. Narrators and Chorus wear short white tunics with blue Greek design on hems, floral wreaths. Later chorus adds gray robes. Demeter wears long green tunic, silver wheat stalk diadem. Later she adds somber gray robe. Persephone wears short yellow tunic, floral wreath. Moth wears gray tunic, wings, short antennae. Shepherd boy wears brown tunic, sheepskin cape, water flask at waist. Hades wears black tunic, boots, cape, crown. Bats wear black tunics, bat wings, hoods. Zeus wears long white tunic, purple and gold cape, crown, white beard. Hermes wears silver cap, short silver tunic, winged sandals, carries caduceus.

Properties: Cornucopia on a tray; basket of flower petals; crook and flute or recorder; large handkerchief; tray of food; pomegranate with seeds on a tray; scroll.

Sounds: Thunder, trumpet calls, Greek style music, flute or recorder solo, vocal spring song.

Lighting: Lights flash as indicated. Strobe light may be used in Scene 2 during the abduction of Persephone.

The King in the Kitchen

by Margaret E. Slattery

Characters

KING
PEASANT
PRINCESS
COOK
DUKE
GUARD
TWO KITCHEN MAIDS

SETTING: *The palace kitchen. Large table with pots and pans is upstage center. Several stools are placed around stage.*

AT RISE: COOK *is standing behind table, fussing with the pots and pans.* 1ST KITCHEN MAID *sits on a stool, peeling potatoes.* GUARD *enters, leading* PEASANT *by the arm. They start to walk across the stage.*

COOK (*Looking up*): Ho, there! You! Guard!

GUARD (*Stopping*): What is it, Cook?

COOK: Where are you taking that man?

GUARD: To the dungeon.

1ST KITCHEN MAID: Oh, my!

COOK: To the dungeon! Why, what's he done, poor fellow?

PEASANT: It was nothing, really. All I did was to ask the King for the Princess's hand in marriage.

GUARD: And him a peasant!

COOK: A peasant! Why, a peasant can't marry the Princess.

PEASANT: I don't see why not. I'm handsome, clever; I can sing—(*Sings*) La-la-la—I can dance, (*Dances around*) and I'm awfully fond of the Princess. She's awfully fond of me, too.

1ST KITCHEN MAID (*Staring*): She is?

PEASANT: Oh, my, yes. I come to the palace every day to deliver vegetables. The Princess thinks I'm wonderful, and I think she's wonderful and the King won't let me marry her just because I'm a peasant. It's a shame!

COOK: The Princess can't marry a peasant, I tell you. She has to marry someone rich and famous and noble and—

1ST KITCHEN MAID: Like the Duke.

PEASANT: The Duke is fifty years old, and stupid too. The Princess will never marry him.

COOK: The Princess will marry whomever her father tells her to marry. I'm sure he'll want a wealthy son-in-law because they say the Royal Treasury is almost empty.

GUARD: Besides, I told you not to ask the King today. If you'd asked him some other time, he might only have exiled you. But he's awfully upset today.

COOK: Why?

GUARD: It was the soup you sent up. He said it was horrible and threw it on the floor.

1ST KITCHEN MAID: Oh, my!

GUARD: Well, come on, peasant. (*Takes* PEASANT'*s arm and starts toward door.*)

PEASANT (*Sings to tune of "London Bridge"*): To the dungeon we must go, we must go, we must go. To the dungeon—(*Exits with* GUARD)

COOK (*Tearfully*): Oh, dear, the King didn't like the soup and I took such trouble with it.

2ND KITCHEN MAID (*Rushing in breathlessly*): Cook, Cook! Something terrible!

COOK: What's the matter?

2ND KITCHEN MAID: It's the King. He's coming here!

COOK (*Flustered*): What?

1ST KITCHEN MAID: The King! But he's never been in the kitchen before.

COOK: This is terrible. Here now, both of you start working. We'll have to straighten this kitchen up. (ALL *rush around, trying to straighten up, bumping into each other and dropping pots and pans.*)

KING (*Striding in*): Well, so this is the kitchen. (*Looks around*)

Hmm. At least you're working. Now, who made that awful soup?

COOK (*Curtseys*): I—I did, your Majesty.

KING: It was horrible! Horrible, do you hear me?

COOK: But, your Majesty, it's really not my fault. The ingredients we've been getting lately have been very inferior.

KING: Stuff and nonsense! I could make a better soup than that with my eyes shut. In fact, I'll do it!

2ND KITCHEN MAID (*Shocked*): Your Majesty!

KING: Yes, that's exactly what I'll do. And with my eyes shut. Now, out of my way, everybody. (*Marches behind table, looking at things on it. Picks up mixing spoon*) What's this?

COOK: A mixing spoon, your Majesty.

KING: Well, I guess I'll need it. Now let me see, what do I want?

2ND KITCHEN MAID: Maybe a bowl, your Majesty? (*Hands him a bowl*)

KING: Of course. The very thing. You're a smart girl. (*Puts bowl on table*) All right, I'm ready. Now, Cook, give me your apron.

COOK: But your Majesty—

KING: Hurry up! (*Takes apron from* COOK *and puts it on*) Now, I'll show you I can do this with my eyes shut. Tie something around my eyes, Cook.

COOK: Your Majesty, I don't really think—

KING: Be quick about it. (COOK *ties dish towel around* KING's *eyes.*) There! I'm ready to begin.

1ST KITCHEN MAID: What will you do first, your Majesty?

KING: Ah, let me see. Have we any water?

COOK: Oh, a nice kettle full, your Majesty.

KING: Well, pour some in the bowl. (COOK *pours some in.*) Now, I think I'd like a little flour. (COOK *dumps some in bowl.* KING *feels about table and picks up a bottle.*) What's this?

COOK: That's sauce, your Majesty. You don't want that for soup.

KING: Silence! That's exactly what I do want.

COOK: But, your Majesty—

KING: Who's making this, you or I?

COOK: You are, your Majesty.

KING: Very well then. (*Pours some sauce in bowl*) Now, what next?

1ST KITCHEN MAID: Maybe a little salt.

KING: That's just what I was about to say myself. Put some in. (KITCHEN MAID *pours a little salt in a teaspoon and dumps it in.*) How much did you put in?

1ST KITCHEN MAID: Oh, just a dash, as the good cookbooks say.

KING (*Screaming*): Cookbooks! Cookbooks! What do I care about cookbooks? You, Cook! Do you use cookbooks?

COOK: Oh, yes, your Majesty.

KING: Then that's what's the matter with your cooking. No imagination. Who ever heard of a dash of salt? We want this to have flavor, don't we? Here, where's that salt shaker? (*Pulls towel off eyes and grabs up shaker*) This is the way to do it. (*Holds salt shaker in both hands upside down over bowl. Shakes it furiously*)

COOK: Your Majesty, stop!

KING (*Putting down shaker*): There, that's better. (*Stirs it vigorously with mixing spoon. Enter* PRINCESS)

PRINCESS: Oh, here you are, Father. I've been looking everywhere for you.

KING: Now, now, my dear, don't bother me. I'm very busy.

PRINCESS: Father, I must talk to you. Have you seen my peasant anywhere today? He's usually here by eleven o'clock with the vegetables.

KING: Oh, him. Yes, I saw him and I threw him in the dungeon.

PRINCESS (*Shrieking*): *What!*

KING (*Looking around at things on table and stroking chin*): Now let me see, what next?

PRINCESS: But, Father, why?

KING: Are you still here? Go away.

PRINCESS: Father, why did you throw him in the dungeon?

KING: Who?

PRINCESS (*Stamping foot*): Father, stop it. You know who I mean.

KING: Oh, that peasant. Yes, I had to throw him in the dungeon. He had the colossal nerve to ask for your hand in marriage.

PRINCESS (*Clapping hands*): He did?

KING: Yes.

PRINCESS: Oh, Father, did he say I was wonderful?

KING: Yes, I guess he did.

PRINCESS: And beautiful?

KING: Yes.

PRINCESS: And perfect?

KING: Yes, yes, yes. Now leave me alone. I'm trying to think.

PRINCESS: You have to let him out of the dungeon. I want to marry him.

KING: Nonsense, you can't marry a peasant and you know it. Why he's as poor as a—a—what's that thing people are always being as poor as?

2ND KITCHEN MAID: A church mouse, your Majesty.

KING: That's it. He's as poor as a church mouse.

PRINCESS: I don't care. There's no one in the whole kingdom as clever and handsome and wonderful as my peasant.

KING: No doubt, no doubt, but he's still a peasant. What this family needs is a relative with some money. Why, just the other day the Prime Minister was telling me that we are as poor as—as—what was that again, Kitchen Maid?

2ND KITCHEN MAID: As church mice, your Majesty.

KING: Yes, as church mice. Now find someone with royal blood and lots of money and you can marry him.

PRINCESS (*Sitting down on chair and crying*): I want to marry my peasant.

KING: There, don't cry. Look at this nice thing Daddy made for you here. See? (*Holds bowl out to her*)

PRINCESS (*Sniffing*): What is it?

KING: I don't know. Why don't you taste it?

PRINCESS (*Peering at it*): It looks awful. What do you suppose it is, Cook?

COOK (*Coming over and taking bowl*): I'm sure I don't know, your Highness. (*Stirs it around a little*) It's not porridge.

KING: Of course it's not porridge. It's—it's—well, don't all of you stand there. What is it?

1ST KITCHEN MAID: I really don't think it's soup.

2ND KITCHEN MAID: Nor stew.

KING (*Stroking chin*): Hmm. This is a problem. (*Paces floor*) I have it! One of my wonderful ideas!

COOK: Oh, dear! (KITCHEN MAIDS *groan.*)

PRINCESS: Oh, Father, what is it this time?

KING: We'll have a contest. Whoever can guess what this is, wins a reward.

COOK: And what will the reward be, your Majesty?

KING: Why, the hand of the Princess in marriage, of course.

PRINCESS (*Jumping up*): Father!

KING: Certainly. You want to have a lovely wedding and get lots of presents, don't you?

PRINCESS: Yes, but—

KING: Now, let me see. Whom shall we have enter the contest?

1ST KITCHEN MAID: What about the Duke, your Majesty?

KING: Of course. Now, Kitchen Maid, run quickly and tell the Guard to tell the Footman to tell the Butler to tell the Chancellor to send the Duke here immediately. (*Exit* 1ST KITCHEN MAID)

PRINCESS: But I don't want to marry the Duke. He's the stupidest man in the palace.

2ND KITCHEN MAID: Or the country.

KING: Quiet, Kitchen Maid.

PRINCESS: She's right. There's no one as stupid as the Duke.

KING: Well he can't be so stupid he won't be able to tell what this is.

PRINCESS: How will you know if he's right anyway? You don't know what it is yourself.

KING: Nonsense! Why, it's—it's—(*Noise outside*) Ah, here comes the Duke now. (*Enter* GUARD *and* DUKE)

DUKE: Ah, your Majesty, good afternoon. Making a little tour of the kitchens, I see? We in this country are so fortunate to have a king who takes an interest in these simple matters. I have always said—

KING: Save that for an after-dinner speech.

DUKE: Ahem, Yes. And, your Highness. (*Bows to* PRINCESS) How beautiful you look today!

KING: All right, all right, let's get on with it. Now, Duke, can you tell me what I've made here in this bowl? (*Points to bowl* COOK *is holding*)

DUKE: Er—what *you've* made, your Majesty?

KING: Yes, of course I made it. And if you can tell me what it is, you win the hand of the Princess in marriage.

DUKE: Well, that would indeed be an honor. (*Takes bowl*) Now let me see. (*Stirs it around*) Ah-er—could it be—pudding?

KING: Pudding! Of course not, you nincompoop! Why would I make a pudding? You must really be stupid.

DUKE: Oh, no, I'm not—not at all, your Majesty. Maybe if I could just taste it—(*Takes some up on mixing spoon*) I'm sure it will be delicious. (*Puts spoon to mouth*)

KING: Well?

DUKE (*Choking and coughing*): Ah—ugh—er (*Claps hand over mouth*)

KING: What? Speak up man!

DUKE (*Muttering through hand over mouth*): Ug—mmph—mm—er—

KING: What is that idiot trying to say?

PRINCESS: I don't know. I told you he was stupid.

DUKE (*Sitting down on stool in corner*): Mmph—er—(*Covers face with hands*)

PRINCESS: Well, there you are, Father. He doesn't know what you've made so I don't have to marry him.

COOK: Congratulations, your Highness.

KING: Well, just because he's stupid doesn't mean everyone is. Let's see, whom shall we ask next. (*Looks about room*) Ah, what about you, Guard?

PRINCESS: Father!

GUARD: Oh, I'm afraid it wouldn't be fair for me to enter the contest, your Majesty. I'm already married.

KING: Well, don't stand there gaping. Go and find someone. (*Exit* GUARD)

PRINCESS: Father, this is so silly.

KING: Not at all. By now I'm curious myself to find out what I've made. It's too thick for soup.

COOK: And too thin for porridge. (*Enter* GUARD)

GUARD: Your Majesty, I have someone for the contest.

KING: Well, send him in, send him in.

GUARD (*Calling offstage*): All right, you. Come on in. (*Enter* PEASANT)

PRINCESS: My peasant! My very own dear peasant!

PEASANT (*Going down on one knee before* PRINCESS): My Princess! My very own dear Princess!

KING: What is all this?

PEASANT (*Rising*): Your Majesty, this is an unexpected pleasure. But you really didn't have to come all the way down to the kitchen to see me. I would have been glad to come upstairs to the throne room.

KING: Who let you out of the dungeon?

GUARD: I did, your Majesty. You said you wanted someone to enter the contest.

KING: Idiot! I didn't tell you to empty out the dungeon. Can't you find anyone in this palace with royal blood?

PRINCESS: Oh, this is wonderful! Father, please let him try. He's so clever!

PEASANT: Ah, thank you my dear. I've always thought so myself.

PRINCESS: You will win the contest so you can marry me, won't you, dear peasant?

PEASANT: Of course. What is the contest?

KING: I've made a perfectly wonderful dish of something or other, and whoever can tell me what it is, receives the hand of the Princess in marriage.

PEASANT: Your Majesty, I didn't know you could cook.

PRINCESS: Go ahead, dear. Guess what Father's made.

PEASANT (*Goes over to bowl. Sniffs. Stirs it a little. Sniffs again*): Ah!

KING: Delicious, isn't it?

PEASANT: Indeed, yes. (*Peers at it*) Let me see. Ah, of course! I have it. (*Sits down on chair*)

PRINCESS (*Excitedly*): What is it? What is it?

PEASANT: Now just a minute—(*Takes off shoe, picks up a little of the liquid on a spoon and drops it on edge of sole. Makes motions of pressing sole tight against shoe*) There!

KING: What are you doing?

PEASANT (*Putting shoe back on*): Now we'll see. (*Gets up and walks around a little. Then bends down and looks at shoe.*) Ah-ha, just as I thought! Congratulations, your Majesty.

KING: What for?

PEASANT: You have just made a bowl of the most wonderful glue I've ever seen.

KING (*Bellowing*): What!

PRINCESS: Glue!

COOK: Glue!

KITCHEN MAIDS (*Together*): Glue!

PEASANT: You are a genius! An absolute genius. Why this glue is strong as iron. See? (*Lifts up foot*) The sole of my shoe was almost falling off. Now it's on tight as new.

PRINCESS: Wonderful!

KING: Thank you, daughter.

PRINCESS: No, I mean my peasant.

KING: Well, I made the glue. (*Turning to* PEASANT) So you think I'm a genius, do you?

PEASANT: Certainly. You'll be famous. Rich, too. We'll put this in bottles and sell it everywhere. Let's see. We could call it King's Glue.

Go out today

And buy King's Glue.

Through thick and thin,

It sticks with you.

PRINCESS: I knew you were clever. We gave some to the Duke and he didn't know what it was.

PEASANT: The Duke ate some? (*Rushes over to* DUKE. *Peers at him*) Just as I thought. His teeth are stuck together.

KITCHEN MAIDS (*Together*): Oh my! (*Hurry over and look at* DUKE)

KING: It serves him right. The stupid fellow ought to have known better than to eat glue. Here, guard, take him off to the Royal Dentist.

DUKE (*Getting up*): Mmph! (GUARD *takes him by arm and leads him off.*)

KING (*Stirring spoon in bowl*): It does look a little like glue. How clever I am.

PRINCESS (*To* PEASANT): You've won the contest! Now we can be married.

KING: This is terrible. What will my Prime Minister say when he hears I am to have a peasant for a son-in-law?

PEASANT: Never you mind. When we tell him how much money will go into the Royal Treasury from your glue, he won't care about anything. Of course, it will mean you will have to spend most of your time in the kitchen.

KING: It's not so bad down here. And I'll always have something to eat. As for you, Cook—

COOK: Y-y-yes, your Majesty?

KING: Off to cooking school you go, and don't come back till you have a diploma. Take the Kitchen Maids with you. (*Exit* COOK *and* KITCHEN MAIDS)

KING: Now you two run along. I want to start working.

PEASANT: All right, your Majesty. See you at the wedding. (*Exit* PRINCESS *and* PEASANT)

KING (*Fussing about with pots and pans*): Now let me see. What did I do first? (*Places pan in front of him and pours some water in*) Did I put one cup of flour in? Or was it two? And how much salt? (*Picks up shaker and shakes some in*) Oh, well— (*Stirs it up, singing*)

Go out today
And buy King's Glue.
Through thick and thin,
It—sticks—with—you!

THE END

Production Notes

THE KING IN THE KITCHEN

Characters: 4 male; 4 female.

Playing Time: 20 minutes.

Costumes: The King, Princess and Duke are dressed as royalty, the Guard wears a soldier's uniform, the Cook and Maids wear huge aprons, and the Peasant a simple but colorful peasant costume.

Properties: Pots, pans, knife, potatoes, spoon, bowl, dish towel, bottle, kettle of water, flour, salt shaker, teaspoon.

Setting: The palace kitchen. A large table loaded with pots and pans is upstage center. Several stools are placed around stage. Other furnishings, such as a stove, cupboards, etc., may be added.

Lighting: No special effects.

The Lake at the End of the World

by Janet Brown

Characters

EMPEROR OF THE INCAS
PRINCE, *his son*
CHANCELLOR, *Emperor's advisor*
TWO MAIDENS OF THE SUN
MOTHER
FATHER
MATA, *their daughter*
CONDOR ⎫
TUPAC ⎭ *their sons*
THE CHASQUIS, *relay messenger*
THREE BIRDS
GIANT CRAB
ALLIGATOR
RED FLYING SNAKE
TWO GUARDS
TOWNSPEOPLE, *extras*
GODS ⎫
MONSTERS ⎭ *offstage voices*

SCENE 1

TIME: *About 1400 A.D.*
SETTING: *Emperor's court. Throne is left; pallet, center; small altar, right.*
AT RISE: PRINCE *lies on pallet as* EMPEROR *kneels beside him, stroking his forehead.* CHANCELLOR *stands nearby.* GUARDS *stand at attention on either side of throne.*

EMPEROR (*Soothingly*): Try to sleep, my son. (*To* CHANCEL-LOR) Is there nothing else you can try?

CHANCELLOR: Your Majesty, we have tried every remedy known to the Incas. Your son's life is in the hands of the gods.

EMPEROR (*Shaking his head*): I have prayed for hours. I have sacrificed llamas on the altar.

CHANCELLOR: Everyone in the Empire fears for the life of your son. If you grow old without an heir, the whole Empire will be in danger. (PRINCE *groans*.) Let us gather all the people in the city to plead with the gods to protect the Inca Empire.

EMPEROR: Very well. Guards, call my people together. And ask the Sun Maidens to come from the Temple of the Sun to lead us in prayer. (GUARDS *bow and exit*. PRINCE *moans*.) Be brave, my son. (TOWNSPEOPLE *enter right and left, kneel or stand near altar, facing audience*. MAIDENS OF THE SUN *enter, go to either side of altar and raise their arms*.)

1ST MAIDEN: Oh, Creator! Pachacamac!

ALL: Oh, Creator! Pachacamac!

2ND MAIDEN: God of the Sun, Goddess of the Earth!

ALL: God of the Sun, Goddess of the Earth!

1ST MAIDEN: Heal our Prince!

ALL: Heal our Prince! (*A cymbal crash is heard offstage. Smoke rises behind altar. [See Production Notes]* TOWNSPEOPLE *murmur in awe and point to altar*.)

GODS (*Offstage; softly*): Drink the water from the lake at the end of the world. (*Louder*) Drink the water from the lake at the end of the world. (*Loudly*) Drink the water from the lake at the end of the world! (*Another cymbal crash is heard, another puff of smoke, and a golden cup appears on the altar.* TOWNSPEOPLE *gasp*. MAIDENS *pick up cup and carry it downstage*.)

2ND MAIDEN: Your Majesty, the gods have answered our prayers. If the Prince drinks the waters from the lake at the end of the world, he will be cured.

1ST MAIDEN: He must drink the water from this sacred cup.

EMPEROR (*Eagerly*): At last, a cure! Chancellor, how can we find this lake?

CHANCELLOR (*Shaking his head; sadly*): No one has ever been there. It does not appear on any map.

EMPEROR (*Desperately*): We must search for it! I will go myself!

PRINCE (*Weakly*): No, Father, please do not leave me!

1ST TOWNSPERSON: We will search for the lake, Your Majesty!

TOWNSPEOPLE (*Ad lib agreement*): Yes! We will find the lake! We'll bring some water to the Prince. (*Etc.*)

EMPEROR (*Pleased*): Yes, that is the best plan. Guards, send my relay runners—my chasquis—all over the Inca Empire. Tell them this: The Emperor offers a great reward to anyone who can find this magic lake and cure my son. (GUARDS *bow and exit. Curtain*)

* * * * *

SCENE 2

TIME: *Mid-afternoon, a few days later.*

SETTING: *Outside, on a farm in the mountains. Backdrop may be painted with mountains, a farm house, and an Inca castle in the distance.*

AT RISE: MATA *and* MOTHER *are planting potatoes.* FATHER *and* TUPAC *are hoeing.* CONDOR *enters, out of breath.*

CONDOR (*Panting*): Father, a chasquis is coming with a message!

MATA (*Excitedly*): Oh, what can it be?

MOTHER (*Continuing her planting*): He is just on his way to meet the next relay runner in the village.

CONDOR: No, Mother, he is coming here. I saw him from the hillside. He turned off the road when he saw our farm! (CHASQUIS *enters, bows.*)

CHASQUIS: Greetings from the Emperor.

OTHERS (*Enthusiastically*): Greetings!

CHASQUIS: The Emperor wishes all his subjects to know that the Prince is very ill. The gods have said that the Prince can be cured, if he will drink the water from the lake at the end of the world.

TUPAC: I have never heard of this lake.

CHASQUIS: No one has ever been there before. The Emperor offers a great reward to anyone who can bring back this water and save the life of his son. Farewell. (*Bows and exits*)

CONDOR (*Excitedly*): A great reward! Tupac, let us go and look for this lake.

FATHER (*Shocked*): Condor, what are you saying? We need you here at home, to work the farm.

CONDOR: But, Father, when we bring back this magic water, the Emperor will make us rich. We will never have to work again!

MOTHER (*Fearfully*): It is too dangerous! Who knows what monsters you might meet at the end of the world!

CONDOR: We are not afraid. We will be heroes!

TUPAC (*Nervously*): Monsters? Well, (*Hesitantly*) I–I do not know, Condor. How will Mother and Father work the farm with only little Mata here to help?

MATA (*Offended*): What do you mean, *little* Mata? Anyway, I am going with you!

FATHER (*Firmly*): No, you are too young, Mata.

MATA (*Pleading*): But think of the Emperor! Think of the little Prince, who may be dying!

MOTHER (*Sorrowfully*): Oh, that poor young boy! (*To* FATHER) If our sons can help the Prince, I think they should try.

FATHER (*Considering*): Perhaps you are right. If the Emperor needs our help, we should not be selfish. (*To* CONDOR *and* TUPAC) Boys, you may go, but be back before the harvest.

MATA: But what about me? Who will keep the boys out of trouble?

MOTHER: Daughter, we need you here. Now come and help me pack some corn and a jug of chicha for your brothers' journey. (MATA, *downcast, follows* MOTHER *off as curtain closes.*)

* * * * *

SCENE 3

TIME: *Early morning, a few months later.*

SETTING: *Same. A basket with a pottery jar and a cloth bag of corn in it are on the floor up left.*

AT RISE: MOTHER *is checking potato crop; she holds potato in her hand*. MATA *enters carrying pail of water*.

MOTHER (*Holding out potato*): Look, the potatoes are ready for harvest. Take the water to the house and bring a basket back with you. Where is your father?

MATA: He is letting the llamas out to pasture. I fed the ducks and geese.

MOTHER (*Shaking her head*): There is too much work to be done around here. (*Sighs*) When will your brothers come home? (FATHER *rushes on*.)

FATHER: A chasquis is coming! Maybe he has news of our sons! (CHASQUIS *enters and bows*.)

CHASQUIS: Greetings.

MOTHER *and* FATHER (*Eagerly*): Greetings.

CHASQUIS (*Matter-of-factly*): Your sons, Condor and Tupac, are at the Emperor's castle. They are locked in the dungeon there.

FATHER (*Shocked*): What?

MOTHER: Are they all right?

CHASQUIS: They are all right. The Emperor was merciful.

MATA: What did they do?

CHASQUIS: They brought water that they claimed was from the lake at the end of the world. But they lied. When the Sun Maidens poured the water into the sacred golden cup, it ran right out again.

FATHER (*In disbelief*): Why would they do such a thing?

CHASQUIS: They were tired of looking. They thought the Emperor might reward them for their efforts, at least, and then they could come home. The lazy foolish boys! The Emperor ordered them locked up until the true water is found.

MOTHER: Oh, this is terrible!

CHASQUIS: I must go now. I have other messages to relay in the village. Farewell. (*Bows and exits*)

FATHER: Our poor, foolish sons!

MATA: Now will you let me go?

FATHER: Go where? You cannot help Condor and Tupac in their dungeon cell.

MATA (*Confidently*): Yes I can. If I find the lake at the end of the world, my brothers will be freed.

MOTHER (*Shaking head*): Oh, no, Mata. We need you now more than ever.

MATA: I will be very careful, and I will come back quickly, whether I find the water or not.

FATHER (*To* MOTHER; *seriously*): She is a wise child. Maybe we should let her try. (MOTHER *considers, then nods solemnly.*)

MATA: Oh, thank you, Mother. Thank you, Father.

MOTHER: Here, Mata, take some chicha to drink, and some dried corn. (*Picks up basket and hands it to* MATA) Be careful and hurry back.

MATA: I will. Goodbye! (FATHER *puts his arm around* MOTHER. *They exit left sadly.* MATA *walks once around stage as if on a journey, then sits, rubs her feet.*) I can't walk any farther today. (*Takes bag of corn from basket.* BIRDS *enter, gather around* MATA.) Oh, what beautiful birds! Here, are you hungry? (*She scatters some corn on stage.*) Have some corn. (BIRDS *peck at corn.*)

1ST BIRD: Thank you, little girl!

MATA (*Amazed*): You can speak!

2ND BIRD: What are you doing alone in these woods, little one?

MATA: I am looking for the lake at the end of the world.

3RD BIRD: You won't find it. Many people have tried and failed.

MATA: But I must try! (BIRDS *huddle together a moment, twittering.*)

1ST BIRD: Little girl, because you fed us, we will help you get to the lake.

3RD BIRD: Each of us will give you a feather. If you put them together, they will make a magic fan that will carry you anywhere you want to go.

MATA (*Delighted*): Oh, thank you! (*Each* BIRD *gives* MATA *a feather.*)

1ST BIRD: Before you go, we must warn you. At the lake, you will meet three monsters.

2ND BIRD: A crab as big as a pig—

3RD BIRD: An alligator—

1ST BIRD: And a red, flying snake.

2ND BIRD: They guard the sacred lake from trespassers.

MATA (*Concerned*): If I meet them what should I do?

2ND BIRD: Just wave the magic fan, and the monsters will go to sleep.

MATA: Will you come with me?

3RD BIRD: No, we must go another way. Just remember what we told you and you will be safe.

MATA: All right. Thank you and goodbye! (BIRDS *exit*. MATA *makes a fan with feathers*.) A magic fan. (MATA *holds up fan and takes basket in other hand*.) Take me to the lake at the end of the world. (*She runs out, waving fan in front of her as if it is pulling her along. Curtain*)

* * * * *

SCENE 4

TIME: *A moment later.*

SETTING: *Lake at the end of the world. Blue throw rug down left represents edge of lake. Backdrop is painted with fanciful plants.*

AT RISE: MATA *runs in right, as though pulled by fan. She stops and looks around fearfully.*

MONSTERS (*Offstage; gruffly*): This is the lake at the end of the world. Keep away! Keep away! (MATA *takes a deep breath*.)

MATA (*Firmly*): But I must take some water for the Emperor's dying child. (*As she puts down basket and takes out jug*, CRAB *enters left, walking sideways*. MATA *jumps back, startled*.) A giant crab!

CRAB (*Unkindly*): Do not approach the sacred lake! (MATA *defiantly takes step forward*. CRAB *comes toward her waving claws menacingly*. MATA *screams, drops feathers, and runs a few steps away*.) Go back! Go back!

MATA: What shall I do? (*She raises her arms; pleading*) Earth Mother, help me! (*As she lowers arms, she spots feathers*.) The feathers! I almost forgot what the birds told me. (*She edges over, picks up feathers as* CRAB *waves claws. He starts for her and she waves fan*.) Sleep, Crab! (CRAB *goes to sleep.* ALLIGATOR *enters right*.) An alligator!

ALLIGATOR (*Harshly*): You put the crab to sleep, but I am not tired!

MATA: Oh, but you are! Sleep, Alligator! (*She waves fan.* ALLIGATOR *sleeps.* SNAKE *enters.*) A red, flying snake.

SNAKE (*Hissing threateningly*): I will succeed where the others have failed. (MATA *waves fan;* SNAKE *sleeps.*)

MATA (*Relieved*): Thank you, Earth Mother! Thank you, little birds. Now, I will fill my chicha jar with water. (*Goes to rug, mimes filling jug. Then she waves fan in front of her.*) Take me to the Emperor's castle! (*Runs out. Curtain*)

* * * * *

SCENE 5

TIME: *A moment later.*

SETTING: *Emperor's castle.*

AT RISE: PRINCE *is lying on pallet.* EMPEROR *is bending over him anxiously.* GUARDS *stand on either side of throne.* MATA *runs into room pulled by fan and carrying jug.*

MATA (*Looking around*): Where is the Emperor? I must speak to His Majesty!

EMPEROR (*Looking up; startled*): Guards, how did this girl get in here? Arrest her! (GUARDS *start to take* MATA's *arms. She waves fan.*)

MATA: Sleep! (GUARDS *fall asleep.*)

EMPEROR (*Shouting*): What have you done? (*Stepping back, fearfully*) What sort of magic is this? (CHANCELLOR, MAIDENS, *and* TOWNSPEOPLE *rush on.*)

MATA: Your Majesty, please! I mean no harm. I have come to help your son. (EMPEROR *holds up his hands, gesturing to others to wait.*)

EMPEROR (*To* MATA; *gravely*): I see that you have great power. But nothing can help my son except water from the lake at the end of the world.

MATA: I have that water, Your Majesty. (*Holds up jug*) Here it is.

EMPEROR (*Doubtfully*): Can it be true? So many have tried to fool us.

PRINCE (*Struggling to sit up*): Father, let me try it.

EMPEROR: Maidens, bring the golden cup. (MAIDENS *bring cup;* MATA *pours water into it from jug.*)

1ST MAIDEN: The water stayed in the cup!

2ND MAIDEN (*Taking cup and kneeling beside* PRINCE): Here, Your Highness, drink! (EMPEROR *helps prop up* PRINCE *so he can drink.* PRINCE *drinks some water, then stops and sits up on his own. He takes another sip and stands up.*)

EMPEROR (*Overjoyed*): How do you feel, son?

PRINCE: I feel much better. I think I must be cured! (*Everyone claps and cheers.* PRINCE *turns to* MATA.) Thank you. You saved my life. Father, she deserves a reward.

EMPEROR (*Happily*): By all means! (*To* MATA) What would you like as your reward?

MATA: You have two young men, Tupac and Condor, locked in your dungeons. They are my brothers, and I would like their release as my reward.

EMPEROR: Guards, go and bring—Guards! (GUARDS *continue to sleep.* EMPEROR *turns to* MATA.)

MATA (*Raising fan*): Awaken! (GUARDS *wake up, shake their heads.*)

EMPEROR: Guards, bring Tupac and Condor from the dungeons. (GUARDS *exit.*)

PRINCE (*To* MATA): Who are you?

MATA: My name is Mata. I am a farmer's daughter. (GUARDS *reenter with* TUPAC *and* CONDOR, *who cower fearfully and do not see* MATA. GUARDS *force brothers to kneel in front of* EMPEROR.)

EMPEROR (*Sternly*): Tupac, Condor, you tried to deceive your Emperor. Do you understand the seriousness of this crime?

CONDOR: I knew it was a terrible idea, Your Majesty, but my brother insisted—

TUPAC (*Shocked*): What! It was your idea!

MATA (*Warningly*): Tupac! Condor!

CONDOR (*Surprised*): Mata!

MATA: Ask the Emperor for forgiveness, and maybe he will release you.

TUPAC (*Imploringly*): Your Majesty, we were wrong. Please forgive us.

CONDOR: We are very sorry, Your Majesty.

EMPEROR: Very well. I release you, if that is Mata's wish. You may rise. (*The brothers stand.*)

CONDOR (*Surprised*): Mata's wish? We are free because of little Mata?

PRINCE: Your sister brought back the *true* water, and cured my illness.

TUPAC (*Sincerely*): You saved our lives, Mata. Thank you.

PRINCE: She saved my life, too. Father, she deserves a greater reward than this.

EMPEROR: You are right, son. What do you ask, Mata?

MATA: A bigger farm for my family, with many llamas and alpacas, and lots of help to work the farm.

EMPEROR: Consider it done! Now, gather everyone in the city for a grand celebration! (*All cheer. Curtain*)

THE END

Production Notes

THE LAKE AT THE END OF THE WORLD

Characters: 5 male; 4 female; 10 male or female for Chancellor, Chasquis,
Guards, and animals; as many extras as desired for Townspeople and offstage voices.

Playing Time: 20 minutes.

Costumes: Simple, belted tunics or oversized t-shirts for men and women.
Emperor and Prince wear gold crowns; others may wear cloth head bands.
Birds wear hats with orange beaks and carry large construction paper feathers in each hand. Three of these feathers become magic fan. Crab, Alligator,
and Snake wear appropriate masks.

Setting: Scenes 1 and 5: Court of the Emperor. A throne is left center. Pallet
is center, and an altar is right center. Scenes 2 and 3: Outside on a farm.
Backdrop may be painted with mountains of Ecuador, farmhouse, and Inca
castle in the distance. Or scenes may be played before curtain, with blackout
between scenes. Scene 4: Lake at the end of the world. Blue rug left suggests
lake waters. Backdrop, painted with fanciful plants, may be used.

Properties: Golden vase; two hoes; bucket; basket with pottery jug and sack
of dried corn in it. NOTE: Stagehand, hidden behind altar, squeezes container
of baby powder to create illusion of smoke, and holds up gold vase to make
it seem to rise from altar.

Sound: Gong or symbol when gods speak. Noises may be used to accompany
entrance of animals: bells for birds; a guiro for crab; wood block for alligator;
maracas for snake.

Lighting: No special effects. If Scenes 2 and 3 are played before curtain, blackout may indicate passage of time.

The Emperor's New Year

by Sheila L. Marshall

Characters

HERALD
SNAKE
DOG
HORSE
DRAGON
TIGER
RAT
RABBIT
ROOSTER
MONKEY
OX
PIG
RAM
CAT
TOWNSPEOPLE, *extras*
STORYTELLER
EMPEROR
PAGE
THREE COURTIERS
OTHER COURTIERS, *extras*

TIME: *Long ago.*
SETTING: *Town square. Played before curtain.*
BEFORE RISE: STORYTELLER *is seated on apron of stage, left.*
  SNAKE, DOG, HORSE, DRAGON, TIGER, RAT, RABBIT,
  ROOSTER, MONKEY, OX, PIG, RAM, CAT, *and* TOWNS-
  PEOPLE *enter right and left. Some* TOWNSPEOPLE *form
  small groups to talk; others stroll back and forth.* CAT *curls*

115

up to sleep far right. DOG *sits howling;* MONKEY *does a somersault; other animals improvise appropriate actions; activity suggests bustling town.*

HERALD (*Entering right, carrying scroll and ringing large bell*): Hear ye! Hear ye! (TOWNSPEOPLE *and animals gather around, except* CAT, *who remains asleep.*) Hear ye! Hear ye! (*Reading from scroll*) His Majesty, the most high Emperor of China, has invited everyone to join him at the palace on Saturday morning to welcome the new year.

ALL (*Ad lib*): Wonderful! What fun! How exciting! (*Etc.* HERALD *exits.* TOWNSPEOPLE *scatter excitedly and exit. Animals cluster before curtain.* CAT *remains asleep.*)

SNAKE: I've never been to the palace before.

DOG: Nor I! I'm going to wear my new collar!

HORSE: And I'll brush my mane to look my very finest.

DRAGON: We'll all want to look our best for the Emperor. It's very gracious of him to invite lowly animals to his feast. How can we thank him?

TIGER: Let's take him a magnificent gift to show how grateful we are for this honor.

RAT: A good idea, my friend, but alas, a poor rat like me has no money to buy gifts and no chance to earn any in time for the feast.

RABBIT: I, too, have no funds to spare. What little I have is spent taking care of my large family. What can we do? (*Animals become quiet and sad.*)

ROOSTER (*Suddenly*): Cock-a-doodle-do! I know what to do!

ALL (*Ad lib*): What? Tell us! Speak up ! (*Etc.*)

ROOSTER: Let's each perform what we do best for the Emperor. (*Preening*) I, for one, have a fantastic voice. Every morning, the whole barnyard wakes up to listen to me. I will sing my most beautiful song for him.

MONKEY: What a good idea. I'm quite an acrobat. I'll do some gymnastic tricks for His Majesty.

OX: I'll perform feats of strength to surprise and delight our host.

PIG: We'd better practice. We have only until Saturday to get ready.

RAM: This is going to be fun. Let's get started. (*Animals spread out, and all begin to rehearse:* OX *lifts weights;* ROOSTER *pantomimes singing, etc.*)

STORYTELLER (*Rising and coming center*): Now, the noise wakened the cat, who had been asleep and had not heard the herald's announcement. She decided to find out why the others were working so hard. (CAT *stretches lazily, slowly ambles over to* DOG.)

CAT: Meow, friend dog. Why is everyone so busy?

DOG (*Not looking up*): Bow-wow, friend cat. We're practicing.

CAT: Practicing what?

DOG (*Putting his hands on hips and looking at* CAT): Why, to entertain the Emperor for his new year's party! Didn't you hear the proclamation?

CAT (*Loftily*): No, I was taking a nap.

DOG (*Annoyed*): Well, you should have been listening! It was very important. Everyone is invited to the new year's party at the palace.

CAT: A royal party. How delightful! What day is it?

DOG (*Impatiently*): Sunday. The party is Sunday. Now, please go away and leave me to my practicing. (DOG *resumes practicing.* CAT *goes right, curls up, and goes to sleep again.*)

STORYTELLER: Neither the cat nor the dog realized that the dog had told the cat the wrong day for the party. On Saturday morning, all the animals lined up to parade to the palace except the cat, who thought the party was the next day. (STORYTELLER *returns to apron, sits.* CAT *remains asleep on stage. Other animals line up in order of Chinese years:* HORSE, RAM, MONKEY, ROOSTER, DOG, PIG, RAT, OX, TIGER, RABBIT, DRAGON, *and* SNAKE. *They parade around stage before stopping, center. Curtain opens to reveal throne room, decorated for party. Throne is on raised platform center.*)

* * * * *

SETTING: *Chinese throne room, decorated for a party.*

AT RISE: EMPEROR *sits on throne.* HERALD *stands on one*

side of throne; PAGE, *holding large red envelopes, stands on the other.* COURTIERS *are lined up next to* PAGE.

HERALD (*Loudly*): Your Majesty! May I present the animals of the city! (*March music is played as animals parade in, each bowing in turn to* EMPEROR. *Then* EMPEROR *stands and holds his hands up for silence. Music stops.*)

EMPEROR (*Grandly*): Welcome, my friends. Welcome to my royal house to celebrate the beginning of a new year.

DRAGON: Your Majesty, we wish you happiness in the coming year and thank you for inviting us to this royal party.

EMPEROR (*Gesturing to* PAGE): These envelopes are New Year's gifts for you. (*Takes an envelope*) This one with a picture of a peach is a wish for long life. (*Takes another envelope*) The second is decorated with a fish, a sign that there will be plenty of food for everyone. (*Sits and gestures to* 1ST COURTIER, *who takes an envelope from* PAGE)

1ST COURTIER (*Holding up envelope*): This one with a picture of bamboo symbolizes a wish for peace.

2ND COURTIER (*Taking envelope from* PAGE *and holding it up*): This picture of a large bat stands for many blessings.

3RD COURTIER (*Taking two envelopes and holding them up*): Each of these envelopes contains money in equal amounts to wish you a prosperous new year.

SNAKE: Your Majesty, we have prepared some entertainment to express our thanks.

EMPEROR: How kind of you. Let the show begin. (*Animals, in turn, introduce themselves and then perform.* HORSE: *prancing or dancing;* RAM: *a show of strength by butting a small punching bag;* MONKEY: *handstands or cartwheels;* ROOSTER: *singing;* DOG: *sitting up, fetching small ball, which* PIG *rolls around with his snout;* OX: *lifting weights;* RABBIT: *hopping;* TIGER *and* DRAGON: *roaring;* SNAKE: *a slow dance emerging from a large tub or basket while* RAT *plays an appropriate tune on recorder or flute. At the conclusion,* EMPEROR *applauds enthusiastically.*)

EMPEROR: Wonderful! Wonderful! Thank you all. This is the nicest party we have ever had in the palace.

RAM: Your Majesty, we again wish you the happiest of new years.

ANIMALS (*Ad lib*): Goodbye! Happy new year! Thank you! (*Etc. Animals again line up in order of Chinese years. As they parade across stage,* CAT *wakes up and stretches. She looks at animals curiously.*)

EMPEROR (*Standing*): Listen to me, everyone! (*Animals, including* CAT, *all turn to listen to* EMPEROR.) Watching all of you loyal subjects has given me an extraordinary idea. From now on, the years in the Chinese calendar will be named after each of the animals who came to my party today. (CAT *hisses and claws the air.*) This year will be the year of the Horse. Thereafter we will have the year of the Ram, the year of the Monkey, the year of the Rooster and so on until each of the animals has been honored in turn. When we have made the full round, we will start over, so that nobody will ever forget the joy you have given me today.

ALL (*Ad lib*): What a wonderful idea! Hurray! Hail to our Emperor! (*Etc.*)

STORYTELLER: And so from that day to this, the years of the Chinese calendar have been named after the animals who attended the Emperor's party on that long-ago New Year's Day. (*Animals parade past* CAT, *who hisses and claws the air. As* DOG *passes her,* CAT *arches her back and tries to scratch* DOG, *who backs up and barks.* CAT *hisses and chases* DOG *offstage.*) It is always easier to blame another for our troubles, so the cat became very upset with the dog. That is why, to this day, cat and dog are not friends.

THE END

Production Notes

THE EMPEROR'S NEW YEAR

Characters: 1 male for Emperor; 19 male or female for other parts; as many male and female extras as desired for Townspeople and Courtiers.

Playing Time: 15 minutes.

Costumes: Emperor, Herald, Page, and Courtiers wear royal attire. Animals wear leotards and appropriate accessories. Storyteller and Townspeople wear peasant costumes with large Chinese hats, fans, etc.

Properties: Bell and large scroll; large red envelopes with pictures on them as indicated in text; ball; other properties as desired for animals' acts.

Setting: Town square is played before the curtain. Behind the curtain is Chinese throne room decorated for a party. Lanterns, fans, and other Chinese accessories are placed around. A throne on a platform is center stage.

Sound: March music is played as animals enter palace. Other music may be played as desired during acts.

Lighting: No special effects.

The Crowded House

by Eva Jacob

Characters

FATHER, *John the Carpenter*
MOTHER
MOLLY
JOAN
MEG
MARY ANN
MARTIN   *their children*
WILLY
TOM
JOSEPH
GRANNY
BARTHOLOMEW, *the Wise Man*
GOAT
6 CHICKENS
DONKEY, *played by two actors*

SCENE 1

SETTING: *The only room of a cottage. Small table is upstage center. To right is butter churn. Rough, unfinished table is left. Exit is right.*

AT RISE: *Everyone is busy and the room crowded. Upstage center, GRANNY is rolling out a piecrust. MARY ANN is churning butter. Downstage right, MOTHER and MOLLY are winding wool; MOLLY holds the skein while MOTHER winds. Downstage center sits MEG, surrounded by her dolls; she is pouring tea for them out of an imaginary teapot. Downstage left, TOM and JOSEPH are sorting apples from one basket*

121

into two others. At left of stage, FATHER *is hammering nails into a table he is making; at rise, he gives a few actual hammer blows, then pantomimes, once others start talking. At center of stage,* MARTIN *and* WILLY *are playing "wheelbarrow";* MARTIN *walks on his hands while* WILLY *holds his ankles.* JOAN *is trying to sweep the floor. Throughout the entire scene, the characters pantomime to each other, as if to say: "You're in my way. Please move aside."*

MEG (*Rescuing her dolls, as* MARTIN *and* WILLY'S *"wheelbarrow" approaches*): Oh me, oh my! I *wish* we weren't so crowded!

WILLY: So do I! There's not even room for the mice in this house. (MARTIN *pads toward butter churn,* WILLY *following.*)

MARY ANN (*Gesturing*): Shoo, Willy! Martin—scat! How can I churn my butter? (MARTIN *pads toward* FATHER, WILLY *following.*)

GRANNY (*Turning around*): Sakes-a-mercy, Mary Ann! Your churn is in my way. (GRANNY *and* MARY ANN *gesture protestingly at each other.*)

FATHER (*To* MARTIN *and* WILLY): Children, don't play here. There isn't any room.

JOAN (*Pausing with broom in front of apple baskets*): Joseph! Tom! Please move aside. How can I sweep? (BOYS *carrying baskets move angrily toward* MEG.)

MEG (*Again rescuing dolls*): No, Tom, you mustn't sit here. You're right in the middle of my tea party! (MEG, TOM, *and* JOSEPH *pantomime a quarrel, pointing to each other angrily, etc. Others all begin talking at once, with heated gestures.*)

ALL (*Ad lib; Loudly, to each other*): You're in my way. Please move over. How can I work? There's no room in this house! Why must we be so crowded? (*Etc.*)

FATHER (*At the top of his lungs*): Quiet! Be still, I say. (*Others are silent.* FATHER *clutches his head.*) Oh my ears and shoe buttons! All this noise! You'll drive me out of my wits! (*A knock is heard at door right.*)

MOTHER: Husband, I hear a knock at the door. (*Knock is repeated.*)

FATHER: Aye, good wife. I hear it. (*Loudly*) Come in.

BARTHOLOMEW (*Entering. Leans on his staff and bows*): Good day to you, my friends.

GRANNY: Why, 'tis Wise Bartholomew himself!

BARTHOLOMEW (*Bowing again*): None other.

MOLLY: Have you come to visit us, good Bartholomew?

BARTHOLOMEW: Nay, my child. I was on my way to the forest, but I heard such a shouting and wailing in this house that I thought there must be some trouble.

MOTHER (*Wiping her eyes with her apron*): Alas, good Bartholomew, we have trouble enough and more.

FATHER: We lead a miserable life.

BARTHOLOMEW (*Astonished*): Dear me! But what is the matter?

MEG: We're so crowded.

JOSEPH: We don't have any room at all.

ALL (*Ad lib; pointing accusingly at each other*): He's in my way. She won't give me any room. How can I work? (*Etc.*)

BARTHOLOMEW (*Raising hand for silence*): Sakes preserve us! Say no more. By all the gray hairs in my long gray beard, you really do have a problem.

FATHER: Dear Bartholomew, you are the wisest man in all the village. Can't you think of some way to help us?

GRANNY: Yes, please help us. There must be some way.

BARTHOLOMEW (*Again raising hand for silence*): Perhaps I can help you. Tell me this, friend John—do you own any animals?

FATHER (*In amazement*): Animals? Yes, we have some animals. We have a goat, six chickens, and a donkey out in the barnyard.

BARTHOLOMEW: A goat, six chickens, and a donkey, you say. Ah, excellent. Fine. Very good. Now I'll tell you what to do.

MOTHER (*Eagerly*): Yes, tell us, good Bartholomew. What must we do?

BARTHOLOMEW (*Raising hand for silence*): John, you must go out to the barnyard and fetch your goat. Bring him into this room to live with you.

FATHER (*In disbelief*): What? A goat in this room?

GRANNY: I never heard of such a thing! (*Others pantomime surprise, disbelief, etc.*)

BARTHOLOMEW (*Severely*): Do as I say,
Or go your own way.
Fiddle-dee-dum
Fiddle-dee-dee
That's all the advice
You'll hear from me. (*Turns, as if to go*)

MOTHER: Please don't go away, Wise Bartholomew. We'll do as you say.

OTHERS (*Ad lib*): Yes, we'll obey. We'll get the goat. (*Etc.*)

BARTHOLOMEW: Very well. In seven days and seven nights, I shall come again, to see how you are faring. Good day, my friends. (*Exits*)

FATHER: I suppose I'd better fetch the goat. (*Exits*)

MOTHER: A goat in this room!

JOAN: What a strange idea!

MEG (*Pulling her dolls close*): I'm scared of goats.

MARY ANN (*Severely*): Fiddlesticks! Old Bartholomew is the wisest man in the village. His advice *must* be good.

FATHER (*From offstage*): Watch out, everybody! Clear the way. Here comes the goat! (*All gather up their possessions, prepare to dodge, crying: "Ooooh! Watch out! The goat!" etc. GOAT rushes onstage, heading straight for TOM and JOSEPH, who run shrieking out of the GOAT's path. FATHER tries vainly to hold GOAT back by rope, but is pulled along instead. NOTE: In order to move faster, GOAT may walk on hind legs, crouched over, front legs pawing the air, horns lowered.*)

ALL (*Ad lib; as GOAT charges around the stage*): Help! Watch out! He's coming this way! Help! (*Etc.*)

MOTHER (*Clutching head*): Oh, dear! Oh, dear!
I very much fear
That inviting this goat
Was a bad idea! (*Curtain*)

* * * * *

SCENE 2

TIME: *A week later.*

SETTING: *Same as Scene 1.*

AT RISE: *All are busy with the same activities as in Scene 1, except for* MARTIN *and* WILLY, *who hold a large red cape between them, flaunting it at the* GOAT.

MARTIN: Here, Billy Goat, Billy Goat, Billy Goat!

WILLY: Here, you old goat—come and play bullfight!

MOTHER: Martin! Willy! Stop that at once! I told you not to tease that goat. (GOAT *seems uninterested in cape.*)

TOM: He'll butt you!

MEG: Or he'll butt me! (*Gathers up dolls and pulls fearfully out of the way*)

MARTIN: Oh, Mother, there's really no harm.

WILLY: It's only *bulls* that charge at red things. Goats don't mind. See? (*Waves cape at* GOAT *again.* GOAT *suddenly lowers horns and charges for cape.*) Help!

MARTIN: Watch out! Help! Help! (MARTIN *and* WILLY, *still holding on to the cape, dash out of* GOAT's *path, run around churn, etc., pursued by* GOAT.)

ALL (*Ad lib*): Watch out! Help! You see? We told you! (*Etc.*) (FATHER *runs after* GOAT, *finally manages to catch him.* FATHER *holds* GOAT *down, succeeds in quieting him.*)

FATHER: There, there, old goat. (GOAT *tries to rise. Others watch nervously.*) No! No! Mustn't chase after nice people. Shhhh! (*Knock at the door is heard.* FATHER *places a hand to forehead, exhausted.*) Come in. (BARTHOLOMEW *enters, bows.*)

BARTHOLOMEW (*Cheerily*): Good day to you, my friends.

OTHERS (*Not too enthusiastically*): Good day, Bartholomew.

BARTHOLOMEW (*Still cheerful*): How are you this fine winter's morning? Has the goat been helpful?

FATHER: It's dreadful! Dreadful!

GRANNY: We're worse off than ever before.

OTHERS (*Ad lib*): This goat is terrible. We've had a dreadful week. Awful! (*Etc.*)

BARTHOLOMEW: Dear me. Dear me! You really do have troubles.

FATHER: Please, good Bartholomew, tell us what to do. We need help very badly.

BARTHOLOMEW (*Stroking his beard*): Very well, friend John. This is what you must do. Go out to the barnyard and fetch your six chickens. Bring them into this room to live with you.

ALL (*Incredulously*): What? The chickens, too? Into this room?

BARTHOLOMEW (*Severely*): Do as I say,
Or go your own way.
Fiddle-dee-dum
Fiddle-dee-dee.
That's all the advice
You'll hear from me. (*Turns, as if to go*)

MOTHER: Oh, dear! Oh, dear! Don't be angry, Bartholomew. We'll do as you say.

BARTHOLOMEW: Very well. In seven days and seven nights, I shall return to see how you are faring. Good day. (*Exits*)

GRANNY: Chickens!

MOLLY: The goat was bad enough!

FATHER: Old Bartholomew is the wisest man in the village. I think we should obey him. I'll go fetch the chickens. (*Exits*)

MOTHER (*Shaking her head*): Oh, dear! Oh, dear!
I very much fear
That we won't like having
Those chickens in here. (*Curtain*)

* * * * *

SCENE 3

TIME: *A week later.*

SETTING: *The same.*

AT RISE: *All are trying to pursue the same activities as before, but now they are more crowded than ever.* GOAT *wanders around the stage, sniffing and butting everyone and* CHICKENS *are hopping, pecking, and clucking everywhere.*

JOSEPH (*Shooing two* CHICKENS *away from his basket*): Shoo! Scat! (CHICKENS *squawk, flutter over to* MEG, *who shoos them away.*)

MARY ANN: Watch out for the goat!

MOTHER: Don't step on the chickens.

WILLY: Oh dear, I think I've stepped on an egg!

ALL (*Ad lib; loudly, at once*): Shoo! Scat! Watch out! Keep that chicken away! Watch out for the goat! (*Etc. A knock is heard.*)

FATHER (*At the top of his lungs*): *Quiet!* (*Silence, except for* CHICKENS' *clucking*) I think I heard a knock. (*Knock is repeated.*) Come in.

BARTHOLOMEW (*Enters, bowing. Cheerily*): Good morrow to you, my friends. My, what lovely chickens!

MEG: They're not lovely—they're nasty!

ALL (*Ad lib*): They're awful! We're so crowded! We've had a terrible week! (*Etc.* CHICKENS *flutter about, clucking.*)

FATHER: Please, good Bartholomew. Help us.

MOTHER: We don't know *what* to do!

GRANNY: But, please, kind sir—no more goats and chickens!

BARTHOLOMEW: Very well, my friends. I'll tell you what to do. John, you must go out to the barnyard and fetch your donkey. Bring him into this room to live with you.

MOLLY (*Protesting*): Oh, no! We *can't* do that!

TOM: Not the donkey, too!

BARTHOLOMEW: Fiddle-dee-dum
  Fiddle-dee-dee,
  That's all the advice
  You'll get from me.
  In seven days and seven nights, I shall return to see how you are faring. Good day, my friends. (*Exits*)

GRANNY (*Indignantly*): Well, I never!

MARY ANN: Don't do it, Papa! We *can't* live with a donkey!

FATHER: Old Bartholomew is the wisest man in all the village. (*Sighs*) Let's try his advice just one more time. I'll fetch the beast. (*Exits*)

MOTHER: The goat is a terror
  The hens are a brawl,
  But a donkey, I fear me,
  Is worst of them all. (*Curtain*)

* * * * *

SCENE 4

TIME: *A week later.*

SETTING: *The same.*

AT RISE: *All are trying to pursue the same activities as before, but with more difficulty than ever:* GOAT *is butting everyone.* CHICKENS *flutter, and squawk and peck.* DONKEY *blunders around the stage, braying loudly.*

ALL (*Ad lib*): Shoo! Scat! Watch out for the goat! Don't step on the chickens! Here comes the donkey! Watch out! Help! Be careful! (*Etc.*)

FATHER: Oh, oh, oh! This is dreadful! I can't bear it another minute! (*A knock at the door is heard.*)

MEG: Papa, I think I heard someone knock.

GRANNY (*Snappishly*): If it's that Bartholomew again, I don't want to see him.

FATHER: Come in. (BARTHOLOMEW *enters, bowing as before. The family is silent, hostile.* DONKEY *brays,* CHICKENS *cluck, and* GOAT *baas.*)

BARTHOLOMEW (*Cheerily*): Good morrow to you, my friends. And how are the animals today?

MOTHER: The animals are fine, good sir, but we're *not!*

GRANNY (*Crossly, to* BARTHOLOMEW): Do you have any *more* good advice, kind sir?

BARTHOLOMEW (*Still cheerful. Stroking his beard*): Fiddledum, fiddle-dee; we'll see.

FATHER: Dear, good Bartholomew, you are still the wisest man in all the village. *Please* help us. We've never been so miserable.

BARTHOLOMEW (*Patting* DONKEY. *Looks up, as if astonished*): Do you mean to say that you don't *like* these nice animals?

JOAN (*Tartly*): Begging your pardon, sir, but you don't have to live with them.

BARTHOLOMEW: You don't like living with them?

OTHERS (*Resoundingly*): NO!

BARTHOLOMEW (*Stroking his beard*): Well now, there's only one thing to do. John—

FATHER (*Fearfully*): Yes?

BARTHOLOMEW: Take all these animals—and put them back in the barnyard where they belong!

OTHERS: Hurray! (*They chase all the animals offstage through the door; animals bray, cluck, and baa as they go off.*)

MOTHER: How wonderful! They're gone!

JOAN (*Puts broom aside. Stretches luxuriously*): Mmmmm! Look at all this room we have now. I'm *so* glad they're gone!

MARTIN: I really think this room has grown bigger.

GRANNY: I never knew before how nice it was *not* to have a donkey in the room.

MARY ANN: Or a goat.

WILLY: Or chickens.

TOM: Come on, Meg. Spread your silly dollies out. There's plenty of room now. (*All turn happily to their tasks.*)

MOLLY: It's so quiet and peaceful.

FATHER: I'm so happy. I never knew how much room we had!

BARTHOLOMEW: Fiddle-dum, fiddle-dee

As I've said thrice before:

I don't think you'll be needing

My advice any more.

Farewell, my friends. (*Walks toward exit, waving*)

ALL (*Waving*): Farewell, good Bartholomew! Farewell! Thank you! (*Curtain*)

THE END

Production Notes

THE CROWDED HOUSE

Characters: 6 male; 6 female; 9 male or female for animals.

Playing Time: 15 minutes.

Costumes: Peasant dress for John and his family. Bartholomew wears a long dark robe belted with rope; he wears a beard and carries a staff. Animals wear appropriate costumes. Donkey is played by two actors, one wearing a donkey head, other holding up the rear.

Properties: Rolling pin for Granny; butter churn for Mary Ann; skein of wool for Molly; dolls and tea set for Meg; apples, three baskets for Tom and Joseph; hammer and nails for Father; broom for Joan; red cape for Martin and Willy.

Setting: The only room of John the Carpenter's cottage. Upstage center is small table. To right of center stage is butter churn. At stage left is rough, unfinished table. Other furniture may be placed around the stage. There is an exit at right.

Lighting: No special effects.

The Forest Bride

by Susan L. Throckmorton

Characters

NARRATOR, *offstage voice*
FATHER
TWO SONS
VEIKKO, *his third son*
MOUSE
MOUSE SERVANTS
STRANGER

SCENE 1

TIME: *Long ago.*
SETTING: *Farm at the edge of the forest. Played before curtain.*
BEFORE RISE: VEIKKO, TWO SONS *and* FATHER, *carrying an axe, enter and walk center.*
NARRATOR: There once was a farmer who had three sons. When they were grown, he said to them:
FATHER: My sons, it is high time you all married. Today I want you to go looking for brides.
1ST SON: But, Father, where shall we look?
FATHER: I want each of you to chop down a tree, and then go in the direction the fallen tree points. If you go far enough in that direction, I'm sure you'll find a suitable bride.
1ST SON (*Taking up axe*): All right, Father, let me try first. (*With much grunting he mimes chopping down a tree; shields his eyes as if watching it fall in the distance*) North! (*Happily*) That suits me. I know a farmer there whose daughter is very pretty! (*Holds axe out to* 2ND SON)

131

2ND SON (*Grabbing axe*): Here, let me try. (*Mimes chopping tree; excitedly*) Good! It's pointing south. I've danced many times with a girl who lives on a farm in the south!

VEIKKO (*Eagerly*): Now it's my turn. (*Mimes chopping down tree; disappointed*) Oh, no!

1ST SON (*Amused*): It's pointing straight into the forest!

2ND SON (*Laughing heartily*): What good is a fox or a wolf for a wife!

VEIKKO (*Bravely*): I'm sure this tree will point me in the right direction.

FATHER: Are you ready to begin your journeys?

TWO SONS (*Eagerly*): We're ready!

VEIKKO (*Soberly*): If they're ready, I'm ready, too.

FATHER: Take care, boys. (*Exits left as others start right*)

1ST SON (*Excitedly*): Just you watch. My wife will bake my bread!

2ND SON (*Boastfully*): Mine will mend my clothes!

VEIKKO (*Softly*): I'll try to make mine happy. (*They exit right. Curtain opens.*)

* * * * *

SETTING: *Deep in the forest. A small hut is up left.*

AT RISE: VEIKKO *enters slowly and dejectedly.*

VEIKKO (*Dejectedly*): How can I find a bride in a place where there are no people? (*Looks around, sees hut; surprised*) Wait! There's a hut. Who could live here so deep in the forest? (*Knocks at door, then pushes door open; calls*) Hello? (*Sadly*) It's empty. No one lives here.

MOUSE (*Scurrying onto stage from door; cheerfully*): I live here!

VEIKKO (*Startled*): You? But you are only a mouse. You don't count.

MOUSE (*Offended*): Of course I count.

VEIKKO: I'm sorry. I didn't mean to be rude. I just meant you weren't what I was hoping to find.

MOUSE (*Kindly*): What were you hoping to find?

VEIKKO (*Sighing*): I was hoping to find a bride. My father told me and my brothers that it was time for us to get married.

One brother went north, one went south, and here I am in the forest. (*Sadly*) My older brothers will find brides easily, but I don't see how I can find one in this forest. (*Forlornly*) I'll have to go home and confess that I've failed.

MOUSE (*Brightly*): I'll be your bride!

VEIKKO (*Laughing*): You! Who ever heard of having a mouse for a bride?

MOUSE (*Smiling*): Take my word for it. You could do a lot worse.

VEIKKO: You are very kind, but—

MOUSE (*Eagerly*): Really! We could have great fun! (VEIKKO *thinks a moment, then laughs.*)

VEIKKO: Very well, little mouse. I'll go home and tell my father the news.

MOUSE (*Clapping her hands*): That makes me so happy! I'll be true to you forever, and I'll wait for you no matter how long it takes you to return. (*Begins to hum happily as* VEIKKO *departs. Curtain*)

* * * * *

SCENE 2

SETTING: *Inside farmhouse. Scene may be played before curtain.*

BEFORE RISE: TWO SONS *are arguing loudly as* VEIKKO *stands dejectedly off to the side.*

1ST SON: My bride has the rosiest cheeks you ever saw!

2ND SON: But mine has the most beautiful golden hair.

1ST SON (*Turning to* VEIKKO): How about your bride, Veikko?

2ND SON: Did you find a sweetheart among the forest creatures? (TWO SONS *laugh.*)

VEIKKO: You needn't laugh. I've found a bride, too.

1ST SON (*Surprised*): You have?

2ND SON (*Trying to contain his laughter*): With pointed ears and sharp white teeth? (SONS *laugh again.*)

VEIKKO: She's a gentle, dainty little thing, dressed in velvet.

1ST SON (*Skeptically*): Dressed in velvet?

2ND SON (*Sneering*): Just like a princess, I suppose.

VEIKKO: Yes, dressed in velvet like a princess. With a nice, bright laugh. We are going to have great fun together.

2ND SON (*Haughtily*): Sounds like a wild tale to me! (FATHER *enters.*)

FATHER: My sons, now that you have found sweethearts, have them each bake me a loaf of bread so I can see if they'll make good housewives.

1ST SON (*Eagerly*): Mine will be able to bake bread, I'm sure of that!

2ND SON (*Quickly*): So will mine!

1ST SON: What about your princess, Veikko?

2ND SON (*Disdainfully*): Yes, do you think the *princess* can bake bread?

VEIKKO (*Uncertain*): I don't know. I will have to ask her. (SONS *laugh heartily. All exit as curtain opens.*)

* * * * *

SETTING: *In the forest; same as Scene 1.*

AT RISE: VEIKKO *trudges wearily onto stage.* MOUSE *enters from hut and goes to him excitedly.*

MOUSE: Veikko! I'm so glad to see you! (*Concerned*) But why do you look so sad?

VEIKKO: My father wants each of our brides to bake him a loaf of bread. (*Sadly*) When I come home without my loaf, my brothers will laugh at me.

MOUSE: But, Veikko, I can bake bread.

VEIKKO (*Smiling*): I have never heard of a mouse who could bake bread!

MOUSE: Well, I can. (*She rings a little bell.* VEIKKO *looks on in amazement as* MOUSE SERVANTS *scurry onto stage.*) My little mousy friends, run and fetch me grains of the finest wheat. (*They titter and scurry off.*) You see, Veikko, it will be no trial to bake you a beautiful loaf of bread. (*Curtain*)

* * * * *

SCENE 3

SETTING: *Inside the farmhouse.*

BEFORE RISE: FATHER *enters left.* VEIKKO *and* TWO SONS *enter right, each carrying loaf of bread. They ad lib greetings.*

NARRATOR: The next day the three brothers presented their father with the loaves of bread.

FATHER (*Taking loaf from* 1ST SON): Very good, my son. For hard-working people like us, rye bread is good. (*Turning to* 2ND SON) And you, my second son? (2ND SON *hands him loaf.*) Ah, yes, barley bread. That is also very good. (*To* VEIKKO) Veikko, what has your bride baked? (*Takes loaf; impressed*) What? White bread? She must be very wealthy.

1ST SON (*Sneering*): Of course, didn't he tell us she was a princess?

2ND SON (*Harshly*): Say, Veikko, when a princess wants fine flour, how does she get it?

VEIKKO: She rings a little bell. When her servants come in, she tells them to bring her grains of the finest wheat.

TWO SONS (*Ad lib; unkindly*): A likely story! He's so full of lies! (*Etc.*)

FATHER (*Putting hands up to silence them*): You mustn't be jealous of Veikko's good luck. Each girl knows how to make good bread. But before you bring them home, I want one more test of their skills. Let each one send me a sample of her weaving.

1ST SON: Easy!

2ND SON: Done! (VEIKKO *looks down sadly.*)

1ST SON (*Disdainfully*): We'll see how well *her ladyship* fares this time! (SONS *laugh. All exit as curtain opens.*)

* * * * *

SETTING: *In the forest.*

AT RISE: MOUSE *sits humming to herself as* VEIKKO *enters.*

MOUSE (*Jumping up*): Oh, Veikko, there you are at last!

VEIKKO (*Brightening*): Are you really so glad to see me?

MOUSE: Indeed I am! I've been waiting and waiting for you,

just wishing you would return. (VEIKKO *looks down sadly.*) Does your father want something more from me, Veikko?

VEIKKO (*Gently*): Yes, little one, and I'm afraid it's something you can't give me.

MOUSE: But perhaps I can. Please tell me what it is.

VEIKKO: It's a sample of your weaving, but I have never heard of a mouse who can weave.

MOUSE (*Confidently*): Tut! Tut! Of course I can weave! (VEIKKO *smiles as* MOUSE *rings bell.* SERVANTS *scurry on.*) My little mousy friends, run and fetch me fibers of good flax. (SERVANTS *titter gleefully and scurry off.*) You see, Veikko, it will be easy to weave you a beautiful piece of linen. (VEIKKO, *bemused, sits while* MOUSE *exits into hut.*)

NARRATOR: After the mice had carded and spun the flax into thread, the little mouse wove a beautiful piece of linen. It was so sheer she was able to fold it and put it into an empty nutshell. (MOUSE *reenters with papier-maché walnut shell.*)

MOUSE (*Giving shell to* VEIKKO, *who rises*): Take this, Veikko. In this little box is a sample of my weaving. I hope your father will like it. (*Curtain*)

* * * * *

SCENE 4

SETTING: *At the farmhouse.*

BEFORE RISE: FATHER *enters left.* VEIKKO, *carrying nutshell, and* TWO SONS, *each carrying piece of cloth, enter right.*

FATHER (*Happily*): You have all returned at last! Let me see the samples of your brides' weaving.

1ST SON (*Proudly*): Here, Father, is a square of cotton woven by my bride.

FATHER (*Studying cloth*): Hmm. Not very fine but good enough.

2ND SON (*Haughtily*): My sample is better. See, a piece of cotton and linen mixed.

FATHER (*Taking cloth and studying it*): Yes, a little better. (*Hands cloth back to* 2ND SON) And you, Veikko, has your bride given you a sample of her weaving? (VEIKKO *hands nutshell to* FATHER.)

1ST SON (*Laughing*): Veikko's bride gives him a nut when he asks for a sample of her weaving! (FATHER *opens shell and takes out a sample of the finest linen.* SONS *look on, stunned.*)

FATHER (*In awe*): Why, Veikko, my boy, how did your sweetheart ever get thread for a such a fine web?

VEIKKO (*Matter-of-factly*): She rang a little bell and ordered her servants to bring her fibers of the finest flax. They did as she commanded, and after they had carded it and spun it, she wove the web you see.

FATHER: Wonderful. (*Studying cloth again*) I have never known such a weaver! (SONS *shake their heads at each other, dejected*) I am anxious to meet her. (*To* SONS) In fact, it's time you all brought your brides home. I want to see them with my own eyes. Bring them tomorrow.

TWO SONS (*Downcast*): Yes, Father. (*They exit right.* FATHER *exits left.*)

VEIKKO: I am truly fond of her, but how my brothers will laugh when they find out my bride is a mouse! (*More boldly*) Well, I don't care if they do! She's been wonderful to me, and I won't be ashamed of her! (*Exits right briskly as curtain opens.*)

* * * * *

SETTING: *The forest. Stone bridge and river are painted on backdrop.*

AT RISE: VEIKKO *enters right, pulling a small coach on a string. He takes a few steps then stops.*

MOUSE (*From offstage; as if from inside coach*): Are we almost there, Veikko? Why are we stopping?

VEIKKO (*Turning and speaking to coach*): The path is narrow ahead, little one, and there is a traveler coming this way. We must wait until he passes. (STRANGER *enters left, sees coach, begins to laugh.*)

STRANGER: What do you have here? (*Stoops and looks closely at coach; laughs*) Look at this foolish mouse coach! There really is a mouse in there. (*Laughing hysterically*) I wonder if it floats. (*He tosses coach offstage. Loud splash is heard.*)

VEIKKO (*Horrified*): What have you done? (*Rushes right, looks off helplessly; to* STRANGER, *angrily*) You have drowned my little sweetheart!

STRANGER (*Gruffly*): Your sweetheart? You must be crazy! (STRANGER *exits, chuckling*)

VEIKKO (*Forlorn*): Oh, you poor little mouse. You were faithful and kind and now that you are gone, I know how much I loved you! (*Covers his face with his hands, weeps;* MOUSE, *dressed as* PRINCESS, *enters right.*)

PRINCESS: Veikko, won't you come the rest of the way with me?

VEIKKO (*Turning; surprised*): Who are you? (*Wipes eyes*)

PRINCESS: You weren't ashamed to have me for a bride when I was a mouse, and surely now that I am a real princess, you won't desert me!

VEIKKO (*Gasping*): Are you—were you the little mouse?

PRINCESS (*Merrily*): Yes, Veikko, but once I was a king's daughter. An evil witch became jealous of my beauty, and when I was fifteen, she changed me and all of my servants into mice. The spell could not be broken until one day a young man would truly love me. (VEIKKO *listens to her, wide-eyed.*) Now the evil spell is gone forever. So, come, let us go to your father. After he gives us his blessing, we will be married and go home to my kingdom. (VEIKKO *nods, dumb-struck, and they start left as curtain closes.*)

* * * * *

SCENE 5

SETTING: *The farmhouse.*

BEFORE RISE: FATHER *and* TWO SONS *enter right and mime conversation.* 1ST SON *stops short as he looks off left.*

1ST SON (*Pointing*): Look, Father! It's a royal coach! (*Others look off.*)

2ND SON (*Excitedly*): And look! A prince and a princess are getting out! (VEIKKO *and* PRINCESS *enter.*)

FATHER (*Bowing*): Your highness, welcome to our humble home.

TWO SONS (*Bowing*): Your highness.

VEIKKO: Don't you know me?

FATHER (*In disbelief*): Why, is it you, Veikko?

VEIKKO (*Laughing*): Of course, Father. And this is the princess I'm going to marry. (PRINCESS *curtsies*.)

FATHER: Why, your bride really *is* a princess! (*Confused*) Where did my boy find a princess?

VEIKKO: Right out there in the forest where my tree pointed.

FATHER (*Nodding*): Where the tree pointed. (*Musing*) I've always heard that was a good way to find a bride.

1ST SON (*Annoyed*): Just our luck!

2ND SON (*Throwing up his hands in exasperation*): If only our trees had pointed to the forest, we could have found princesses instead of plain country girls!

PRINCESS: Oh, no. It wasn't because Veikko's tree pointed to the forest that he found a princess. It was because he was good enough to love and be kind even to a little mouse.

FATHER (*Raising his arms*): Bless you, my children. Let us prepare for a grand royal wedding! (*Others gather around excitedly*.)

NARRATOR: And, of course, after they were married, Veikko and the princess were as happy as they should have been, for they were good and true to each other and loved each other deeply for the rest of their lives. (*Curtain*)

THE END

Production Notes

THE FOREST BRIDE

Characters: 5 male; 1 female. Male or female for narrator and male and female extras as desired for Mouse Servants.

Playing Time: 15 minutes.

Costumes: Male characters wear vests, tunics tied at waist, and boots. Father and Stranger have beards. Mouse and servants wear mouse ears and tails. Princess wears gray velvet cloak and tiara.

Properties: Axe; small bell; 3 loaves of bread; papier-maché walnut shell large enough to hold square of cloth; 3 samples of cloth, one lighter and finer than the others, if possible; small cardboard coach on a string.

Setting: All scenes at farmhouse can be performed before curtain. Forest scenes: Small cardboard hut with working door stands at one side of stage. Tree stump or bench is center. Scene 4 forest: bridge and river can be painted on backdrop.

Sound: Splash of water.

Strongman Meets His Match

by Veronica Hughes

Characters

NARRATOR
FOREVER-MOUNTAIN, *famous wrestler*
MARU-MAE, *teenage girl*
YASUKO, *her mother*
GRANDMOTHER
THE EMPEROR
LADIES AND GENTLEMEN OF THE COURT
AMAZING WHALE, *wrestler*
FIVE WRESTLERS, *extras*

SCENE 1

BEFORE RISE: *A bookstand is down right in front of curtain.*
NARRATOR enters, carrying large book under his arm. He
bows deeply, then goes to bookstand and opens book.
NARRATOR: Greetings. Today we have the most distinct honor
of presenting for you a Japanese folktale about Forever-
Mountain and the three strong women. We hope you enjoy
it. (*Reading*) Long, long ago, in Japan, there lived a famous
wrestler named Forever-Mountain. Everyone knew his
strength. He had entered many contests and had won them
all. On the day of our story, Forever-Mountain was on his way
to the capital city of Tokyo, where he was invited to wrestle
in a tournament given by the Emperor. It was three months
away, and he was sure he would be the champion. (NARRA-
TOR *exits, as curtain opens.*)

* * * * *

TIME: *Springtime, many years ago.*

SETTING: *The Japanese countryside. Trees are down left, up center, and up right, suggesting a pathway through the mountains.*

AT RISE: FOREVER-MOUNTAIN *enters down left, strutting back and forth along "path." He stops center and turns to audience.*

FOREVER: It is easy to walk a long time when you are as strong as I am. (*Thumps chest and inhales deeply*) The air is cold, but this thin robe is all I need because I am so healthy. I am exceedingly strong and a very great wrestler. I am also extremely brave, but I am far too modest to talk about all that. (MARU-MAE *enters right, carrying a water bucket on her head, steadying it with her left hand. As she passes in front of* FOREVER *she smiles and giggles at him. She stops left under tree.*) That young girl looks very happy. I'll bet she would squeal if I tickled her! (*Looks at her again, then back at audience*) Maybe she will drop the bucket of water, and that will be even funnier! Then I can run and fill it up and carry it home for her. That's just what I'll do! (FOREVER *tiptoes up behind* MARU-MAE, *who is facing left, and pokes her lightly at the right side of her waist with his right hand.*) Kocho-kocho-kocho! (MARU-MAE *squeals and slams her elbow down hard over his hand, pinning it against her waist.* FOREVER *yelps and tries to pull his hand away.*) Ho, ho! You've caught me, you little trickster. I can't get my hand free.

MARU-MAE (*Laughing*): I know!

FOREVER: Now, young lady, I must warn you, you must let me go right now. I am a very powerful man, and if I pull too hard, I might hurt you.

MARU-MAE: Oh, I admire powerful men! And you may call me Maru-Mae. (*With the bucket still balanced on her head, she turns upstage and begins to walk along path, pulling* FOREVER *behind her.*)

FOREVER (*With irritation*): Stop! I beg you! (MARU-MAE

stops, facing him. Firmly) Now, see here! I am the famous
wrestler Forever-Mountain. I am on my way to Tokyo to show
my impressive strength to the Emperor. (*Upset*) And you're
hurting my hand!

MARU-MAE: Oh, poor Forever-Mountain! Are you tired? Shall
I carry you? I can leave the water here and come back for
it later.

FOREVER (*Angrily*): No, I don't want you to carry me! I want
you to let me go, and then I want to forget that I ever saw
you! Why are you tormenting me?

MARU-MAE: I am sorry, sir. I'm sure that when you get to
Tokyo, you'll do very well. (FOREVER *nods and smiles.*) And
even if you lose, you probably won't get hurt.

FOREVER (*Offended*): I am a very strong man! (*Tugs on his
arm, which is still pinned; weakly*) Really, I am. (*Whimpers*)
You are hurting my hand!

MARU-MAE: If you lose, I'm sure no one will laugh at you.

FOREVER (*Upset*): Maybe they would call me "Not-Much-Of-
A-Mountain" or "Puny Little Hill"!

MARU-MAE: Why don't you come along to my mother's house
and let us make a strong man out of you. The wrestling tournament in Tokyo is still three months away.

FOREVER (*Surprised*): How do you—a simple country girl—
know when the Emperor's tournament is?

MARU-MAE: Well, my sweet old grandmother told me. She's
been thinking of entering it herself. (FOREVER *looks astonished.* MARU-MAE *exits left, dragging him behind her.
Curtain*)

* * * * *

SCENE 2

BEFORE RISE: NARRATOR *reenters and goes to bookstand.*

NARRATOR: Maru-Mae took Forever-Mountain off to meet her
mother and grandmother. The great wrestler was very glad
the road was deserted so no one could see that a young country
girl had overpowered him. He was also very curious to know

how the girl planned to make him stronger. (NARRATOR *exits, as curtain opens.*)

* * * * *

SETTING: *Maru-Mae's family's farm. One tree is up center. Simple white farmhouse is up left.*

AT RISE: GRANDMOTHER *is hidden behind house.* FOREVER *and* MARU-MAE *enter left and stop center. His hand is still pinned under her arm.*

MARU-MAE: Here we are. (*Lets go of his hand and* FOREVER *rubs it*) Grandmother is at home, but she is very old and is probably sleeping. Mother should be bringing our cow back from the field soon—there she is now! (*Points off right. A loud thump is heard.*)

YASUKO (*Offstage*): There you go, Cow, off to the barn. That's a good girl. (YASUKO *enters right, brushing off her hands and shoulders.*) Ah, Maru-Mae, who is this nice young man? Sir, you must excuse the dust on my clothes. The mountain paths are full of sharp stones, and they hurt our cow's feet, so I always carry her back and forth to the pasture. (FOREVER *stares in amazement.*)

MARU-MAE: Mother, this is the famous wrestler Forever-Mountain. He has agreed to stay with us to prepare for the Emperor's tournament. Forever-Mountain, this is my mother, Yasuko. (*They bow.*)

YASUKO: Well, three months isn't a very long time, but we may be able to help him a little. (*Walking around him, sizing him up*) He *does* look terribly frail. He'll need lots of good food and exercise.

MARU-MAE: Perhaps, when he gets stronger, he'll be able to help Grandmother with some of the chores around the house. (GRANDMOTHER *enters from farmhouse, leaning heavily on cane.*)

GRANDMOTHER: What's all this noise out here? (*Stumbles over "roots" of tree and nearly falls*)

MARU-MAE (*Rushing to her*): Are you all right, Grandmother?

GRANDMOTHER: Of course, child. But, you know, my eyes

aren't as sharp as they used to be. That's the third time I've stumbled over that silly tree today. Here, hold this. (*She hands cane to MARU-MAE, then wraps her arms around tree trunk, pulls up tree, and lays it on its side.*) There, that's better. (*Takes cane back*) Yasuko, be a good girl and throw that tree away, so no one else will fall over it.

YASUKO: Yes, Mother. (YASUKO *picks up tree and carries it offstage right. A loud crash of cymbals is heard. She reenters brushing the dirt off her hands casually.*)

FOREVER (*In disbelief*): I can't believe the strength of these women. I'm feeling faint. (*Faints*)

MARU-MAE: This poor, feeble man must be very tired. Let's take him inside and give him some rice and tea. I'll carry him.

YASUKO: No, I'll carry him.

GRANDMOTHER: No, let me! (*They continue to argue over who will carry him as curtain closes.*)

* * * * *

SCENE 3

BEFORE RISE: NARRATOR *reenters and goes to bookstand.*

NARRATOR: For the next three months, the women worked to make Forever-Mountain into the strong man they knew he could be. They fed him the simplest food, and made it as tough as possible. Each day they prepared his rice with less and less water, until no ordinary man could have chewed or digested it. (MARU-MAE *enters right, crosses stage briskly, carrying pot and spoon, stirring "rice."* FOREVER *follows, carrying bowl and chopsticks, chewing with difficulty. Both exit left.*) Every day the women made him do the work of five men, and every evening he practiced wrestling. (MARU-MAE *and* YASUKO *enter left and stop center.*)

MARU-MAE: Which of us should he practice with?

YASUKO: Well, we certainly don't want to hurt him.

MARU-MAE: That's right. Perhaps he should wrestle Grandmother. She is the least likely to hurt him accidentally.

YASUKO: And the exercise will be good for her arthritis. (*They exit right.*)

NARRATOR: And so each night Grandmother taught Forever-Mountain new ways to wrestle. (GRANDMOTHER *and* FOREVER *enter right. She has him in a headlock and drags him along. They do not stop, but continue crossing as they speak.*)

GRANDMOTHER: Very good. Now do what I told you—try to escape.

FOREVER: I'm doing it. I'm doing it!

GRANDMOTHER: Well, try harder, young man! (*They exit left.*)

NARRATOR: Forever-Mountain gained much strength, but he didn't know it. Grandmother could still throw him easily into the air and catch him again. (*Loud thump and cry of pain is heard off.*) Most of the time. (FOREVER *enters, rubbing his head, and stops center.*)

FOREVER (*To audience*): I have never trained so hard for any other tournament. But I don't think I'm getting any stronger. No matter what I do, those women do it better and faster. (*Shakes his head, dejectedly*)

NARRATOR: Sometimes Forever-Mountain did an exercise that Japanese wrestlers do, raising one foot high above the ground and bringing it down with a crash. (FOREVER *does this with one foot, then the other, and we hear loud cymbals and drums each time.*) The people in nearby villages looked up into the sky and told each other that a big thunderstorm was coming. (FOREVER *smiles proudly and exits.*) Soon he could pull up a tree as well as Grandmother. He could even throw one, but not very far. And one evening near the end of the third month, he wrestled Grandmother and held her down for a whole minute! (NARRATOR *exits as curtain opens.*)

* * * * *

SETTING: *Same as Scene 2.*

AT RISE: YASUKO, MARU-MAE, FOREVER-MOUNTAIN *and* GRANDMOTHER *are standing in front of house. The women are congratulating* FOREVER, *slapping him on the back and laughing.*

GRANDMOTHER: Very good! And I didn't just *let* you win this time!

YASUKO: I never would have believed it!

FOREVER: Thanks to you I am now truly the strongest person in Japan! Uh, I mean, the strongest *man!*

MARU-MAE: Now you are ready to show your strength to the Emperor!

YASUKO: Yes, you are right, Maru-Mae. He is ready.

GRANDMOTHER (*To* FOREVER): You must leave for Tokyo tomorrow. We will miss you.

FOREVER (*Surprised*): But Grandmother, aren't you going to the tournament with me? Aren't you going to enter, too?

GRANDMOTHER (*Shaking her head*): Why would I want to do that? I have just been beaten by the one who will be champion. (*Pats his shoulder.*) Besides, wrestling is beginning to bore me. I've been thinking of taking up something more lively. Pole-vaulting, maybe.

YASUKO: Forever-Mountain, you must take our cow along with you. Sell her and buy a silken belt. Get the most beautiful belt you can find. You will look very handsome when you appear before the Emperor.

FOREVER: Oh, I could not take your only cow! You've already done too much for me.

GRANDMOTHER: Please take her. As a good-luck gift from us.

FOREVER: But how would you plow the fields? (*The women laugh.* GRANDMOTHER *laughs so hard she coughs and chokes.* MARU-MAE *slaps her on the back.* FOREVER *looks confused.*)

YASUKO: Oh, that was a good one! We don't use our cow for work! Why, Grandmother here is stronger than five cows! (*They laugh again.* FOREVER *smiles, nods.*)

MARU-MAE: The cow is our pet. We baby her. She has such lovely brown eyes and such a soft hide.

YASUKO: But I am getting tired of carrying her back and forth, back and forth to that pasture each day. No, we insist. You take her.

FOREVER: All right, but then you must let me give you all the prize money that I win.

MARU-MAE: Oh, no! We could never do that! (*Suddenly shy*) It's not proper to accept gifts of money from strangers.

FOREVER: That is true. (*Thinks*) Then I won't be a stranger! I will ask your family's permission to marry you and become a member of this fine family!

MARU-MAE (*Dancing for joy*): Oh! I am going to be a bride! I will make a beautiful dress and be ready for our wedding when you return! (*Stops dancing*) That is—if your proposal is acceptable to my mother and grandmother . . . (YASUKO *and* GRANDMOTHER *whisper, then turn and smile.*)

YASUKO: Yes! We agree. You may marry our beloved Maru-Mae. Let's go inside and celebrate! (*They exit into house. Curtain*)

* * * * *

SCENE 4

BEFORE RISE: NARRATOR *enters and goes to stand.*

NARRATOR: The next morning Forever-Mountain said goodbye to the three women. Then he picked up the cow, put her on his shoulders, and started on his journey. He sold the cow in the next town. She brought a good price because she was unusually fat—after all, she had never worked a day in her life. With the money, Forever-Mountain bought the most beautiful silken belt he could find. When he had walked a few more days, he reached the palace grounds. (*Curtain opens.*)

* * * * *

SETTING: *The palace courtyard. Risers are along right side. Large translucent folding screen is down left.*

AT RISE: LADIES AND GENTLEMEN OF THE COURT *sit on risers, chatting quietly among themselves.* EMPEROR *sits behind screen, strongly backlit, so only his shadow is visible through screen. Shadow of a sack of money is visible at his side.* FOREVER, *wearing his new belt,* AMAZING WHALE *and other* WRESTLERS *sit on floor near center flexing their muscles.*)

NARRATOR: All the ladies and gentlemen of the court were

waiting in the courtyard for the wrestling to begin. The Emperor watched from behind a screen, because he was far too noble for ordinary people to look at. Soon it was time for the wrestling to begin. In Japanese wrestling, the competitors try to force their opponents out of a circle painted on the floor. Forever-Mountain was selected to fight in the first match. His opponent was Amazing Whale, who was one of the finest wrestlers in the land. (FOREVER *and* AMAZING *go to opposite sides of a "circle" and pretend to sprinkle salt from small bowls into the ring*.) Japanese wrestlers sprinkle salt in the ring to drive away evil spirits. Then they stamp their feet very loudly to frighten each other. (AMAZING *stamps foot. Small drum sounds*)

AMAZING (*To* FOREVER): It is your turn to stamp, if you are not too frightened!

FOREVER: Ha! We will see who will be frightened. (*He stamps his foot and loud drum and cymbal clashing sounds are heard.* LADIES AND GENTLEMEN *and* WRESTLERS *cry out and tremble, topple over, etc., from the "earthquake" effect.* EMPEROR *nearly falls out of his chair.* AMAZING *shakes and falls backward out of circle.*)

AMAZING (*Crawling over to* EMPEROR, *bowing, still on floor*): The spirits must be angry. Or maybe there is something wrong with my salt. I don't think I'm going to wrestle today after all. (*Crawls out left*)

NARRATOR: Seeing Amazing Whale so easily defeated, the other wrestlers were not eager to enter the ring.

FOREVER: Who is my next opponent? (WRESTLERS *mumble to each other, then push* 1ST WRESTLER *into circle*) Very well. We begin. (1ST WRESTLER *trembles as* FOREVER *raises one foot high, but brings it down very lightly, so as not to frighten him.* FOREVER *and* WRESTLER *put hands on each others shoulders.* WRESTLER *tries to push* FOREVER. FOREVER *does not budge.* WRESTLER *finally gives up, exhausted.*) Are you finished? (WRESTLER *nods.* FOREVER *smiles.* WRESTLER *bows to* EMPEROR, *then limps off, embarrassed.*) Is there another who wants to wrestle me? (*One by one* WRESTLERS *move into ring and attempt to budge*

FOREVER *across the line. They butt him, tackle his legs, hang on to his arms. Nothing works, and each in turn bows to the* EMPEROR *and scurries off.*)

NARRATOR: Finally, all the wrestlers had been defeated.

EMPEROR: There is only one real wrestler here. (*Standing, still behind screen*) I hereby declare that Forever-Mountain is the winner of the tournament! Here is the prize money. (*Holds sack of money out beyond screen;* FOREVER *goes to* EMPEROR, *bows deeply and takes sack.*)

FOREVER: Thank you, Your Majesty. (LADIES AND GENTLE-MEN *clap politely, then exit right.*)

EMPEROR: Forever-Mountain, I must ask you not to enter any more tournaments. We do not want to hurt the feelings of the other wrestlers. They like to win sometimes, too.

FOREVER: I will do as you ask, Your Majesty. I've been thinking about becoming a farmer, anyway. (FOREVER *steps forward. Curtain closes behind him.*)

* * * * *

NARRATOR: Forever-Mountain walked back to the valley. (FOREVER *crosses to center.*) Maru-Mae was waiting for him. When she saw him coming, she ran down the mountain to meet him. (MARU-MAE *enters right and runs to him. They bow to each other. She takes sack of money and throws it lightly over her shoulder. They exit right.*) Maru-Mae was so happy to see him that she carried him halfway home. Then she put him down and let Forever-Mountain carry *her* the rest of the way, to show respect for her new husband-to-be. Forever-Mountain kept his promise to the Emperor and never competed in wrestling tournaments again. In the big city, his name was forgotten. But up in the mountains, sometimes the earth shakes and rumbles. It is then that the people say Forever-Mountain and Grandmother are practicing wrestling in the hidden valley far away. (*Closes book*) The end. (*He bows, and exits.*)

THE END

Production Notes

STRONGMAN MEETS HIS MATCH

Characters: 3 male; 3 female; male or female for narrator; at least 8 male and female extras for ladies and gentlemen of the court and other wrestlers.

Playing Time: 20 minutes.

Costumes: Robes with colorful sashes, sandals; Forever-Mountain wears a brightly colored belt in last scene.

Properties: Large book; water bucket; cane; pot and spoon; bowl and chopsticks; two bowls for "salt"; bag of money.

Setting: Bookstand is down right, in front of curtain. Scene 1: Japanese countryside. Trees are down left, up center, and up right, suggesting a path through the mountains. Scenes 2 and 3: Clearing in the woods. Simple white farmhouse is up left. Easily moveable tree is up center in Scene 2. Scene 4: Palace courtyard. Risers are along right side. Large translucent folding screen is down left.

Sound: Drums and cymbals as indicated; other rhythm instruments may be used to accent action on stage, if desired.

Lighting: Strong backlighting for screen.

The Leopard's Noisy Drum

by Janice Kuharski

Characters

NYAME, *the sky god*
ELEPHANT
LION
BEAR
TURTLE
LEOPARD

SCENE 1

TIME: *Long ago.*
SETTING: *Tropical forest in western Africa. Tall stool is center.*
AT RISE: *Sound of rhythmic drumbeats is heard offstage.* NY-
AME, *carrying staff, enters and sits on stool.*
NYAME (*Yelling over sound of drum and pounding ground with
staff*): Where is everyone? I called a meeting over an hour
ago! (LION *and* BEAR *rush on.*)
LION: Good morning, Nyame. Sorry we're late.
BEAR: I was nearly caught in a trap. Thank goodness Lion
came along when he did! (*They sit on floor, center right, facing*
NYAME. ELEPHANT *rushes on, followed by* TURTLE, *who
moves slowly.*)
ELEPHANT: Am I late? Did I miss anything? (*Sits*)
NYAME (*Shouting over drum, which gradually fades out*):
Something must be done about Leopard's noisy drum! (TUR-
TLE *finally reaches center and sits.*) The drum keeps everyone
in the forest awake, and what's worse, everyone complains to

me about it. How can I work on a rainstorm when my time is taken up with silly complaints?

LION (*Apologetically*): But, Your Majesty, we've already tried to steal the drum and we've had no luck.

NYAME (*Pounding staff angrily*): Then you must try again! All of you together will go this evening at sunset.

BEAR (*Quickly*): I—I'm afraid I can't go this time. I've got a terrible stomach ache. (*Holds stomach and groans*) Until my stomach is better, I couldn't possibly go on a long trip through the forest.

NYAME: Very well. If Bear cannot go, then Lion and Elephant will go.

LION: Unfortunately, Your Majesty, I can't go either—at least not until my paw has healed. (LION *holds up front paw*.) I stepped on a huge thorn and walking even a short distance is terribly painful. (*Puts paw to ground and winces*)

NYAME (*Poking* ELEPHANT *with his staff*): Then Elephant must go alone. After all he is bigger and stronger than either Lion or Bear.

ELEPHANT (*Stands, takes a step back*): I, Your Majesty? Go alone—by myself? (*Backing toward exit*) I'm afraid I can't go. Without company, I'd probably fall asleep. Leopard's noisy drum kept me awake all last night. (*Yawns loudly*) In fact, I must go take a nap right now.

NYAME (*Bellowing*): Forget the nap, Elephant! (ELEPHANT *jumps, startled.*) Get back here at once.

ELEPHANT (*Quickly returning and sitting down*): Yes, Your Majesty.

NYAME (*In commanding voice*): I am the sky god! I have things to take care of—thunder, lightning, rainbows, et cetera et cetera. And if I don't get back to work soon, the rain forest will have no rain. (*Pounds staff on ground; firmly*) One of you must go—and that is final.

BEAR (*Matter-of-factly*): I was the first to go last time. This time, either Lion or Elephant should go first.

LION: Excuse me, Bear, but *I* was the first to go last time.

ELEPHANT (*Indignantly*): You both have short memories. I went first. Then Bear went, and Lion went last.

NYAME (*Waving staff at them; angrily*): Stop this ridiculous quarrel! I'm tired of excuses. (*Bellows*) Bring me the drum—now!

LION (*Cowering*): Your Majesty, if I may suggest—

TURTLE (*Inching closer to* NYAME): Excuse me for interrupting, Nyame, but I think I have a solution to everyone's problem. I will go get the drum.

BEAR, ELEPHANT, *and* LION (*Amused; ad lib*): What? You're joking! No way! (*Etc.*)

ELEPHANT: If *we* couldn't get Leopard's noisy drum—and we're a hundred times stronger and faster than you—how could you possibly get the drum?

LION (*Boasting*): I'd say we're a *thousand* times faster and stronger! Maybe a million times—

NYAME (*Shouting and pounding staff*): Silence! (LION *trembles.*) It's Turtle's turn to speak. (*Kindly*) Well, Turtle, what is your plan?

TURTLE: It's true that Elephant, Lion, and Bear could not steal Leopard's drum, but that's because he was expecting them. He would not be expecting me.

NYAME (*Stroking chin and nodding*): An excellent point! But even if you do catch Leopard off guard, how do you plan to steal the drum?

BEAR (*Skeptically*): You couldn't even *lift* the drum!

ELEPHANT (*Haughtily*): It's *much* too big and heavy for you.

TURTLE: If my plan works, my part of the task will be easy. Leopard will do the hard part—all by himself!

NYAME: Well, then, it's settled. Turtle will steal the drum.

TURTLE: Thank you, Nyame. (*Turning and starting slowly toward exit*) I will leave now to get a head start.

OTHERS (*Waving to* TURTLE; *ad lib*): Good bye, Turtle. Good luck. (*Etc. Curtain*)

* * * * *

SCENE 2

TIME: *One month later.*

SETTING: *Deep in the forest. Tall stool is center; shorter stool is left.*

AT RISE: LEOPARD *is seated on tall stool, beating drum.* TUR-
TLE *enters left and slowly moves to center and sits on
smaller stool.*

LEOPARD (*Pounding drum and chanting*):
The forest is mine
all night and all day.
The sound of my drum
keeps others away.
Let the Lion or Bear
or the Elephant come;
each one of them fears
the sound of my drum.
My music is magic;
my singing is grand.
While I have a drum,
I'm king of the land.

TURTLE (*Shouting over drum*): Good morning, Leopard. I've
been listening to your music. You have a fine sounding drum
and a fine voice as well. (LEOPARD *stops pounding drum and
looks up.*)

LEOPARD (*Flattered*): Why, thank you, Turtle. (*Boasting*) I do
have the best and biggest drum in the forest.

TURTLE: Without a doubt, you have the best sounding drum
I've ever heard—but not the biggest.

LEOPARD (*Irritated; stepping down from stool*): How can you
say that? There is no drum in the forest bigger than mine!

TURTLE: That would be true—if the great Nyame did not have
an even bigger drum.

LEOPARD: Impossible! No drum is bigger than this. (TURTLE
gets up and inspects drum.)

TURTLE: It's a fine drum, indeed. But Nyame's drum is so large
that he can fit inside his—with room to spare! Can you do
the same?

LEOPARD (*Quickly*): Of course I can! (*Considering*) I mean, I'm
sure I could if I tried.

TURTLE (*Shaking his head*): No, I don't think you could fit in
this drum. (*Smugly*) I don't think this drum is even half as
big as Nyame's. (TURTLE *sits again.*)

LEOPARD (*Upset*): If Nyame can fit inside his drum, then I can fit inside my drum as well.

TURTLE: I've *seen* Nyame get inside his drum.

LEOPARD (*Hotly*): Then you shall see me get inside my drum, as well! (*Puts drum on its side*) But you will need to tell me when I am completely inside. (*Begins to crawl into drum head first*)

TURTLE (*Going to drum*): It would be a great honor.

LEOPARD (*Wiggling forward inside drum*): How am I doing, Turtle?

TURTLE: Your hindquarters are still showing, Leopard.

LEOPARD (*Inching forward*): Am I inside the drum yet, Turtle?

TURTLE (*Smiling broadly*): Almost, but your tail is still showing.

LEOPARD (*Pulling tail inside drum*): I can't see a thing—it's dark in here. Can you see me now?

TURTLE: Not even a speck of you is showing now.

LEOPARD (*Panicked*): Help me, Turtle. I'm stuck. I can't turn around in here! Get me out!

TURTLE: I will let you out, Leopard, but not until I've brought you to Nyame. (*Aside*) Thank goodness much of the way back is downhill this time. Leopard's drum should roll nicely—all the way home.

LEOPARD (*Pounding frantically*): Let me out! Let me out or you'll be sorry, Turtle!

TURTLE: My advice to you, Leopard, is to stop complaining and make yourself comfortable. You'll have plenty of time for a nice long nap. (*Curtain*)

* * * * *

SCENE 3

SETTING: *Same as Scene 1. Tall stool is center.*

AT RISE: NYAME *sits on stool.* ELEPHANT, BEAR, *and* LION *sit on floor.* TURTLE *stands next to drum, center left. Sounds of banging and pounding from inside drum are heard intermittently.*

ELEPHANT: It's been so long since you left, Turtle. We didn't think you were coming back.

TURTLE (*Proudly*): I am not only back, but I have the drum as well.

NYAME: How were you able to bring Leopard's drum back all by yourself?

TURTLE: That was easy. Many animals in the forest wanted to get a closer look at Leopard's wonderful drum. So they were only too happy to help me push.

NYAME (*Admiringly*): Ah! A very clever plan, indeed, my friend!

LEOPARD (*From inside drum; furious*): Let me out! Let me out!

NYAME: What is that horrible racket?

TURTLE: It's Leopard, and except for when he's sleeping, he's been screaming like that since we started out. What should I do with him, Nyame?

ELEPHANT: The only thing you can do, Nyame, is banish Leopard from the forest.

LION (*Eagerly*): Yes, yes. Banish him—and the sooner the better! (*Boastfully*) Then I will be the undisputed king of the forest.

BEAR (*Scornfully*): That's not true, Lion. I should be the one to rule the forest, not you.

ELEPHANT: *I* should be the king of the forest. After all, I'm the tallest, the heaviest, and the strongest.

TURTLE: Your Majesty, I have a suggestion. If Leopard is not around, these three will never agree on who should be king of the forest. And the noise from their endless squabbling will be even worse than the sound of Leopard's drum.

NYAME (*Gets down from stool and paces; stroking his chin*): An excellent point, Turtle. I could not stand another commotion. Leopard is free to return to his home in the forest. (ELEPHANT *helps* LEOPARD *climb out of drum.*)

LEOPARD (*Shaking himself out; indignantly*): It's about time! (*Fluffing himself*) Look! My fur is all matted! (*Grumbling as he exits*) I'm still king of the forest, you know!

TURTLE (*Gestures toward drum*): And here is the drum you asked for, Nyame. What will you do with it?

NYAME (*Setting drum upright*): Leopard's drum is just what I need to make loud rolls of thunder. Listen! (NYAME *beats drum, as thunder is heard offstage.* ELEPHANT, BEAR *and* LION *cower and cover ears.* NYAME *turns toward* TURTLE; *pleased.*) You have done what Elephant, Bear, and Lion could not do. What reward shall I give you?

TURTLE (*Thinking*): Well . . . I have always wanted a house that I could carry on my back when I travel.

NYAME (*Nods*): A fine idea! That is exactly what you shall have. (*Exits and returns carrying shell; ties shell on* TURTLE's *back*)

ELEPHANT (*Walking around* TURTLE, *inspecting shell*): It's magnificent! Look at the colors—olive green and yellow, even a bit of red.

BEAR (*Looking at shell*): And it has a nice design around the edge.

LION (*Nodding*): The shape fits his body perfectly.

ELEPHANT (*Thinking*): I could use something like that—only bigger, of course.

BEAR: How ridiculous! You don't need a shell. But I could certainly use one.

LION: And so could I. (*Eagerly*) Let's ask Nyame. (*Turns toward* NYAME) Your Majesty, do you think each of us could have a shell just like Turtle's?

NYAME (*Stroking chin*): Perhaps we should ask Turtle what he thinks of your request. (*Turns to* TURTLE) Well, Turtle, what do you say?

TURTLE: I think that if Lion, Elephant, and Bear each had a shell, they would be even stronger than they already are. It would not be fair to give them shells . . . unless each one agrees to give up something that makes him strong.

NYAME: I see your point. What do you think a fair exchange would be?

BEAR, ELEPHANT, *and* LION (*Excitedly*): Yes, tell us! (*Each in turn looks taken aback as* TURTLE *speaks.*)

TURTLE: Well, Elephant could give up his strong tusks. Lion could give up his strong teeth, and Bear could give up his mighty claws.

NYAME (*Pounding staff*): A splendid idea! Shells in exchange for tusks, teeth, and claws. I'll do it at once!

BEAR, ELEPHANT, *and* LION (*Ad lib; alarmed*): No! Wait! We can't do that!

ELEPHANT: I really don't need a shell after all!

LION: Nor do I. A shell would cover my beautiful mane.

BEAR: I don't need one either. A heavy shell would just slow me down.

NYAME (*Firmly*): Then stop wasting my time with your foolishness! I have work to do! (NYAME *beats drum, and thunder is heard off.*) A rain forest must have rain, you know! Now that I have Leopard's drum, I'll shake the skies open and *let the rain come!* (*Lights dim. Thunder is heard and lights flash.* BEAR, LION, *and* ELEPHANT *cower and cover ears.* TURTLE *pulls head under shell and moves toward exit. Curtain closes.*)

THE END

Production Notes

THE LEOPARD'S NOISY DRUM

Characters: 6 male or female.

Playing Time: 20 minutes.

Costumes: Nyame wears gray beard, colorful African robe and hat, sandals. Appropriate animal costumes: Elephant has tusks and trunk; Bear has claws; Lion has large teeth, and Leopard has spotted coat. Turtle wears green body stocking. All wear face paint.

Properties: Tall drum painted with colorful African design. Must be large enough for Leopard to crawl inside. Staff or walking stick. Large papier-maché turtle shell that can be tied onto Turtle.

Setting: Forest. Backdrop depicts tall trees, vines, monkeys, colorful birds, snakes, etc. Tall stool is center in Scenes 1 and 3. Second, shorter stool is next to it in Scene 2.

Sound: Recorded African drum music; thunder.

Lighting: Lights dim at the end of the play, followed by flashes of lightning.

The Maharajah Is Bored

by Barbara Winther

Characters

HERALD
GOPAL, *tailor*
PANDIT, *scholar*
SITARA, *poor girl*
RADHA, *rich girl*
MERCHANT
SNAKE CHARMER
COBRA
MAHARAJAH
SERVANT
VILLAGERS, *extras*

BEFORE RISE: HERALD, *carrying a scroll, enters before curtain to the sound of drum roll.* VILLAGERS *enter from both sides of stage.*

HERALD (*Calling in loud voice*): Dhian deejai! Dhian deejai!*
I bring a message from The Magnificent Hindu Prince of Maharastra to the villagers of Rajapur. (VILLAGERS *murmur eagerly among themselves. Then quiet down as* HERALD *begins to read.*) "I, the Maharajah, Prince of Maharastra, am extremely bored! Therefore, I will conduct a contest tomorrow at noon under the banyan tree near the village well. If anyone knows how to make my life more interesting, let him appear before me. The person with the best suggestion will be awarded a thousand rupees, two white elephants, and my

---

*Rough translation: "Hear ye! Hear ye!"

160

eternal gratitude." (HERALD *exits, followed by* VILLAGERS, *ad libbing excitedly. Curtain opens.*)

* * * * *

TIME: *The next morning.*
SETTING: *Street in Rajapur, India. Down left, canopy erected on poles represents tailor's shop. Money box and Radha's sari are on table under canopy. Patchwork sari is in basket on floor beside table; stool stands next to it. Down right is banyan tree; up center a stone well.*
AT RISE: GOPAL, *seated on stool, is sewing industriously on jacket. Scraps of cloth are scattered about.* PANDIT *enters left, reading book. He crosses right, sits on ground, lotus-style, under banyan tree, and continues to read.*
GOPAL: Good morning, Pandit.
PANDIT (*Not looking up from book*): Good morning, tailor Gopal.
GOPAL: Why is it that each day you sit under the banyan tree and read?
PANDIT: Because I am a learned scholar. I shall not stop until I have read every book in the world.
GOPAL: Is that possible?
PANDIT: I will answer that question after I have read the last book.
GOPAL: But why must you read so much?
PANDIT (*Loftily*): Everything important has been recorded. The answers to all problems are in books.
GOPAL: Indeed! What problem are you solving today?
PANDIT: I am seeking ways to cure the Maharajah's boredom. In so doing, I have come upon other problems to which I must find answers.
GOPAL: It is good to study, but I believe many problems can be solved through experience.
PANDIT: That, sir, is complete nonsense. (SITARA *enters and crosses to well, carrying a water jar.*)
SITARA (*Calling happily*): Good morning, Gopal! Your shop is open early.

GOPAL: Yes. I must finish this jacket for a wealthy merchant.

SITARA (*Running over to him*): Let me see. Oh, lovely! Such soft silk!

GOPAL (*Gently pulling jacket away*): No, no, Sitara. You will get it dirty, and there is no time to clean it. The merchant will come soon.

SITARA (*Noticing material on table*): Ah-h! What is this?

GOPAL: It is a dress for the rich girl named Radha.

SITARA (*Seeing more material*): And this? (*Awestruck*) Gold threads all over! (*Reaches for material*)

GOPAL: Ah, ah, don't touch. These are fine clothes for people to wear before the Maharajah today. A poor, ragged little girl like you must only look at them from a distance.

SITARA (*Backing away*): If I were rich, Gopal, I'd have you make me a sari, so I, too, could appear before the Maharajah. I would win the contest, and my mother and father would ride the white elephants to the Arabian Sea and back again. And I would run beside them making up songs about the forest.

GOPAL (*Laughing*): You have such an imagination, little one. Do you really think you could win the contest!

SITARA: Of course!

GOPAL: And what would you tell the great Hindu prince so that he would no longer be bored? (*Bites off thread, having finished jacket*)

SITARA: I would say—(*Thinking*) I would say—(*Hangs head and sighs*) I don't know what I would say.

GOPAL (*Smiling, as he folds jacket and puts it on table*): I am afraid you are full of childish dreams. (*Stuffs scraps into basket*) How is your mother today?

SITARA (*Sadly*): She is no better. If only we had the money to take her to a doctor, she might get well. (*With spirit*) Someday, Gopal, someday I am going to find a hidden treasure chest on the banks of the Krishna River. Then, my mother will grow well, and we will never be hungry again. I will find enough to make everyone happy, someday! (GOPAL *carries basket to right exit.*)

GOPAL (*Turning*): I hope you will have a good "someday," Sitara.

SITARA (*Calling after him*): What do you have in the basket?

GOPAL: Scraps of material from the clothes I make.

SITARA: What are you going to do with them?

GOPAL: Throw them away.

SITARA (*Running to him; shocked*): All those silks and satins and velvets? Those embroideries?

GOPAL: They are only small pieces.

SITARA: How pretty they are!

GOPAL: They are too little to make into anything.

SITARA: Gopal, wouldn't it be splendid if all the scraps were sewn together into a brilliant sari?

GOPAL (*Shaking head*): Your head is full of coconuts. A patchwork sari?

SITARA: Why not?

GOPAL (*Patiently*): It is not the style.

SITARA: I do not care about style.

GOPAL (*Teasing her*): Aha! You wish to wear the patchwork sari *yourself!*

SITARA: Yes, for then I could appear before the Maharajah.

GOPAL (*Laughing*): Go home, child. You have too many ideas. (SITARA *crosses to well and fills water jar.*)

SITARA (*Sadly*): If I had no ideas, Gopal, there would be little in life for me. (*Exits.* GOPAL *again starts to exit, stops, looks at scraps in basket, then walks back into shop.*)

GOPAL: I will throw these away later. (*He puts down basket, as* RADHA *enters and crosses to shop.*)

RADHA (*Haughtily*): Tailor, have you finished my gown?

GOPAL (*Picking up folded sari and spreading it out for* RADHA *to see*): Here is your sari, Mistress Radha. (RADHA *walks back and forth, looking critically at sari.*)

RADHA (*Decisively*): I don't like it!

GOPAL (*Startled*): It is the material you chose. (*Bringing sari closer to her*) And, you see, I made it exactly as you commanded.

RADHA (*Pacing in front of shop in annoyance*): I don't care. (*Furious*) It isn't elegant enough. (GOPAL *sighs and folds sari, replacing it on table.*) If I am going to win the Maharajah's contest, I must be better dressed than anyone. (*Stamping her foot with rage*) You are a stupid tailor! You sew no better than a monkey! (*She gives an exclamation of disgust.*) Oh, well, at least it's something new to wear. (*Rudely snatches sari, then takes coins from pocket and flings them at* GOPAL's *feet.*) Here are your rupees, old man. (GOPAL *crouches down and picks up coins.*) It amuses me to see how the poor will grovel in the dust for a few rupees. (*Tosses her head arrogantly and exits.* GOPAL *rises, and puts coins into money box.*)

GOPAL: Radha is a cruel woman. I hope she will not win the Maharajah's contest. (MERCHANT *enters and strides to* GOPAL's *shop.*)

MERCHANT (*Bruskly*): Good morning, tailor. Is my jacket finished?

GOPAL (*Bowing to* MERCHANT): It is finished, sir. (*Takes jacket from table and holds it up*) Do you wish to try it on?

MERCHANT (*Imperiously*): Of course. Help me with it. (GOPAL *helps him into jacket.*)

GOPAL: The jacket is a perfect fit. It makes you look so impressive that the Maharajah will surely listen to every word you say.

MERCHANT: He will listen anyway. I am the wealthiest merchant in the village. Here is your money. (*Takes coins from pocket, hands them to* GOPAL)

GOPAL (*Counting*): Excuse me, good sir, but you owe me ten more rupees.

MERCHANT (*Waving* GOPAL *aside*): I have paid you enough.

GOPAL: We agreed on the price before I made the jacket. It was understood that—

MERCHANT (*Interrupting*): If you do not feel I have paid you enough, take back the jacket. (*Starts to remove it*) I shall pay no more.

GOPAL (*Protesting*): But, sir, the jacket was made to fit *you*. It would not look right on anyone else.

MERCHANT (*Sarcastically*): What a pity. Then you'd better keep the money I have given you and say nothing more. (*Strides right, snickering*) Hmph! It pleases me to make a good bargain, especially at another's expense. (*Exits, rubbing hands together greedily*)

GOPAL (*Putting coins in box*): I think that merchant is a snapping crocodile, not fit to live with people. (*Sits on stool*) Sitara should win the contest. She is more deserving of the prize than any of these disagreeable people. (SNAKE CHARMER *enters right, playing flute. He sits on ground cross-legged and keeps playing.* GOPAL *nods to music, smiles, picks up scraps from his basket, sewing them together and chanting.*) A little bit of this, and a little bit of that. A sari for Sitara. Yama tali tat. (*Neither* CHARMER *nor* GOPAL *sees* COBRA *rising out of well, swaying with music, slithering over edge, still swaying and crossing to center.* COBRA *speaks in hissing manner.*)

COBRA (*Rising up behind* CHARMER *and peering down at him*): Stop playing that flute! (CHARMER *stops, eyes wide with alarm. He looks up slowly, sees* COBRA *and shrieks. Terrified, he stumbles to well, hides behind it.* GOPAL, *seeing* COBRA, *drops sari, leaps to his feet and runs behind table in fright.*)

GOPAL: By the Taj Mahal! A giant cobra!

COBRA (*Moving toward him*): Sh-h-h. Be still! I am sick to my hood from waving around to music. What is your name?

GOPAL (*Nervously*): G-g-gopal.

COBRA: The tailor?

GOPAL: Y-yes.

COBRA: I'm sorry.

GOPAL: Why?

COBRA: I'm looking for someone named Sitara.

GOPAL: The girl? She was here a moment ago.

COBRA: Find her. Be quick, before some villager comes along and throws stones at me.

GOPAL (*Concerned*): You won't hurt her, will you?

COBRA: Of course not. I am here to help her. Run, run. (*Hisses at him.* GOPAL *runs off right.*)

GOPAL (*From offstage; calling*): Sitara! Sitara!

COBRA (*Rummaging around in basket*): S-scraps! (*Looks around on ground and spies sari; stares at it, waving head*) This must be the sari for Sitara. What *charming* colors! (CHARMER *crawls over for closer look.* COBRA *sees him.*) I

don't find you charming at all. (*Darts at him*) Shoo!
(CHARMER *shrieks and runs to* PANDIT, *shaking his arm.*)

PANDIT (*Not looking up*): My good man, will you please leave
me alone so that I may read this important book? (CHARMER
makes exited noises, pointing to COBRA.) How am I going to
find out about anything unless you let me read? (CHARMER
shrugs and runs behind well. GOPAL *reenters, followed by*
SITARA.)

GOPAL (*Shouting excitedly*): There it is—a giant cobra! (SI-
TARA *crosses to center and falls to her knees.*)

SITARA (*Hands together, respectfully*): Great Cobra, I am
Sitara.

COBRA: Good. I have been sent here by the Goddess of the
Krishna River.

SITARA: Why?

COBRA: She merely said I must tell you to appear before the
Maharajah at noon to inform him how his life can become interesting.

SITARA (*Surprised*): Me? I have nothing to wear and nothing
to say.

COBRA: The tailor is making a sari for you.

GOPAL (*Hurrying into shop*): Yes. It is almost finished. (*He sits
on stool and starts to sew feverishly, casting furtive glances
at* COBRA.)

COBRA: And you, Sitara, should know what to say.

SITARA (*Perplexed*): But I don't.

COBRA: Come closer, and I will hiss a hint.

SITARA (*Fearfully*): You will bite me.

COBRA: I bite only evil people. Don't be afraid.

SITARA (*Taking deep breath*): All right. I will trust you.
(*Moves closer*)

COBRA: You must tell the Maharajah what makes you happy.

SITARA: He is a great man, Cobra. Do you think what makes
me happy would ever interest him?

COBRA: Yes! Deep inside, you humans are quite alike, you
know.

SITARA: No, I don't know. (*She looks around thoughtfully; then
suddenly determined.*) I will tell him. (*To* COBRA) Oh, Cobra,

may you have a long life and shed many skins! (*Impulsively hugs* COBRA)

COBRA: Shoo! You are messing up my scales. (*Flustered*) By all the muggy monsoons, I've never been hugged before. My friends will never believe this. (GOPAL *bites off last thread, rises, holds up sari to full length.*)

GOPAL: Here, Sitara. The sari is done. (SITARA *takes sari.*)

SITARA (*Overwhelmed*): How beautiful! Gopal, you are the greatest tailor in all of India. (GOPAL *smiles.*)

COBRA: Run, run, Sitara. Get ready, for it is almost noon.

SITARA (*Bowing, touching fingers to forehead*): Thank you, thank you. (*Turns and exits right, running*)

COBRA (*Yelling*): Where is that silly snake charmer? (CHARMER *peeks over edge of well, groaning.*) Play your flute, little man. It is time for me to return to the well. (CHARMER *nods nervously and sits center as before, playing flute, while* COBRA, *swaying to music, slithers into well and disappears.* CHARMER *stops playing, runs over to look into well, sighs in relief, and retreats to banyan tree. Sound of drum roll off left.* HERALD *enters.*)

HERALD (*In loud voice*): Dhian deejai! Dhian deejai! The Maharajah is approaching. All those entering the contest, come to the banyan tree by the well. (CHARMER *looks about nervously, then quickly retreats into shop.* RADHA, MERCHANT, *in clothes Gopal made, and* VILLAGERS *enter, ad libbing excitedly.*)

MERCHANT (*Pointing left*): Look! His elephant is covered with gold and silver. (*All turn, look off left.*)

RADHA: The elephant kneels. The Maharajah steps down.

HERALD (*To* PANDIT): You with the book, go someplace else. (*Shakes* PANDIT's *arm*)

PANDIT (*Grandly*): Sir, I am solving the world's difficulties.

HERALD: That is all very well (*Pulling* PANDIT *to his feet*), but you cannot sit there and do it.

PANDIT (*Crossing to well*): I am finding more problems and more answers than I ever dreamed existed. In fact, each problem has so many solutions, that I cannot decide which solution is right for which problem. (*Sits at foot of well.* SERVANT *enters left, places chair under tree, and quickly exits.* MAHA-RAJAH *enters left to slow drumbeat, followed by* SERVANT *waving fan. All except* PANDIT *fall to knees, touching foreheads to ground.* MAHARAJAH *sits in chair.*)

MAHARAJAH (*Sitting; yawning*): Rise, villagers of Rajapur. (VILLAGERS *rise, move right and left, some sitting.* SITARA, *in patchwork sari, hurries in.*) The contest will begin. Who wishes to be first?

RADHA (*Crossing center*): I am called Radha, the daughter of Sankar Lal. My father owns more water buffalo than any man in Rajapur, and he is—

MAHARAJAH (*Interrupting*): I do not care what your father owns. (*Yawns and stretches*) Just tell me, Radha, how can my life be interesting?

RADHA: Great Prince, you are far too kind to your subjects. If you spend your time being a tyrant, going about telling everyone what they do wrong, punishing them for their faults, making them work twice as hard to please you, surely your life would become more interesting.

MAHARAJAH: Ho-hum. It is true that there are no perfect people in my state. I could spend a lifetime correcting everyone. I shall take your suggestion under consideration. (*Gestures her away*) Next! (*She moves to one side.*)

MERCHANT (*Crossing to center*): Oh, mighty Hindu Prince, I am the wealthiest merchant in Rajapur, Karad, and Sangli. I sell teak and rosewood carvings, brass and ivory statues, jeweled necklaces—

MAHARAJAH (*Interrupting*): I do not care what you sell. (*Sighs deeply*) Do you know how to make my life interesting?

MERCHANT: It is my suggestion that you spend your time buying the most expensive items in the world and building bigger and better and more beautiful palaces to house your treasures. Furthermore, I am experienced in obtaining the best prices and would be pleased to assist you—for a small fee, of course.

MAHARAJAH: Ho-hum. It's true that there are many fascinating objects in the world. I could spend a lifetime collecting them for my personal enjoyment. I shall take your suggestion under consideration. (*Gestures him away.* MERCHANT *crosses back to crowd*) If that is all, then I will return to the palace and decide. (GOPAL *pushes* SITARA *forward.*)

SITARA (*Crossing to center; shyly*): Maharajah, I am a poor girl by the name of Sitara.

MAHARAJAH (*Surprised*): You are poor? What qualifies you to give advice?

SITARA (*Humbly*): Only that I am a human being, and we are all that.

MAHARAJAH (*Smiling*): True. (*Kindly*) Tell me, child, how do you propose to make my life interesting?

SITARA: See the little things in life, meditate on them, then use them to create beauty.

MAHARAJAH: Such as?

SITARA: Look at my sari. It was sewn from pieces of leftover cloth.

MAHARAJAH: Hm-m-m! Who made this?

SITARA (*Pointing*): My friend, Gopal. (GOPAL *bows.*) He is an excellent tailor and a kind man.

MAHARAJAH: I must agree your sari is pleasing to the eye and most original. Tell me more.

SITARA (*Pointing to leaves on tree*): Have you noticed how delicate are the veins in the leaf of a banyan tree? And yet, the tree is so big, a hundred men could hide behind its roots. Is it not wonderful to see what nature forms? (*Enthusiastically*) There is so much, Prince! (*Points off right*) See, there, how softly the butterfly rests on the jasmine flowers? (*Kneels, pointing*) And, here—how industriously the tiny ant marches about his business. (*Rises; with an expansive gesture*) There is music in the sounds of the wind and the river. You could write poems and songs, whole books about the little things around you.

MAHARAJAH (*Picking up leaf and inspecting it*): I have never really stopped to look before. It is indeed wonderful to observe how a leaf is formed. But how does one learn to know about such things?

SITARA: You listen to what your heart says, Prince.

MAHARAJAH: Continue, little girl.

SITARA: A piece of discarded wood can make a crutch to help an old, lame man. Clay on the banks of the Krishna River can form a water jar. Small stones joined together will build a strong wall for a neighbor's house. There are many little things that can help people and make them happy.

MAHARAJAH: How do you know what will make others happy?

SITARA: Again, I say you listen to your heart.

MAHARAJAH: I am deeply moved by your words. There are those around who desire wealth and power. (*Gestures at* MERCHANT *and* RADHA, *who look away*) How can the greedy and cruel ever see beauty? (*Crosses to center*) There is no need to continue this contest. Sitara, you have shown me the way to true happiness. I award you a thousand rupees, two white elephants, and my eternal gratitude. I shall spend the rest of my life trying to create beauty out of little things, and I do not believe I shall ever be bored again. (*Returns to chair; sits.* GOPAL *and* VILLAGERS *rush forward to congratulate* SITARA. MERCHANT *and* RADHA *exit angrily.* CHARMER *runs to side of well and plays flute.* VILLAGERS *break into small groups right and left.* SITARA *dances joyfully around well, while* GOPAL *claps time.* PANDIT *sits reading.* COBRA *rises in time to music. Curtain closes.*)

THE END

Production Notes

THE MAHARAJAH IS BORED

Characters: 4 male; 2 female; 4 male or female for Herald, Snake Charmer, Cobra, and Servant; as many extras for Villagers as desired.

Playing Time: 25 minutes.

Costumes: Indian dress. Cobra, dressed as snake, keeps hands at waist. Arms and upper body are covered to give appearance of a hood. He slides about on knees, waving body back and forth. Sitara changes from ragged clothing to bright, patchwork sari.

Properties: Scroll, book, sewing supplies, large basket with patchwork sari in it, scraps of material, small money box, jacket, Indian sari, water jar, coins, wicker chair, fan with long handle.

Setting: Village street in Rajapur, India. Poles in cans of sand hold up shop canopy. Under canopy are small coffee table, foot stool. Up center is garbage can surrounded with paper and painted to look like stone well (must be large enough to hide cobra). Cardboard cutout of banyan tree is down right. Upstage, dark backdrop curtain or painted street scene.

Lighting: No special effects.

Sound: Drum and flute music.

Panic in the Palace

by Martha Swintz

Characters

CHANCELLOR
UPPER SECRETARY
LOWER SECRETARY
LORD SPLOTZ
LADY SPLOTZ
PAGE
KING
QUEEN
PRINCESS HELEN
PRINCESS MARGARET
NURSE
GUARD
COURTIERS
LADIES

SETTING: *Throne room in the palace of Eidelwitz. Two thrones with pillows on them are upstage center.*
AT RISE: CHANCELLOR *is pacing the floor.*
CHANCELLOR: I wish they would hurry and come. It must be at least twenty minutes since I sent for them. (UPPER *and* LOWER SECRETARIES *enter.*)
UPPER SECRETARY: You sent for the Upper Secretary, and here I am.
LOWER SECRETARY: Likewise, the Lower.
CHANCELLOR: You gentlemen should have been more prompt. We have very important business to arrange. As you know, today is the first birthday of the Princess.
BOTH: Long live the Princess!

CHANCELLOR: It has been declared a legal holiday. The King will read a proclamation this afternoon concerning the birthday celebration.

BOTH: Long live the Princess!

CHANCELLOR: Yes, yes. But he has also ordered a session to give reports on the state of the kingdom. This is to be done before the festivities for the Princess.

BOTH: Long live the Princess!

CHANCELLOR: Oh, forget it! Upper Secretary, have you your report ready?

UPPER SECRETARY: All the upper business is functioning quite smoothly and in the highest order.

CHANCELLOR: Excellent! Lower Secretary?

LOWER SECRETARY: All the lower business is functioning quite smoothly and in the lowest order. Somehow that doesn't sound just right.

CHANCELLOR: Never mind. Hurry now and put your reports to the King in writing.

BOTH: At once. (*Exit*)

CHANCELLOR: I must go get my report ready too. But I hate to leave the throne room very long. I'm so afraid something will happen to spoil the celebration. (*Bustles over and plumps up pillows on thrones.* LORD *and* LADY SPLOTZ *enter.*)

LADY SPLOTZ: A-choo!

LORD SPLOTZ (*With hand to ear, indicating deafness*): What's that, my dear?

LADY SPLOTZ: I'm still sneezing, George. If this hay fever doesn't let up it will drive me mad.

LORD SPLOTZ: Cad? Who's a cad? Anyone we know?

LADY SPLOTZ: Not cad—mad! M-a-d!

LORD SPLOTZ: I'm sorry to hear that. Hope it was nothing I said.

LADY SPLOTZ: Never mind, dear. (*Shouts*) Why don't you turn up your hearing aid?

LORD SPLOTZ: I can't. The battery is dead.

LADY SPLOTZ: What a pity. On such an important occasion, too. (*Noticing* CHANCELLOR *for the first time*) Oh, my goodness! I didn't see you over there. You must be the Chancellor.

CHANCELLOR: Yes, I must—King's orders—or, believe me, I wouldn't bother with the job. It isn't worth having. Who are you?

LADY SPLOTZ: We are Lord and Lady Splotz; we come as good-will ambassadors from your neighbor, the King of Danderhoff.

CHANCELLOR (*Bowing*): We are honored to greet you and your husband. I shall show you to your apartment, where you may await your audience with the King.

LADY SPLOTZ: Thank—a-choo! Do excuse me. I have hay fever.

CHANCELLOR: I understand. Now, if you will please come this way I will show you to your rooms. You will find that you have been honored with an apartment between the sisters of the King and Queen.

LADY SPLOTZ: How perfectly—a-choo!

CHANCELLOR: Just come this way. (*Starts toward exit*)

LORD SPLOTZ: Pay? You expect us to pay? Most extraordinary!

LADY SPLOTZ (*Taking* LORD SPLOTZ *by the arm*): Come along, George. The Chancellor will show us to our room.

LORD SPLOTZ: Broom? My word! Do we have to sweep the floor too? (CHANCELLOR, LORD *and* LADY SPLOTZ *exit right.* PAGE *enters left.*)

PAGE: By order of his Majesty, let all the court assemble! (KING, QUEEN, COURTIERS *and* LADIES *enter, followed by the* UPPER *and* LOWER SECRETARIES *carrying large books.*)

KING (*After he and* QUEEN *are seated on thrones*): You may now read the proclamation.

PAGE (*Reading from large scroll*): By order of the King! This day shall be celebrated throughout the land of Eidelwitz as a holiday in honor of the first birthday of our fair Princess! So be it!

ALL: Long live the Princess!

KING: That's a very good proclamation. Who wrote it?

PAGE: You did, sire.

KING: Oh, I can't be bothered with writing proclamations. I hire ghost writers. All the famous dignitaries have them.

Look at the bottom corner of the page and see whose initials are there.

PAGE (*Examining paper*): It says S. U.

KING: Ah, that's Spiritus Unus. A great writer, that old boy.

QUEEN: I've never seen any of your ghost writers around here.

KING: Certainly not. I have a new angle. I'm the only king in the world who uses real ghosts.

QUEEN: Real ghosts?

KING: To be sure. Think of the savings. No food—no shelter. Just an occasional sheet now and then.

QUEEN: Don't they make the proclamations too grave?

KING: Oh, no. As writers they are out of this world. But now, let's hear the reports of the Secretaries. Upper?

UPPER SECRETARY (*Clearing throat*): Your Majesty, the statistical implications of this report are substantially factual rather than sublimated to coincide with the views of your humble servant, the Upper Secretary.

KING: Yes, yes, of course. But, just a moment before we wade through all this. Do we owe anyone any money?

UPPER SECRETARY: No, sire.

KING: Does anyone owe us any money?

LOWER SECRETARY: No, sire.

KING: Good. That's all I really wanted to know. Let's skip the rest of the report. Where is the Chancellor?

CHANCELLOR (*Running in*): Here, sire.

KING: Have any of the guests arrived?

CHANCELLOR: They certainly have—with a battery that doesn't run and a nose that does.

KING: Please explain yourself.

CHANCELLOR: Lord and Lady Splotz, ambassadors from Danderhoff, have arrived, sire. The battery to his hearing aid has burned out, and she sneezes all the time. Whew, what a pair!

KING: Yes, I was expecting them. (*Enter* LORD *and* LADY SPLOTZ.) Who are these people?

CHANCELLOR: These people, your Majesty, are Lord and Lady Battery—I mean Nose—that is—Splotz!

QUEEN: We are happy to have you with us, Lord and Lady Splotz.

LADY SPLOTZ: A-choo! Oh, dear, my hay fever is terrible.

LORD SPLOTZ: If we may be excused, we would like to return to our room.

QUEEN: Of course. I know Lady Splotz is tired and needs rest. I hope her hay fever will improve.

CHANCELLOR: Improve? It's perfect now.

LADY SPLOTZ: A-choo!

LORD SPLOTZ: Yes, adieu. Come, my dear. (*They exit.* PAGE *follows them.*)

QUEEN: I wonder why they were in such a hurry to leave.

KING: Probably sensitive about their conditions. He can't hear and she can't smell. Perhaps we could help some way. Upper Secretary, is there anything in the Upper State Department concerning batteries?

UPPER SECRETARY (*Rummaging frantically through his book*): I'm sorry, sire, I can find nothing here.

KING: Lower Secretary, do you have anything on noses in your book?

LOWER SECRETARY: The nose being located where it is on the body, sire, it would not come under the jurisdiction of the Lower State Department.

KING: You are no help at all. You may both leave. (SECRE-TARIES *exit.*) Chancellor, try to find a new battery for Lord Splotz. Try to do something about Lady Splotz's nose, too.

CHANCELLOR: A clothespin, perhaps? Oh, me! Why didn't those people stay at home? Batteries, noses. Noses, batteries. What next? (*Exits*)

KING: I don't blame him much. They *are* difficult guests.

QUEEN: Speaking of difficult guests, I understand you expect your sister, the Princess Helen, to arrive soon.

KING: Yes, and she's bringing Horace with her.

QUEEN: Horace? I didn't know your sister had married.

KING: She hasn't. (*Laughs.* PAGE *enters.*)

PAGE: The Princess Helen has arrived, sire.

KING: Show her in at once. (PAGE *exits.*)

QUEEN: I'm certainly anxious to see this Horace person.

KING: You may be disappointed. He isn't very handsome. (PAGE *enters.*)

PAGE: The Princess Helen! (PRINCESS HELEN *enters with covered basket over her arm.* PAGE *exits.*)

KING: Welcome to the Court of Eidelwitz, Helen. I would like to present you to my wife, the Queen.

QUEEN: I am glad to have you with us for the celebration.

HELEN: Thank you. I am honored to be invited.

QUEEN: Did you bring Horace with you?

HELEN: Oh, my, yes, but I imagine he is still asleep. I'm afraid he got awfully tired in his basket on the trip.

QUEEN: His basket? How quaint.

HELEN (*Opening lid of basket*): Horace, are you awake?

QUEEN: You mean he—he is really in that basket?

HELEN: Of course he is. Come on, Horace, wake up and meet these nice people. (*Approaches* QUEEN's *throne*) He's rather shy around strangers. (*Holds basket toward* QUEEN)

QUEEN (*Leans forward warily, peeks into basket, shudders and recoils*): He's—he's green! And he's a frog!

HELEN: Frogs are usually green, my dear. You didn't expect a red one, did you?

QUEEN: I didn't expect a frog at all. (*Commotion is heard offstage.* PRINCESS MARGARET *enters carrying a basket over her arm.* PAGE *is trying to hold her back by the other arm.*)

PAGE: I tried to keep her out, your Majesty.

MARGARET: He certainly did. But, after all, I *am* the Queen's sister. I don't understand how he dared to come close to me.

KING (*Covering his nose with large handkerchief*): I don't understand that, either. What perfume do you use? Chaperone No. 85? The court has my permission to use their handkerchiefs. (COURTIERS *and* LADIES *hold large handkerchiefs to noses.*)

QUEEN: I am glad to see you, Margaret, and it is quite obvious you brought Felicity with you.

KING: Felicity? Who's she? I've never heard of her.

QUEEN: I've never heard of Horace either, my dear. You see, my sister has her pets the same as yours. Margaret, I want to present you to my husband, the King. I hope you will become close friends. (MARGARET *starts toward* KING's *throne.*)

KING (*Holding up hand*): That's close enough.

CHANCELLOR (*Running in*): Something terrible has happened! Some old witch with a skunk has gotten into the palace and (*Points to* MARGARET) there—there she is now!

QUEEN: She is my sister, Chancellor, and you are being rude to her.

MARGARET: This is Felicity, my skunk, Chancellor. You are also being rude to her. (*Pushes basket toward* CHANCELLOR, *who faints*)

HELEN: I'm glad Horace never makes himself so unwelcome.

MARGARET: Do you collect skunks, too?

HELEN: Decidedly not. I have a pet frog. He's a smart one, too, and can talk to me. Whenever I ask him a question, he has learned to thump out the answer.

MARGARET: You should put him on a quiz program. But I don't believe a word of it.

HELEN: All right, I'll prove it to you. Horace dear, how much is two and two? (*Four distinct thumps are heard.*)

CHANCELLOR (*Raising head from floor*): I hear jungle drums. I'm going mad, absolutely mad.

KING: Get up off the floor. It's only Horace.

CHANCELLOR: Who, pray, is Horace?

KING: My sister Helen's frog.

CHANCELLOR: O-o-h n-o-o. (*Drops back again and groans*)

KING (*Standing*): Page, get everybody out of here. This has gone far enough. Show the ladies to their rooms. Call the Secretaries. I have an emergency on my hands. Be gone, all of you! (*All exit except* KING, QUEEN *and* CHANCELLOR, *who remains on floor.*)

QUEEN: We really should do something to bring the Chancellor around. Our throne room doesn't look very tidy with him sprawled on the floor.

KING: Let him lie. He's the only one in the palace getting any peace. (SECRETARIES *come running in, stop suddenly and start to sniff.*)

UPPER SECRETARY: What is that strange aroma? It can't be flowers.

LOWER SECRETARY: There is no glue factory near the palace.

QUEEN: You have just missed our uninvited guests, the King's sister and her pet frog.

KING: And the Queen's sister and her pet skunk.

UPPER SECRETARY: Did they attack the Chancellor?

KING: He was overpowered, shall we say, by their personalities. Revive the Chancellor. We must get down to business. (SECRETARIES *shake and slap* CHANCELLOR.)

CHANCELLOR (*Getting up*): Batteries! Noses! Frogs! Skunks! Please knock me out again.

KING: No. We must decide what to do about this unexpected menagerie.

UPPER SECRETARY: I will be glad to dispose of the frog.

LOWER SECRETARY: I will be glad to dispose of the—wait! What am I saying?

CHANCELLOR: Now I would suggest—(NURSE *enters in very starchy uniform on which are pinned many medals.*)

NURSE: Your Majesty! Pardon my breaking in on your conversation like this, but never in all my experience, which is considerable, have I ever known of anyone robbing a Princess.

KING: What do you mean, Nurse?

NURSE: Someone has stolen the Princess's formula. I have guarded the Princess with my life, but I never thought it was necessary to stand guard over her bottle too.

LOWER SECRETARY: A baby-bottle snatcher! There's nothing lower, not even in my department.

KING: It comes at a very bad time. Because of the celebration, I have given the cows the day off. Tell us what happened.

NURSE: I had just taken out a bottle of milk to warm it when a strange woman came in and started talking to me. Before I realized what was happening, she had snatched up the bottle of formula and disappeared.

UPPER SECRETARY: The case of the filched formula! (*Commotion offstage.* LORD *and* LADY SPLOTZ *are brought in by* GUARD, *bound and with handkerchiefs tied over their mouths.*)

GUARD: Your Majesty, this woman was caught in the act of destroying a bottle of milk and we suspected that—

NURSE (*Pointing*): That's the woman! That's the woman who stole the baby's bottle.

GUARD: While we were searching her room, her husband was seen throwing a piece of paper out the window. One of our men caught it before it touched the ground. I have it here. (*Hands paper to* KING)

KING: This is just a blank piece of paper.

GUARD: It looks that way, sire, but it must be important. Lord Splotz wanted to make sure we didn't see it.

KING: Then it must be *very* important. (*Turns paper over and over*) Hm, I wonder if this could be some sort of ghost writing. It's invisible but it might be a ghost code of some sort. Perhaps old Spiritus Unus could read it.

UPPER SECRETARY: He wouldn't know anything about it. A code calls for a very high degree of intelligence. I'm sure I can solve it, your Majesty.

LOWER SECRETARY: On the other hand, sometimes a code concerns matters of the lowest nature. I am sure I can handle it, your Majesty.

KING: It makes no difference to me who solves it, just so we figure it out.

CHANCELLOR: Shall I prepare for a thinking session?

KING: By all means, at once.

CHANCELLOR (*Claps hands and* PAGE *enters*): Page, arrange for setting up the thinking equipment. (PAGE *bows and exits.*) Secretaries, clear your minds of all other business. This is most important. Prepare to think. (SECRETARIES *close eyes and rub their heads with their hands.* PAGE *enters, carrying a stepladder, a tall dunce cap, a cushion and a beret.*)

UPPER SECRETARY (*Indicating place on floor*): Place my equipment there and hand me my thinking cap, please. (*Seats himself on top of stepladder and puts on dunce cap*) Now the paper, please. (PAGE *gets paper from* KING *and hands it to* SECRETARY.) This may take a little time. (*Turns paper at all angles and bites one corner*) Hm, very clever work indeed. Quite a professional job.

KING: But what does it say?

QUEEN: Surely there must be something written there.

UPPER SECRETARY: Well now, a few of these words are a little hard to make out.

QUEEN: Skip the hard words and read us the rest of them.

UPPER SECRETARY: Yes, but there aren't any others. In fact, there aren't any at all. It is my official opinion as Upper Secretary that this is just a blank piece of paper.

QUEEN: You're the biggest fool in the kingdom!

LOWER SECRETARY: Just a moment, your Majesty. Remember I am here too. (*Indicates place on floor for cushion to be put*) My thinking cap, please. (*Puts on beret*) Now to assume the proper position for deep thought. (*Lies flat on stomach on cushion*) We'll soon have this matter settled once and for all. (*Stretches out hand*) The paper please, Chancellor. (CHANCELLOR *hands him the paper.*) Now, let me see.

UPPER SECRETARY: You can't see anything. There's nothing there.

LOWER SECRETARY: Don't be too sure, Upper. (*Takes pair of dark glasses from his pocket and puts them on*) I can see that this paper has no concern whatever with the Lower Department. I suggest that we simply dismiss it from our minds.

KING (*Jumping up*): Minds? Minds? Why, you pair of stupid fools. You can't dismiss it from your minds. You don't have any! I wish there were someone in this kingdom who could think.

PAGE: Please, your Majesty, may I interrupt?

KING: Might as well. We're getting no place this way. What's on your—no, you probably don't have one either. What have you to say?

PAGE: I am a Junior Detective, and in volume one, page 16, of my Junior Detective Handbook there is a section on invisible ink. It says that milk can be used in writing secret messages.

KING: What difference does that make in this? Wait a minute. The nurse identified Lady Splotz as the woman who stole the baby's milk. And Lord Splotz threw the paper out the window. A note could have been written in milk on that paper.

PAGE: I'm sure it was, your Majesty.

KING: And the white milk on the white paper—

PAGE: Exactly, sire. It doesn't show!

CHANCELLOR: So what? We're right back where we started.

QUEEN: Perhaps not. Page, do you know how to read the message?

PAGE: It says in my Junior Detective Book that if the paper is smoothed with a hot iron, the message can be read.

QUEEN: Good. We'll try it. Chancellor, take the paper to the royal laundress and tell her to smooth it carefully with a hot iron.

CHANCELLOR: Yes, your Majesty. (*Exits with paper*)

KING: Page, if the information you have given us proves to be correct, you shall have a medal.

PAGE: Thank you, sire. But—there is something I would much rather have.

KING: Something more important to you than a medal?

PAGE: Oh, yes, sire. I'd much rather have Volume Two of the Junior Detective Book.

KING: Then by all means you shall have it. (CHANCELLOR *enters, waving paper*.) Here comes the report. Chancellor, what have you found out?

CHANCELLOR: It worked! The writing is clearly visible!

QUEEN: What does it say?

CHANCELLOR (*Reading*): "To our noble King: Lord and Lady Splotz beg to report a situation of utmost danger to the kingdom of Danderhoff."

QUEEN: Why, that's impossible. Are you sure that's what it says?

CHANCELLOR: Absolutely, your Majesty. But there is more. Listen to this. (*Reads*) "Lord Splotz, with his delicate sense of smell, has discovered a room in the palace where poison gas is being manufactured, while Lady Splotz, whose hearing is most acute, has detected the rhythmic beat of time bombs. The seeming friendliness of the kingdom of Eidelwitz is only a ruse to disguise obvious preparations for war." And it's signed, Lord and Lady Splotz.

KING: What a mess! Why wasn't I informed? When did we start preparing for war?

CHANCELLOR: I didn't order preparations. (*Goes to* LADY

SPLOTZ) What do you mean by writing such a note? (*Removes handkerchief from her mouth*) Now tell the truth.

LADY SPLOTZ: A-choo! (*In terror to* LADY HELEN, *who is just entering with her basket*) Don't bomb us! Please, have mercy!

HELEN: What's the matter with her? (*Thumps are heard.*) She's disturbing Horace. (*More thumps*) He's becoming very nervous. (*Thumps*)

LADY SPLOTZ: You have a time bomb in that basket! I can hear it!

HELEN: There is nothing in this basket but Horace.

LADY SPLOTZ: Call it what you will—but it is going to explode!

CHANCELLOR: No such luck. (LADY MARGARET *enters with her basket.* LORD SPLOTZ *struggles violently at his bonds.*)

MARGARET: What's going on in here? Why all the commotion? (LORD SPLOTZ *struggles and points at* MARGARET.)

KING: I'm beginning to see through all this now. Remove the handkerchief from Lord Splotz's mouth. Let's hear what he has to say. (CHANCELLOR *removes handkerchief.*)

LORD SPLOTZ: There it is! That basket is full of poison gas! Run for your lives! (*Tries to get away*) Get out of here quickly!

CHANCELLOR: I wish I could.

KING: Well, well, well, I understand it all now. Page, assemble the court. (PAGE *runs out.*)

QUEEN: It's all on account of Horace and Felicity.

KING: Exactly. Time bombs and poison gas. That's good! (*Laughs.* COURTIERS *and* LADIES *enter.* PAGE *follows them in.*)

CHANCELLOR: Ladies and gentlemen, a frog and a skunk have caused an emergency.

LADY SPLOTZ: I have never been so insulted in all my life. George, can you hear what he is calling us?

KING: Just a moment. I can explain everything, Lady Splotz. You heard Horace, Princess Helen's pet frog, tapping out messages and thought it was a time bomb. Your husband noticed the presence—or, shall I say essence—of Felicity, a pet skunk belonging to Princess Margaret, and jumped to the conclusion that it was poison gas. I might add that he did not miss the mark as far as you. However, we are not preparing for war.

LADY SPLOTZ: I don't believe a word of it. You'll have to prove it.

KING: Very well. During the remainder of your stay in Eidelwitz you shall keep Horace, the frog, with you at all times. Helen, give her your basket. (HELEN *hands basket to* LADY SPLOTZ, *who peeks inside and shudders.*)

LADY SPLOTZ: A-choo! I'm so allergic to frogs!

KING: Lord Splotz shall be required to carry Felicity, the skunk, with him as long as he stays in the palace. Margaret, give him your basket. (MARGARET *hands basket to* LORD SPLOTZ.)

LORD SPLOTZ: Gassed! I knew it was coming. (*Sinks to the floor*)

CHANCELLOR (*Rubbing his hands in glee*): This is wonderful—wonderful! The old boy flat on his face, and his wife reduced to a frog-sitter.

NURSE: Frog-sitter! Oh, that reminds me. All this time I've left the baby Princess all alone—and on her birthday, too! (*Exits, running*)

BOTH SECRETARIES: Long live the Princess!

KING: And now on with the celebration!

ALL: Long live the Princess! (*Curtain*)

THE END

Production Notes

PANIC IN THE PALACE

Characters: 2 male; 5 female; 5 male or female for Chancellor, Upper Secretary, Lower Secretary, Page, and Guard; male and female extras.

Playing Time: 25 minutes.

Costumes: All of the characters can wear elaborate costumes of make-believe royalty. The Nurse should wear a highly starched white uniform with many medals pinned on it.

Properties: Large scroll, books, covered baskets for Princess Helen and Princess Margaret, large handkerchiefs, paper, stepladder, cushion, dunce cap, beret, dark glasses.

Setting: The throne room. Two thrones with pillows on them, upstage center.

Lighting: No special effects.

The Tiger and the Brahman

by Shirley Simon

Characters

TIGER
BRAHMAN
TREE
ELEPHANT
JACKAL

SETTING: *Roadside in India.* TREE *is standing upstage left. Cage is upstage center.*

AT RISE: TIGER *is in his cage, pacing about, growling softly.* BRAHMAN *enters left.*

TIGER: Brahman! (*Pleading*) Brahman!

BRAHMAN: Who is calling me?

TIGER: Help, Brahman. Help! It is I, the Tiger. The poor Tiger who is caught in this cage.

BRAHMAN (*Sees* TIGER. *Without enthusiasm*): Oh, you. Hello there, Tiger. How are you?

TIGER: How am I? I am caught in this cage, that's how I am. How would you like to be caught in a cage like this? Trapped—like a tiger in a cage.

BRAHMAN: Oh, I am sorry for you, Tiger. Indeed I am.

TIGER: Sorry? Of what use is your pity? Now if you could help me—

BRAHMAN: I could not be of help to you, Tiger. I am only a poor Brahman.

TIGER (*Impatiently*): Of course, you can help me. All you have to do is unlock the door to this cage, and I will be free as a bird—free as you are now.

BRAHMAN (*Frightened*): Oh, no, Tiger. I could never do that. No. No.

TIGER: Why do you say that, Brahman?

BRAHMAN: Because if I were to let you out, you would—you would eat me.

TIGER (*Shocked*): Oh, no, kind Brahman! After you had done me such a kindness? Oh, no, good Brahman! I would never be such a beast as to eat you!

BRAHMAN (*Hesitates*): Well—(*Goes to door of cage, draws back*) No. No, I would not feel safe in letting you out. (*Firmly*) No, I will not do it.

TIGER (*Wheedling*): Please, please, Brahman. Good Brahman. Kind Brahman. Pious Brahman. Can you refuse to do a good deed for a fellow creature?

BRAHMAN: Well—

TIGER (*Pressing his advantage*): Please, please, please. (*Begins to cry*) If you have a heart, kind Brahman, please let me out of this terrible cage.

BRAHMAN (*Hides his face*): I can't bear to see a creature in distress. (*Looks at* TIGER) Will you give me your word that if I let you out you will not eat me?

TIGER (*Puts his paw on his heart*): My word as a gentleman. Upon the honor of my soul.

BRAHMAN: All right. (*Opens door.* TIGER *comes out, pounces upon* BRAHMAN, *and holds him by the shoulders.*)

TIGER: You were a fool to let me out. I am going to eat you for dinner.

BRAHMAN (*Frightened*): But you promised! You promised! (*Pulls away from* TIGER)

TIGER: Bah. What do promises mean? I am hungry as a tiger from being cooped up in that cage, and I intend to eat you for dinner. What's more, dinner will be in a few minutes.

BRAHMAN: After what I did for you, you should at least give me a chance. Let us ask someone. Let someone else judge whether you are acting fairly.

TIGER: You and your fancy ideas! If you hadn't been such a

soft-hearted fool, you would never have let me out of the cage.
All right. We'll ask someone. Then you will see that I am
right. You will see that everyone is out for himself and that
no one will stand up against me for a poor fool like you.

BRAHMAN: I don't believe you. I don't believe that everyone
is hard-hearted and cruel like you. A promise is a promise,
and everyone will agree with me.

TIGER: All righty. We will ask the first three things we see.
(*Leaves of* TREE *rustle in the wind.*) Ask that tree, why
don't you?

BRAHMAN (*Goes up to* TREE): Tree? (*Clasps hands in front of
him, pleading*) Tree, we are appealing to you. You see, the
Tiger was in the cage, and I came along—

TREE (*Waving branches as he talks*): I heard it all, Brahman. I
agree with the Tiger. You were very foolish to expect anything else.

BRAHMAN (*Sadly*): After what I did for him!

TREE: So? Don't I give shade to everyone? What thanks do I
get? (ELEPHANT *enters, sits down in shade of* TREE.) They
tear down my branches to feed their cattle. (*Looks at* ELE-
PHANT) See what I mean? He enjoys my shade, and what
thanks do I get?

ELEPHANT (*Stands, waves his trunk indignantly*): What
thanks do *you* get? Men ride on my back all day; I carry
princes and rajahs. Do I get a word of thanks? Not I.

BRAHMAN: Please, Mr. Elephant.

TIGER (*Jumping up and down for joy*): Ask him! Ask him! You
agreed to ask the first three things we see. Ask *him*.

BRAHMAN (*Drops to his knees in front of* ELEPHANT): Please,
Mr. Elephant.

ELEPHANT (*Gruffly*): What is it?

BRAHMAN: You see, the Tiger was in that cage, and he begged
and pleaded, and I let him out. Now he wants to eat me for
dinner.

ELEPHANT: Well?

BRAHMAN: Do you think that's fair? I surely deserve better
for being kind to him.

ELEPHANT: Fair? What is fair, and who gets what he deserves?

My dear Brahman, you should know better than that. It is everyone for himself. You should expect no more than that. If you were not a foolish dreamer, you would not have let the Tiger out in the first place. (*Sits down under* TREE)

BRAHMAN (*Shaking his head*): I cannot believe it! I cannot believe that no one will help me.

TIGER: It *is* true, Brahman, whether you believe it or not. (*Takes napkin out of pocket and ties it under his chin*) Now for dinner. That's you, Brahman.

BRAHMAN: Not yet, Tiger. Not yet. (JACKAL *enters, clowning and playing as he walks along.*) I was to ask the first *three* things I saw. I have only asked two. (*Notices* JACKAL) I will ask him.

TIGER (*Growls*): A waste of time. He will say the same as the others. But if you insist, let's get on with it.

BRAHMAN: Jackal, wait a bit. You must decide something for us. (JACKAL *is still playing, making funny faces, etc.*) It is very important, so try to concentrate.

JACKAL (*Looks around*): I'll try.

BRAHMAN: It was this way, Jackal. The Tiger was in the cage, and I came walking by. He begged and pleaded with me to let him out. I did, and now he wants to eat me.

JACKAL (*Suddenly serious, puts his paw to his head*): Now let me see if I can understand this. My poor, weak brain! You were in the cage, and I came walking by.

BRAHMAN: No, Jackal. The Tiger was in the cage, and I came walking by.

JACKAL (*Claps his paws with delight*): Now I have it. I was in the cage, and *you* came walking by.

TIGER (*Angry*): No, no, no, you fool! You are delaying my dinner with your stupidity. I was in the cage, and the Brahman came walking by.

JACKAL (*Trembling with fright*): Please don't be angry with me. I'm *trying* to understand. (*Paw to head again*) Now I think I have it. The Tiger was in the Brahman and the cage came walking by.

TIGER: No, no, no, you idiot! (*Jumps up and down in rage*)

JACKAL: My poor brain. I just can't understand.

TIGER: I'll *make* you understand. I am the Tiger. See? (*Beats his breast*) Me. Tiger.

JACKAL (*Meekly*): Yes, sir. You are the Tiger.

TIGER: And this is the Brahman. (*Pushes* BRAHMAN, *who almost falls over*) See? Him. Brahman.

JACKAL (*Eagerly*): Yes, yes. I've got that part quite well. He is the Brahman. (*Begins to dance a bit*) And I am—Oh, I've got it! I am the Jackal. Right?

TIGER (*Angry*): Yes, of course, you are the Jackal. That's not important.

JACKAL: To me it is very important.

TIGER (*Impatiently*): Let's get on. I am the Tiger, and he is the Brahman. You've got that much? (JACKAL *nods.*) Now I was in the cage.

JACKAL (*Bewildered*): Cage?

TIGER (*Yelling*): Yes, cage. Cage! (*Goes over to cage*) This is the cage, and I was in the cage.

JACKAL (*Holding his head*): That's the part I don't understand. You were in the—oh, yes, you were in the—No, I can't understand it!

TIGER (*In a rage*): Oh, you stupid Jackal! (*Jumps up and down*) Look at me! I am the Tiger! I was in the cage. Like this. (TIGER *jumps into the cage.* JACKAL *immediately closes the door. There is a loud click as the door locks.*)

JACKAL (*In a firm, clear voice*): I understand now, Tiger. Perfectly. You *were* in the cage; you *are* in the cage; you shall *stay* in the cage.

TIGER (*Screaming and sobbing*): Let me out! I've been tricked! Let me out! It's not fair! Let me out!

BRAHMAN (*Embraces* JACKAL): Thank you! Thank you! (*Turns to* TREE *and* ELEPHANT) You were wrong! You were wrong! (*To* JACKAL) These two were trying to tell me that no one would help me. They said that everyone is out only for himself.

JACKAL (*Dancing*): They were wrong! They were wrong!

ELEPHANT (*Shyly*): Tree?

TREE: Yes?

ELEPHANT: Thank you for the shade.

TREE: Oh, it's nothing, Elephant. Elephant?

ELEPHANT: Yes, Tree?

TREE: We both owe the Jackal thanks. He showed us how wrong we were. Do you know something, Elephant? I'm glad we were wrong.

TREE *and* ELEPHANT: Thank you, Jackal.

TIGER: Let me out! Let me out!

OTHERS: No. Not on your life. You got what was coming to you.

BRAHMAN: You see, Tiger, every once in a while we do get what we deserve.

THE END

Production Notes

THE TIGER AND THE BRAHMAN

Characters: 5 male or female.

Playing Time: 15 minutes.

Costumes: Tiger wears tan and black striped costume with long mane. Brahman wears white pajamas and turban. Tree wears brown costume with leaves covering arms and hair. Elephant wears gray costume with long trunk. Jackal has yellowish-brown outfit and long tail.

Setting: A roadside in India. Tree and cage are on stage at rise. There may be additional trees, rocks, etc., as desired.

Properties: Napkin, for Tiger.

Lighting: No special effects.

The King's Bean Soup

by Sally Werner

Characters

KING
FOUR ATTENDANTS
COURT JESTER
PALACE COOK
THREE COOKS
PAGE
BEGGAR

SETTING: *Throne room of the King's palace. Throne is on a raised platform at center. Exits are left and right.*

AT RISE: FOUR ATTENDANTS *are pacing back and forth across the stage.*

1ST ATTENDANT: The King has lost his appetite. He refuses everything. He wants nothing but bean soup.

2ND ATTENDANT: If it were only as simple as that. It must be a special kind of bean soup—an old-fashioned kind of bean soup.

3RD ATTENDANT: Made from an old recipe his great-grand-mother, the Queen of the North Country, once had.

4TH ATTENDANT: We have searched through all the cook-books in the palace. We have tried all the recipes for bean soup. His Majesty insists that we have not found the right recipe.

1ST ATTENDANT: Oh, dear, something must be done. The King must have his bean soup. He has scarcely eaten any-thing for a week.

PAGE (*Rushing in*): The cook has found it! He has found the lost recipe for bean soup!

1ST ATTENDANT (*To* 2ND ATTENDANT): They have found
the recipe.

2ND ATTENDANT (*To* 3RD ATTENDANT): They have found
the recipe.

3RD ATTENDANT (*To* 4TH ATTENDANT): They have found
the recipe.

ALL: They have found the recipe! The King shall have his
bean soup!

JESTER (*Comes in dancing and singing*): Bean soup! Bean soup!
The King shall have his bean soup! (*Dances out again*)

PALACE COOK (*Comes in carrying old cookbook*): Alas and
alas! The recipe is old and torn. One ingredient is missing.

1ST ATTENDANT: Ssh! Not so loud. The King must not know.
Prepare the soup anyway. Perhaps he will not notice. Make
haste! (COOK *hurries away.*)

4TH ATTENDANT: Meanwhile, we must try to find the missing
ingredient. I will send word to all the best cooks in the land.
Surely someone will know what is missing.

ALL: Yes—yes. Make haste. (4TH ATTENDANT *hurries away
as* KING *enters and sits on throne.* ATTENDANTS *bow.*)

KING (*Shakes head sadly*): Oh, I feel weak—I feel faint. Oh,
that I could have but one sip of my favorite bean soup.

1ST ATTENDANT: We have good news, your Majesty.

2ND ATTENDANT: Very good news, your Majesty.

3RD ATTENDANT: Excellent news, your Majesty.

1ST ATTENDANT: The lost recipe has been found.

KING (*Very excited*): You mean my great-grandmother's bean
soup recipe?

2ND ATTENDANT: Yes, your Majesty. The recipe has been
found.

KING: And I am to have my bean soup today?

ALL (*Bowing*): Yes, your Majesty—today.

KING: Ah! At last! At last! My favorite bean soup. Ah! (PAL-
ACE COOK *enters, carrying bowl and spoon on tray. Places it
before* KING. *He tastes it, smacks, rolls eyes upward, frowns,
shakes head.*) No—no—no! Something is missing. It is not the
same, I tell you. It lacks something. Why, oh why, can't I have
my favorite bean soup? (*Puts head in hands and groans*) Take

this soup out and give it to the beggars at the roadside. Take it away! (PALACE COOK *takes tray and exits with* 2ND AT-TENDANT.)

1ST ATTENDANT: Your Majesty, let me explain. The recipe was found at last, but it was in a very old book and one ingredient was torn away. We thought it was some small item of little importance, so the soup was made anyway.

KING: The missing ingredient must be found, I tell you! It must be found! Why don't you do something?

3RD ATTENDANT: We—we have, your Majesty. We have sent word to all the best cooks in the land. They should be here very soon and someone will know what is missing from the recipe.

KING: Whoever finds the missing ingredient shall be well rewarded.

4TH ATTENDANT (*Entering and bowing before* KING): The very best cooks in the land have come, your Majesty. First comes the cook from the Hill Country.

1ST COOK (*Enters carrying bowl of soup on tray*): Your Highness, I have prepared bean soup from the lost recipe and added a very special herb which grows only in the Hill Country. I am the only one who knows about this herb, sire, and I believe it is the missing ingredient. (KING *tastes soup, frowns and shakes head.*)

KING: Take it away! That is not the bean soup I am longing for. You have not found the missing ingredient. (1ST COOK *takes tray and leaves.*)

4TH ATTENDANT: The very best cook from the Low Country is here, your Majesty.

2ND COOK (*Enters, carrying bowl of soup*): Your Highness, I have prepared bean soup from the lost recipe and added a very special herb which grows only in the Low Country. I am the only one who knows about this herb, sire. I am sure it must be the missing ingredient. (KING *tastes soup, frowns and shakes head.*)

KING: Take it away! That is not the missing ingredient. (2ND COOK *takes tray and leaves.*) Why, oh why, can't I have my favorite bean soup?

4TH ATTENDANT: Your Highness, the very best cook from the Island Country is here.

3RD COOK (*Enters, carrying bowl of soup on tray*): Your Highness, I have prepared bean soup from the lost recipe and added a special plant which grows only at the bottom of the sea. Only I know about this plant and I am sure it is the missing ingredient, sire. (KING *tastes soup, frowns and shakes head.*)

KING: No—*no*—*no!* This is not right. (*Gives bowl back.* COOK *leaves.*) Is there no one in the world who knows what the missing ingredient might be? Why, oh why, can't I have my favorite bean soup? Oh, that my royal great-grandmother were here. Only she would know what is missing. (*There is a great noise offstage and* 2ND ATTENDANT *comes in dragging a ragged* BEGGAR, *who carries a pot of soup.*) What is this great commotion?

2ND ATTENDANT: We found this beggar, your Majesty, begging for food on the palace grounds. That is quite against the rules, sire.

KING: Did you not give him the bean soup my cook prepared?

2ND ATTENDANT: We did, your Majesty, but he will not go away. He says he wishes to talk to the King. What shall we do with him, sire?

KING: Beggar, what have you to say for yourself?

BEGGAR (*Bowing in front of* KING): Your Majesty, they said they brought me bean soup. I think you should know, your Highness, that there is one ingredient missing.

KING (*Jumps up*): And do you know what that ingredient might be? What is wrong with this bean soup they keep bringing me? Speak up, beggar.

BEGGAR: They have forgotten to add the beans, sire.

ALL (*Repeating one after the other*): No beans? No beans?

BEGGAR: Your Majesty, may I add that the soup is made from a very old and very tasty recipe. I have added the beans and I would feel greatly honored to have your Majesty taste the soup now.

KING: Indeed I will. Here—let me try it. (BEGGAR *comes forward and bows.* KING *tastes soup, rolls eyes, smacks his lips and then smiles.*) Ah-h-h!

ALL: Ah-h-h!

KING: My great-grandmother's bean soup! This is it! This is it! You have found the missing ingredient. Beggar, you shall be my royal cook. You shall have fine clothes and gold and you shall ride in a fine chariot. You shall be very happy. (BEGGAR *looks sad*.) What is the trouble, beggar?

BEGGAR: Your Majesty, you are much too kind. I cannot accept.

KING: Nonsense! I insist!

BEGGAR: I couldn't think of it, your Majesty.

KING: Don't be silly. It's all settled.

BEGGAR: But, your Majesty—the only thing I can cook is bean soup.

KING (*A little worried*): Only bean soup?

BEGGAR (*Nodding*): Only bean soup.

KING: Hmm. That means we would have to eat bean soup every day. (BEGGAR nods. KING *shakes his head, then smiles*.) I have it! You shall be royal cook for Saturdays. Every Saturday you shall come to the palace and make bean soup for me.

BEGGAR: I would be happy to do that, your Majesty. (*He bows low*.)

JESTER (*Dancing about and singing as the curtains close*): Saturday, bean soup—all you lucky people, I wish the same to you.

THE END

Production Notes

THE KING'S BEAN SOUP

Characters: 1 male; 11 male or female.

Playing Time: 10 minutes.

Costumes: The King wears a long robe and a crown. The cooks are dressed in white and wear aprons and chef's hats. The Jester and Page wear typical costumes, while the Attendants may be dressed in red, white and blue uniforms. Beggar wears any ragged clothes.

Properties: A bowl, a spoon and a tray will serve for the four appearances of the soup on the stage; cookbook; pot and spoon.

Setting: Throne room of the King's palace. There are entrances at right and left. A throne on a raised platform is at center and there are several chairs, at right and left, on each side of the throne. The room may be decorated as elaborately as desired.

Lighting: No special effects.

The White Spider's Gift

by Jamie Turner

Characters

WHITE SPIDER, *Offstage voice*
KUMA, *Guarani boy*
TWO GIRLS
OLD WOMAN
PIKI, *Guarani boy*
MOTHER, *Piki's mother*
TUKIRA, *Chieftain's daughter*
CHIEFTAIN
MESSENGER
DIKA
DABU
KINTA } *Guarani boys*
MUNGA
VILLAGE PEOPLE, *extras*

SCENE 1

TIME: *Long ago.*
SETTING: *Forest of Paraguay. Played before curtain. Murals on walls flanking stage depict trees and undergrowth. One large bush, displayed on right wall outside curtain, represents spider's home. Bush must be visible throughout the play. A large spider's web of white yarn covers most of the bush.*
BEFORE RISE: KUMA *enters left, and runs toward spider's web.*
SPIDER (*From offstage*): Help me! Please, I am over here in the spring!
KUMA (*Stopping; irritably*): What? Who are you? (*Peers over stage apron*)

197

SPIDER: Please, will you bend down here and lift me out? I have fallen into the spring.

KUMA: What? Help a spider? I cannot stop for such a small matter. I must go find tea leaves for my father. I have already wasted much time, and he will be angry.

SPIDER (*Pleading*): Oh, please. I would not trouble you if I were not so tired. The water bubbles up so, and I cannot reach the edge.

KUMA (*Looking up at sky*): I must hurry. Father is waiting. (*Runs out. 1ST GIRL enters at side, looks along floor as if hunting.*)

SPIDER: Please, little girl, help me! See, I am here in the spring.

1ST GIRL (*Stooping*): Where? Oh, I see—why, you are a spider! I am afraid of spiders! And you are a white one, besides; I have never seen a white spider. You must be ill. I cannot help you; I might get hurt.

SPIDER: I am harmless, little girl. Please do help me. My strength is almost gone.

1ST GIRL: Oh, but I could not bear to touch a spider. Swim to the edge and climb out yourself. Spiders are good climbers.

SPIDER: I cannot! The water swirls around me with great force; it is stronger than I am.

1ST GIRL: If I remember, I will send a friend to help you when I get back to the village. I am looking for the beautiful *nand-ari* flower now. I cannot stop. (*Exits, humming and stooping to examine flowers. OLD WOMAN with walking stick enters, shuffling toward spider web, dragging burlap sack behind her.*)

SPIDER (*Calling*): Kind woman! Please help me! (OLD WOMAN *cocks head, puts hand to ear*)

OLD WOMAN: What is it that I hear?

SPIDER: It is I, the little white spider who lives in the *yerba* bush beside the spring.

OLD WOMAN (*Looking up at web*): Eh? Who? Where?

SPIDER: No, no, not up there. I am down here in the water! I fell from my web and cannot get out. Please help me!

OLD WOMAN (*Looking over edge of stage; shaking head, sadly*):

Ah, yes, life is full of trouble, little spider. And the older one gets, the more burdened with care he becomes.

SPIDER: But will you not help me, Guarani woman? Will you not hold your stick down and let me crawl upon it so that you may lift me out?

OLD WOMAN: I am old, little spider. I must help myself. I must look for twigs so that I may have a fire tonight. (*Exits, mumbling*) Trouble, trouble. Life is full of trouble. (PIKI *and* MOTHER *enter, carrying large earthen jars, and walk across stage.*)

SPIDER: Help! Oh, please! I am growing weak! Please help me!

PIKI: Do you hear a cry for help, Mother?

MOTHER: Yes, Piki, I do. (*Calls*) Where are you?

SPIDER: Here in the spring! (*Voice grows fainter.*) I cannot swim any longer. My legs are . . .

PIKI (*Dropping to knees and looking over edge of stage*): Oh, Mother, it is a spider. She is sinking! (*Reaches down. "Spider"* [*see Production Notes*] *may be concealed in* PIKI's *hand when he first enters or hidden on ledge near spring.*)

MOTHER: Can you reach her, Piki?

PIKI (*Rising, cupping hand gently*): Yes. Oh, I hope she's still alive!

MOTHER: Oh, Piki, see—she opens her eyes!

PIKI (*Patting inside hand with finger*): Little spider, are you really alive? I am so happy I could catch you before the water pulled you down.

MOTHER: Is this the little white spider who lives in the *yerba* bush there beside the spring? (*Looks up at web*)

PIKI: Yes. I see her each day when I come to fill the water jars. She lives so quietly and peacefully, spinning her beautiful web of silk. I am pleased that I could help her.

SPIDER (*Weakly*): Thank you, kind Piki. You are a good, strong young Guarani.

PIKI: Strong? But it does not take strength to lift a small spider.

SPIDER: No, it does not take a strong body, Piki, but it takes a strong heart. A selfless heart is the strongest of all. I am feeling better now. Will you please place me back in my web so that I may rest?

PIKI: Certainly. (*Places* SPIDER *in center of web*) Rest quietly, little friend. I will visit you tomorrow to see if you are well. Goodbye.

SPIDER: Goodbye, Piki. Someday I shall help you as you have helped me this day. (PIKI *stoops as if filling jar with water.* MOTHER *takes it from him and gives him another to fill.* TUKIRA *enters at side, pretending to gather berries, placing them into basket.* PIKI *looks up and sees her; he stands slowly, gazing in wonder.* TUKIRA *sees him, looks down quickly, turns and runs off.*)

PIKI: Mother! Who is she?

MOTHER: She is Tukira, the chieftain's daughter.

PIKI: But why have I never seen her before?

MOTHER: When Tukira was a small child, her mother died, and the chieftain sent her to live with an aunt in a distant village. She is sixteen now and has come back to our village to live. The chieftain will soon choose a husband for her.

PIKI: How will he do that?

MOTHER: Tomorrow he will assemble the young men from our village and announce his plan. You will be among them.

PIKI (*Lifting jar to his shoulder*): Tukira . . . what a beautiful name.

MOTHER (*Lifting other jar*): Yes. A beautiful name for a beautiful princess. Let us start home now, Piki. It is growing late. (*They exit. Curtain*)

* * * * *

SCENE 2

TIME: *The next day.*

SETTING: *Chieftain's home. Clothcovered wooden frame center has leafy branches laid across the top. Large earthen jars, weaving frame, and wood for fire are on either side. Background mural shows forest.*

AT RISE: CHIEFTAIN *sits on floor beneath frame.* 1ST WOMAN *pretends to cook over open fire.* 2ND WOMAN, *carrying earthen jar, crosses stage and exits.* CHILDREN *run across, laughing as they play tag.* 3RD WOMAN *pretends to weave on loom.* MESSENGER *enters and bows before* CHIEFTAIN.

CHIEFTAIN: Have the six youths received my message to come today?

MESSENGER (*Bowing*): Yes, Chieftain. They come now. (PIKI, DIKA, DABU, KINTA, MUNGA, *and* KUMA *enter, carrying bows and arrows. All but* CHIEFTAIN, MESSENGER, *and boys exit. Boys stand on either side of* CHIEFTAIN, *with backs to audience.*)

CHIEFTAIN: I have chosen you six youths to have a contest. The winner of the contest may have the hand of my daughter Tukira in marriage and perhaps may rule our village when I grow old. (*Speaks to each of six in turn*) You, Kuma, are tall and strong. Dika, you swim and fish with the skill of your father. With your swift arrows, Dabu, you have fed your family well. You, Kinta, have the wisdom of your ancestors. Munga, you are brave in times of war. And you, Piki, are good and noble. The contest will begin now and will end in three days. Today you will compete in running, shooting, and wrestling. First will be the foot race. The course is clearly marked through the forest and back to our village. You may take a moment to prepare. My messenger will signal the start. (MESSENGER *sits, beats on small drum. Boys lay down bows and arrows and prepare to run.*)

KUMA (*Boastfully*): I shall surely win the race, for I am the oldest.

DABU: You may be the oldest, but I have seen young Piki run— and he is very fast. He saves his energy by running steadily, and then his feet seem to grow wings as he nears the end of a race.

KUMA: He will not pass me. You will see. (*Boys line up in front of* MESSENGER, *facing left. Drum grows louder.* MESSENGER *shouts, and race begins. Boys run offstage and follow prescribed course through audience, with* KUMA *in the lead. With* PIKI *right behind,* KUMA *returns to stage slightly ahead of others.* KUMA *glances back and deliberately trips* PIKI. CHIEFTAIN *stares straight ahead, apparently not seeing the incident.* PIKI *rises, brushes off knees and hands.* KUMA

looks exultant. Other boys return to stage, panting, and
CHIEFTAIN *motions for all to sit.*)
CHIEFTAIN: You all ran well, but you, Kuma, finished first.
(PIKI *drops his head briefly but raises it again.*) Next is the
shooting contest. (*Points off left*) Do you see the red feather
on the trunk of the old tree beside the river? (*Boys nod.*) The
one whose arrow pierces the tip of the feather will win this
contest. (MESSENGER *stands far left, announcing results of
each boy's shot.*) Munga, you may try first. (*One at a time boys
stand, facing left, and raise their bows slowly as if to aim
an arrow.*)
MUNGA (*Shooting*): How close is it?
MESSENGER: It is very close, only a hand's length from the
feather's tip. (MUNGA *runs out left.* KINTA *shoots next and
runs out left.*) That was a good shot, but the first arrow is
still closer.
DABU: Surely I can shoot closer. I will pretend the feather is
the forehead of a wild boar. (*Shoots*)
MESSENGER: Dabu's arrow is only a finger's width from the
tip of the feather! (DABU *shouts joyfully as he rushes off left.*)
DIKA: Save your joy, Dabu. There are three more of us to try.
(*Shoots*)
MESSENGER: Your arrow did not fly true, Dika. It fell far
beneath the feather. (DIKA *exits, disappointed.*)
KUMA (*Boastfully*): With my new bow I can easily win. Watch
how straight my arrow will fly! (*Shoots*) I won, did I not?
MESSENGER: No, Kuma, your arrow has fallen near the bot-
tom of the feather's stem, not its tip. Now, Piki, it is your
turn. (KUMA *stalks angrily right and sits, sulking.*).
KUMA: *You* will never win, Piki. You are the youngest of us.
Have you ever even held a bow before?
PIKI: I have held a bow for many years, Kuma. This was my
father's bow, and it has never failed me. (*Shoots. Boys and
MESSENGER shout excitedly and run back onstage, with
MESSENGER holding feather aloft. Feather is large and may
be made out of red construction paper, cut partway down the
middle as if split by the arrow.*)
MESSENGER: See, Piki, your arrow pierced the feather's tip,

dividing it exactly in half. You have won! (KUMA *scowls angrily.*)

CHIEFTAIN: Kuma has won the foot race, and Piki has won the shooting contest. Now you will all wrestle. (MESSENGER *hands* CHIEFTAIN *a stick.*) You will hold this stick between you, and you must keep both hands on the stick at all times. You may not move your feet once the contest begins. The one who can force the other to lose his balance will win. Kuma and Dika will fight first. (KUMA *and* DIKA *stand facing each other with stick between them, each grasping it with both hands. They plant their feet firmly.*)

MESSENGER: Begin. (KUMA *and* DIKA *begin their "fight." After brief struggle,* DIKA *loses balance, and* KUMA *wins. Next,* DABU *and* KINTA *fight, and* DABU *wins. Then* MUNGA *and* PIKI *fight, and* PIKI *wins.*)

CHIEFTAIN: Now the three winners will fight. First, Piki and Dabu. (PIKI *and* DABU *face each other and begin. Others form semicircle behind them, upstage, facing audience, but* KUMA *stands in back of others, drops to ground, takes tube out of his waistband, and aims at* PIKI's *ankle, as if blowing stone or dart.* PIKI *winces and grabs his ankle, losing his balance. No one else appears to see what* KUMA *did.*) Dabu has won. Now, Dabu, you and Kuma will fight. (DABU *and* KUMA *fight, and* DABU *wins after a struggle.*)

KUMA (*Throwing stick down angrily*): It was not fair! I was not ready to start!

CHIEFTAIN: Dabu is the winner. (*Looks around at boys*) You have all done well today, but only three have won. Kuma, Piki, and Dabu will now compete in another contest, which will end in three days. The winner will marry my daughter Tukira on that day. (DIKA, KINTA, *and* MUNGA *exit;* CHIEFTAIN *addresses remaining three.*) Each of you must find a beautiful gift to present to my daughter. Return in three days with your gifts, and she will choose the best. Go now and may your search be rewarded. (*Drum beats as* KUMA, DABU, *and* PIKI *exit. Curtain*)

* * * * *

SCENE 3

TIME: *Two days later.*
SETTING: *The forest; before curtain.*
BEFORE RISE: PIKI *enters, carrying jar. He approaches spring, kneels down as if to fill jar, then sets jar beside him and sits, looking sad.*
SPIDER (*From offstage*): Piki, Piki, why do you look so sad?
PIKI (*Looking up at bush in surprise*): Oh, it is you, little spider. (*Sighs*) My heart is heavy because I shall not win the beautiful Tukira for my wife. I ran well, I shot well, and I fought well. But now I have no hope. Tukira will surely become the wife of Kuma or Dabu.
SPIDER: You can win the final contest with my help.
PIKI: Do you know of the contest?
SPIDER: Yes. I listen as I sit quietly in my *yerba* bush spinning my web. The women talk as they come to fill their water jars. I heard them speak of the gifts for the lovely princess.
PIKI: Yes, the lovely princess . . . but she will never be mine. Tomorrow we must present our gifts. It is said that Dabu will bring a headdress woven of colorful feathers from rare birds. And Kuma boasts openly of his gift, a necklace of gold, encrusted with the lovely topaz stones of the highlands. But I . . . I have nothing. My mother and I are poor, unlike the families of Dabu and Kuma.
SPIDER: Piki, did you not hear me? I shall help you win Tukira's hand.
PIKI: But how can you help, little spider?
SPIDER: Go home to your mother, Piki, but return to the spring at sunrise. Your special gift for Tukira will be ready. Be joyful, Piki, for the morning will dawn bright.
PIKI (*Puzzled yet hopeful*): I shall do as you say, little friend. Bless you for giving me hope.
SPIDER: Bless you, Piki, for taking time to save me from the bubbling spring. I promised on that day to repay your kindness, and I will. (PIKI *exits, looking back in wonder at spider's bush. Lights dim and music plays softly, indicating nighttime.*) I will spin my most delicate thread and sprinkle it with

moon dust. In the center I will form the beautiful *guava* flower
. . . the loveliest I have ever spun. And then, rare orchids of
many designs. Then I shall spin stars to twinkle around the
edges, and then I shall weave all the designs together with a
fine, intricate lace. Now I will begin my work, for I must finish
before the sun reaches the horizon. (*Music continues for 30
seconds, with lights gradually coming up. Music stops.*)

PIKI (*Entering left, approaching bush*): The new day has
dawned, and I have returned as you said, friend.

SPIDER: Look beneath the bush, Piki. I have finished your gift.

PIKI (*Removing lace mantle from bush; holding it up*): Oh, it is
beautiful! Never have I seen such delicate lace! It is fit for
a princess.

SPIDER: It will be Tukira's bridal veil. Now, hurry home to
show it to your mother, and then take it to the chieftain at
the appointed time.

PIKI: How I thank you, White Spider! (*Gently folds lace and
turns to exit, but KUMA enters, blocks his way. PIKI hides
lace behind his back.*)

KUMA: Piki, what makes you rise so early? Surely you are not
still searching the forests for a gift worthy of the princess?
(*Laughs*)

PIKI: No, Kuma, I am no longer searching. But I cannot talk;
I must go now. (PIKI *starts to move on, but* KUMA *stops
him roughly.*)

KUMA: The women of the village say you have no gift to bring.
(*Laughs rudely*) *I* have fashioned gold into a necklace for
Tukira.

PIKI: Yes, Kuma, I have heard of it. The whole village has
heard.

KUMA: And soon Tukira will wear my necklace and become
my bride. What will you bring, Piki? Perhaps a bowl of tea
leaves? (*Laughs*) Or a dish of berries? (*Laughs harder*) Or
perhaps the lovely princess would like a new mat woven from
dried grass. (*Laughs more*) Go, Piki, and I shall meet you soon
as we stand before the chieftain—unless you decide not to
come. I would not blame you.

PIKI (*Passing* KUMA): I shall be there, Kuma. (*Exits, followed by* KUMA, *laughing. Curtain rises.*)

* * *

TIME: *Later that morning.*
SETTING: *Chieftain's home.*
AT RISE: CHIEFTAIN *and* TUKIRA *sit side by side.* 2ND GIRL *combs and arranges flowers in* TUKIRA's *hair.* MESSENGER *sits behind them, tapping a drum as they talk.*
CHIEFTAIN: The morning has come, daughter. Soon the three young braves will hear the drum and arrive to present their gifts.
TUKIRA: Father, what if I cannot decide which is the most beautiful gift?
CHIEFTAIN: You will know. Your heart will tell you. And after you choose, I shall give one final test to prove the worthiness of your husband. Stand, now. Here come the youths. (CHIEFTAIN *and* TUKIRA *stand as* DUBA, KUMA, *and* PIKI *enter, carrying gifts behind their backs.* MESSENGER *stops beating drum, and* VILLAGE PEOPLE *enter, gather around.* CHIEFTAIN *addresses boys.*) The three days have ended, and now Tukira will choose among you. Present your gift first, Duba. (DUBA *steps forward, kneels, holds out feathered headdress.* PEOPLE *murmur approval.*)
TUKIRA (*Taking headdress; with admiration*): It is lovely. Such rare feathers and such brilliant colors! Thank you, Dabu. (TUKIRA *hands headdress to* 2ND GIRL. DABU *rises and moves back.*)
CHIEFTAIN: Now your gift, Kuma. (KUMA *steps forward, kneels, presents necklace to* TUKIRA. PEOPLE *murmur even louder and lean forward for closer look.* KUMA *glances back at* PIKI *scornfully.*)
TUKIRA (*In admiring tone*): What fine gold! And such glowing topaz stones! Thank you, Kuma. (TUKIRA *hands necklace to* 2ND GIRL.)
KUMA (*Pompously*): The topaz stones do not compare to the beauty of your eyes, lovely princess. (TUKIRA *lowers her eyes,*

and CHIEFTAIN *motions* KUMA *back.* KUMA *speaks to* DUBA *and* PIKI.) I can see in her eyes that she admires the necklace above all else.

CHIEFTAIN: Piki, you may present your gift now. (PIKI *steps forward, kneels, and presents lace mantle.* PEOPLE *gasp, reach forward to touch it, murmuring loudly at its beauty.* TUKIRA *takes mantle, unfolds it, studies it silently.*)

TUKIRA (*After a moment*): Never have I held such beautiful lace. It is clearly a miracle, for no hands could spin such glistening threads and intricate patterns—so delicate yet so strong. I choose Piki's lace mantle as the best gift, Father. (PIKI *bows head gratefully, rises, steps back.* KUMA *scowls angrily.*)

CHIEFTAIN: You have chosen well, daughter. (*Addresses boys*) Before I give up my daughter, however, there is one final test.

KUMA (*Aside*): Aha! Perhaps I shall win yet!

CHIEFTAIN: It is said that the spirit of a great tiger roams throughout our forest. Only the wisest and noblest among the Guaranis can see the spirit. (*Motions toward audience*) Look into the forest and tell me what the tiger wears around his neck. (PEOPLE *murmur.* DABU, KUMA, *and* PIKI *gaze out silently.*)

DABU (*Questioningly*): I believe he wears around his neck a . . . a cord of twisted vines?

KUMA (*Boastfully*): Yes, yes, I see the spirit clearly, but you are wrong, Dabu. He wears about his neck a beaded leather strap. He turns his head now and gazes at me, recognizing me as one of the wise and noble. (*Kneels and bows toward "spirit"*)

CHIEFTAIN: Piki, what can you see?

PIKI (*Puzzled*): I have looked and looked, Chieftain, but I see no tiger spirit at all. (PEOPLE *murmur.*)

CHIEFTAIN: You have shown yourself worthy, young Piki, for it is also said that the tiger spirit never reveals himself where many people are gathered. I do not know what you saw, Dabu, nor you, Kuma, but it was not the great tiger spirit. You alone, Piki, have been truthful. Surely you are the wisest and noblest of all the young Guaranis. You have competed with

honor and have won the hand of my daughter in marriage.
Let us make ready for the ceremony. It will be tonight.

TUKIRA: And I shall wear the lovely lace mantle for my veil.

PIKI: Yes, you shall. Just as my friend said you would. (PIKI
gently places mantle over TUKIRA's *head as curtain falls.*)

THE END

Production Notes

THE WHITE SPIDER'S GIFT

Characters: 6 female; 7 male; 1 male or female for Messenger; male and female extras.

Playing Time: 20 minutes.

Costumes: Girls wear simple "sack-style" dresses with wooden beads or colorful sashes. They may also wear flower wreaths or headbands. All characters
are barefoot or wear simple leather sandals. Boys wear loose shorts of solid
color. Some may also wear capes, headbands, and beaded ankle bands. Piki
and Kuma each wear some distinguishing item, such as colorful armband
or headpiece.

Properties: Walking stick; burlap sack; two large water jars; spider made of
large cotton ball sprinkled with glitter, with eight small pipe cleaner legs;
basket; bows and arrows; drum; large feather made of red construction paper, cut partway down the middle as if split by arrow; sturdy stick or dowel;
blowtube; comb; flowers; feathered headdress; gold necklace; lace mantle.
Note: Lace mantle should already be hidden somewhere around the bush
at beginning of Scene 3.

Setting: Before Rise, forest of Paraguay. Murals on walls flanking stage depict
trees and undergrowth. One large bush, displayed on right wall outside
curtain, represents spider's home, and must be visible throughout the play.
Large spider's web of white yarn covers most of the bush. At Rise, Chieftain's Home. Cloth-covered wooden frame center has leafy branches laid
across the top. Large earthen jars, weaving frame, and wood for fire are on
either side. Background mural shows forest.

Lighting and sound: In Scene 3, lights dim, then come up, and soft music is
played, to indicate passage of time.

The Girl Whose Fortune Sought Her

by Patricia Clapp

Characters

MELINDA
WIDOW
CLOWN
PEDDLER
GIRL
MAN

TIME: A *spring morning.*
SETTING: *The yard in front of the Widow's cottage. The cottage stands upstage center, and there is a bench on either side of working door. Everywhere one looks, beautiful flowers grow.*
AT RISE: MELINDA *comes out of the front door, carrying small gardening tools and starts to prune the flowers in the window boxes, and carefully to loosen the earth around them. A moment later* WIDOW *comes out door.*
WIDOW: That's right, be gentle with them. Careful of those new little leaves.
MELINDA: Yes, Mother.
WIDOW: We must be gentle with all living things, Melinda, whether they're plants or people.
MELINDA: Yes, Mother.
WIDOW: You have a nice touch with flowers, child.
MELINDA: Thank you, Mother.
WIDOW: What's the matter, child? You don't seem very happy. Is something wrong?
MELINDA: No, Mother.

WIDOW: "Yes, Mother; no, Mother; thank you, Mother"—what is it, Melinda? It isn't like you to be so quiet. Tell me what the trouble is.

MELINDA (*Suddenly throwing down her trowel and shears*): I'm just tired of staying home all day, day after day, doing nothing but tending the flowers and sweeping the floors and drying the dishes. I want to go away, to find something *big* to do. Mother, I want to go to seek my fortune!

WIDOW: But, child! A girl can't do that. It isn't right! You can't go wandering off alone.

MELINDA: If I were a boy I could. Boys always go off to seek their fortunes.

WIDOW: But you're *not* a boy. You're my only daughter. I can't let you go traipsing off around the world by yourself.

MELINDA: Why must boys have all the fun? Why can't girls do anything? It isn't fair!

WIDOW: You're not the first to say that, nor the last, I'll wager. But until you marry and have a home of your own, your place is here.

MELINDA: Mother, if I can't go off to seek my fortune may I sit here, and perhaps my fortune will seek me?

WIDOW: Whatever do you mean, Melinda?

MELINDA: I don't quite know, Mother. But people go by here all day on their way to the big cities. Perhaps if I sat here and talked to some of them, one of them could help me, could give me excitement, or something important to do, or big pieces of gold—or—or—well, whatever it is that boys find when they go to seek *their* fortunes. There must be something more for me than just snipping leaves off the flowers.

WIDOW: Why must you be so discontented, Melinda?

MELINDA: I don't know, Mother. I just want to *do* something, something that will be important, that will really matter. Please, Mother, just let me sit here and talk to the people who go by. I won't go away, I promise.

WIDOW: Well, I guess there's no harm in that.

MELINDA: Then I may? Oh, thank you, Mother. (*She settles herself on one of the benches and folds her hands expectantly.*)

WIDOW: But mind you, stay here in the yard.

MELINDA: I will, Mother. I'll stay right here. I'll just let my fortune find me.

WIDOW (*Shaking her head*): Such a strange girl! Your fortune, indeed! (*She goes back into cottage and closes the door behind her.* MELINDA *leans forward to peer up and down the road, suddenly sees someone coming and smooths her skirts neatly around her, touching her hair and generally putting herself in readiness to meet her fortune.* CLOWN *enters, singing loudly and happily, doing a little dance step as he approaches.*)

MELINDA: Hello.

CLOWN (*Coming to a stop and making a low, exaggerated bow*): Madam! Good day to you!

MELINDA: Where are you going?

CLOWN: To work, dear madam, to work.

MELINDA: Do clowns work? I thought it was all play for them.

CLOWN: Play? Madam! (*He does a few acrobatics.*) Does that look like play?

MELINDA: Well, yes. It does. Isn't it?

CLOWN: Madam, I will have you know that even those few simple movements took months to learn. And every day I must find new ways to amuse people, new ways to make them laugh. Alas and alack, it is work, dear madam. (*Cheerfully*) But I like it.

MELINDA: Where are you going now?

CLOWN: To town to join a traveling troupe. We will go round the countryside, visiting fairs and little villages, making the children laugh and the grownups tap their toes to our music. (*Offering his arm*) Will you join me?

MELINDA: Join you? (*She laughs*) What could I do? I can't stand on my head, nor spin like a top!

CLOWN: You can sing, perhaps?

MELINDA: Not very well.

CLOWN: Dance?

MELINDA: Hardly at all.

CLOWN: Juggle?

MELINDA: I'm afraid not.

CLOWN: Dear, dear! You *are* limited! If you don't mind my asking, what *can* you do?

MELINDA (*Hanging her head*): Nothing, I'm afraid.

CLOWN (*Sitting down on the ground and absently picking one of the flowers*): Nonsense! Everyone can do something. This flower, for instance. It not only looks beautiful, but it also smells delightful. (*He sniffs it with a comical expression of ecstasy.*) Think of the people to whom this flower could bring pleasure.

MELINDA: For instance?

CLOWN: Me, for instance. (*He tucks it behind his ear.*) There! You see? Now it will bounce along beside me, reminding me of this lovely garden, and the pleasant rest I found in it.

MELINDA: If only I could go with you! I want to see the cities and the fairs and the other villages. I want to see the people and hear the children laughing.

CLOWN: And leave this quiet place? Leave this for noise and dust, and the long roads and the pushing crowds? Leave all these beautiful flowers for tinsel and shabby costumes? Leave this perfumed place for the smell of canvas and cheap powder? Oh no, madam! Stay here, this is the right place for you.

MELINDA: Then why do *you* go?

CLOWN: Because I am a clown. It is all I know. It is the way I live. Everyone has something he can do, and I can be a clown. I can bring a few minutes of laughter every day to people who do not laugh enough. That's why I must go. (*He bounces to his feet.*) But I thank you for the flower. It is beautiful, like you. (*He bows deeply again, and starts off down the road, skipping a little and sniffing the flower.*)

MELINDA: Goodbye, Clown.

CLOWN: Farewell, madam. Stay with your flowers. Farewell. (*He exits.* MELINDA *settles back, and as she waits for someone else to appear she reaches down and idly picks a dead leaf from one of the plants. In a moment* PEDDLER *appears, a heavy pack strapped to his back and a string of bells around his neck that ring as he plods along.*)

MELINDA: Hello.

PEDDLER (*Stopping*): Hello, young lady. A good day to you.

MELINDA: Thank you. (PEDDLER *takes a large handkerchief*

from his pocket and wipes his face and forehead.) Are you hot? Won't you sit down and rest a moment?

PEDDLER: Why, thankee, young lady. That's very kind of you. (*He unslings his pack and lets it fall to the ground.*) Such a lovely place to rest in. You must be very happy here.

MELINDA: Not really. I should like to travel as you do, to see the world.

PEDDLER: The world? (*He sits down, rubbing his shoulders which are tired from the heavy pack.*) But it is all the same. Some places a little prettier—like this; some places a little uglier. But all about the same. (*Hopefully*) Perhaps I could show you a few trinkets while we sit here? A comb for your pretty hair, perhaps? A ribbon for your bonnet?

MELINDA: I am sorry. I have no money for such things. We are very poor, sir.

PEDDLER (*Looking around him*): Poor? In this place? But you have a wealth of beauty here. No one can be poor in such a place.

MELINDA: It is only the flowers. And I cannot buy your wares with flowers.

PEDDLER: And why can't you? Give me some of your flowers and I will let you choose whatever you like from my pack.

MELINDA: But what good are the flowers to you? They are worth nothing.

PEDDLER: Ah, there you're wrong. There is a little girl in the next village. She is ill. She has lain in bed for months, never able to see the world outside. The place she lives in is shabby. There is nothing near it that is beautiful. I told you some of the world was ugly, remember? She lives in an ugly place.

MELINDA (*Sympathetically*): The poor little thing! And you would take the flowers to her?

PEDDLER (*Nodding*): They would mean more to her than anything I carry in my pack.

MELINDA: But why can't she have flowers of her own? Surely someone could grow them for her.

PEDDLER: Not everyone can make flowers grow like this, young lady. And so many people don't care about them. You will let me take her some?

MELINDA: Of course! There is a bunch I cut this morning, just a little while ago. I laid them in the shade with damp moss around their stems to keep them fresh till I could take them in the house. And then I forgot them. Wait, I'll fetch them for you. (*She disappears around the corner of the house, and comes back immediately with a gay bunch of flowers.*) Here, take her these.

PEDDLER: Oh, young lady, thank you! (*He takes the flowers and lays them on the bench beside him while he reaches for his pack and opens it.*) Here, make your choice. Anything you want.

MELINDA: But it doesn't seem right, just for a bunch of flowers.

PEDDLER: No—for a handful of beauty. And beauty is beyond price. It is something there is not enough of in the world. Those people are blessed who can create it. Here, what will you have? (*As he holds up various items*). This pin, perhaps? Or this gleaming bracelet? Or, wait—perhaps these beads?

MELINDA: No, none of those, though they are pretty things. (*She reaches deep into the bag and pulls out a shawl.*) Oh, this! How warm it feels! How soft! My mother would be so happy to have this around her shoulders when the evenings are cool. (*She stops suddenly.*) But surely this is not a fair trade? Far too much in exchange for those few flowers?

PEDDLER: No! It is yours. I told you beauty is beyond price. Take the shawl and may it bring your mother one half the pleasure these flowers will give the little girl. (*He sighs and shoulders his pack again, then picks up the flowers.*) Thankee, young lady, and bless you for these. (*He touches his hat and starts slowly down the road.*)

MELINDA (*Clutching the shawl happily and waving to him*): Goodbye, Peddler. Give the little girl my love when you give her the flowers. Thank you for the shawl.

PEDDLER: Thankee, young lady, goodbye. (*He exits.* MELINDA *holds the soft shawl against her face and then folds it carefully and places it on the bench beside her. There is the sound of gay singing, and a* GIRL *steps lightly along the road. She carries a tray held around her neck with a ribbon. It is covered with a white cloth. As she approaches,* MELINDA *calls to her.*)

MELINDA: Hello.

GIRL: Hello. What are you doing?

MELINDA: Waiting for my fortune to seek me. Won't you sit down for a moment and rest?

GIRL: I'm not tired, but I'll sit down for a minute. What do you mean, waiting for your fortune to seek you?

MELINDA: Well, I want to *do* something in the world, not just stay here at home doing nothing. What do *you* do?

GIRL: I bake. Cakes and tarts and buns and cookies. Then I sell them in the town. That's where I'm going now. I guess my baking is my fortune, but I never thought of it like that. It's just the only way I know how to earn money for pretty things to wear.

MELINDA: You like pretty things?

GIRL: Of course. Doesn't everyone? My young man likes to see me in gay colors and pretty clothes when we go walking together. He would love those flowers, as he is so fond of pretty things.

MELINDA: Would you like some of my flowers? I'll pick you some.

GIRL: But I'll have no money till I have sold these cakes on my tray. I could not pay you for them.

MELINDA: I don't want money—they are just flowers.

GIRL: Such beautiful ones! I know, I could give you a cake for them, if you would take that. They're very good cakes.

MELINDA: Oh no, you can sell your cakes for money. My flowers are worth nothing.

GIRL: Worth nothing! But that's not so! My young man's eyes would brighten and he would smile when he saw me wearing them. That's worth everything to me. Here, take one of my cakes. Please.

MELINDA: Well, thank you very much. Oh, how wonderful they look! How pleased Mother will be with a cake for supper! Wait, I'll fix the flowers for you. (*She carefully selects a small bunch, and using a few large leaves and strands of heavy grass makes it into a bouquet. As she works, the two girls talk.*)

GIRL: How can you raise such beautiful flowers? I think they are the loveliest I've ever seen.

MELINDA: I don't know. I just tend them as carefully as I know how.

GIRL: Many people raise flowers, but few are as large and bright and fragrant as these. How clever you are!

MELINDA: Clever? Oh, no. There is really nothing I can do. I can't bake very well, and I can't sing, or dance, or juggle—

GIRL (*Laughing*): Why should you want to juggle?

MELINDA (*Laughing too*): I don't really know, but there was a clown here who asked me if I could. I was unhappy because it seemed I could do nothing.

GIRL: What a silly you are! Why, you can grow the most beautiful flowers in the world. You should be proud!

MELINDA (*Handing her the finished bouquet*): I am beginning to be. What a delicious cake I have earned for my few flowers. Perhaps there *is* something I can do.

GIRL: Of course there is. (*She rises and adjusts her tray, smoothing down the cloth that covers it and gently laying the flowers on top.*) And now I must go on. Thank you so very much for these. My young man will be proud when he sees me wearing them tonight. I hope you like the cake.

MELINDA: I know we will. Have a lovely time.

GIRL: I will—I always do. Goodbye.

MELINDA: Goodbye. (GIRL *exits.* MELINDA *admires the shawl and the cake, touching them gently. Then she picks up her trowel and the shears from where she dropped them earlier and bends to tend some of the flowers. Presently* MAN *appears. He is obviously a gentleman, and has a fat money bag hanging from his belt. He pauses to look at the flowers, and* MELINDA *looks up and smiles at him.*) Hello.

MAN: Good day, my dear. What a lovely garden!

MELINDA (*With a little pride*): Thank you, sir.

MAN: Do you grow the flowers yourself?

MELINDA: Yes, sir.

MAN: They are beautiful!

MELINDA: Thank you, sir. Won't you come in for a moment and look at them.

MAN: With pleasure. (*He steps into the garden and looks admir-*

ingly around.) How happy you must be to work with these gorgeous flowers all day.

MELINDA (*Truthfully*): I never used to be, sir. I wanted to get away and do something big and important in the world. But somehow suddenly I seem to like my flowers better than I did.

MAN: I'm glad, because this is a big and important thing that you are doing. Anyone who can create the beauty that grows here has a wonderful gift, and is to be envied.

MELINDA: Envied? Me? Just for growing flowers? Oh, no, sir.

MAN: Oh, yes, my dear. There are few in the world who can do with a small piece of ground what you have done here. I wonder—

MELINDA: Yes, sir? What do you wonder? Whether I would give you some? But of course.

MAN: No, not whether you would give me some, but whether you would sell me some—every day, all summer long, as long as they grow.

MELINDA: My flowers grow all winter too. I have them in pots in our kitchen where the sun shines warmly on them through the window, and they are just as lovely when the snow flies outside as they are now.

MAN: Better and better! All the year round then. Will you let me buy flowers from you all the year round? Great bunches of them?

MELINDA: But, sir, what can you do with flowers every day? That's so many!

MAN: I want them for my wife. She is a beautiful lady who loves beautiful things. It would be a constant reminder of my love for her if she were surrounded by such beauty every day. Will you? I'll pay you well.

MELINDA: You mean you would really pay money just for my flowers?

MAN: Gladly.

MELINDA: I was given a soft warm shawl today for them, and a feather-light cake. But money? I don't know. They don't seem worth it.

MAN: To me they are, and to my wife they will be. I will send a servant every day to get them. Will you?

MELINDA: Of course, sir, if you really want them.

MAN: I really want them. It's a bargain, then. I cannot take them now. I have business to do in the city and they would wither before I reached home. But tomorrow my servant will come. And every day after that.

MELINDA: I can't believe it! Money for my flowers! How much this will mean to my mother!

MAN (*Taking a coin from his purse*): Here, this will seal the bargain. Tomorrow then, you will have them ready. It is agreed?

MELINDA (*Taking the coin*): Oh, yes. And thank you, sir, so very much. (*She curtseys.*)

MAN: Thank you, my dear, for giving me such beauty. Goodbye.

MELINDA: Goodbye, sir. I'll send the loveliest flowers I can grow. And I hope they make your wife very happy.

MAN: They will. Goodbye. (*He strides off down the road.* ME-LINDA *stands a moment fingering the coin he has given her and then runs to the door of the cottage and opens it.*)

MELINDA: Mother, Mother, come here at once. Hurry, please, Mother, hurry!

WIDOW (*Running out of the house*): Whatever is the matter, child? Has something happened to you?

MELINDA: Oh yes, something wonderful! My fortune has found me, Mother. See, see what I have for you! (*She shows her the shawl, the cake and the coin.*)

WIDOW: Melinda! Where did you get these things?

MELINDA: Well, Mother, first there was a clown, and then came the peddler. He gave me the shawl, and then the young girl with the cakes and then the man. He must be very rich—he wants me to sell him some every day!

WIDOW: Some what, child? What are you talking about?

MELINDA: My flowers, Mother. My flowers! They all wanted them, and they gave me these things for them.

WIDOW: But I don't understand, Melinda. Your flowers are lovely, but what exactly are you talking about?

MELINDA: It's my fortune, Mother. The flowers are my fortune. Oh, I must work so hard with them. I must raise such lovely ones! Oh, come inside, Mother, and we'll fix supper. See, we'll have our cake for supper. And then you'll sit here in the garden. You can put the shawl around you if it's cool, and I'll work with my flowers. Come now—

WIDOW: I declare, I don't know what you're talking about, child.

MELINDA: Just come in, Mother. I'll tell you all about it while we fix our supper. It's the flowers, Mother—they're my fortune! And it *did* seek me! Don't you see? (*They turn and go toward the house as the curtains close.*)

THE END

Production Notes

THE GIRL WHOSE FORTUNE SOUGHT HER

Characters: 3 male; 3 female.

Playing Time: 15 minutes.

Costumes: Modern, everyday dress. Clown wears a colorful clown costume. The Peddler is dressed in old, dusty-looking clothes. Girl wears a brightly-colored skirt and a peasant blouse. Man is dressed in a business suit.

Properties: Gardening tools, trowel, shears, single flower for Clown, peddler's pack, string of bells, large handkerchief, bunch of flowers for Peddler, shawl, tray of cookies for Girl, flowers and grasses to be made into a bouquet, cake, coin.

Setting: The yard in front of the Widow's cottage. The cottage, made of cardboard or painted on a backdrop, stands upstage center. If possible, it has working door. There is a bench on either side of the door. Above benches are window boxes filled with colorful flowers. There are other flower beds placed about the stage, and a large trellis at left covered with roses. The flowers may be real or made of crepe paper.

Lighting: No special effects.

Rapunzel

Adapted by Adele Thane

Characters

WITCH
FRANZ, *a dollmaker*
EMMA, *his wife*
RAPUNZEL, *their daughter*
PRINCE FREDERICK
BOY
GIRL

SCENE 1

TIME: *A day in summer.*

SETTING: *Witch's garden and front yard of Franz's cottage. Garden, left, is separated from yard, right, by stone wall which extends a short way from back down center, ending in high iron gate. Wall continues along back of garden, in the center of which is a bed of lettuce. Oddly-shaped rocks are scattered about. In Franz's yard are bench and work table, strewn with material and tools for making dolls. Down right is sign:* FRANZ—DOLLMAKER.

AT RISE: FRANZ *is seated on bench, humming to himself as he paints doll's face.* WITCH *enters garden left with watering can and trowel. She goes to bed of lettuce and sprinkles it.*

WITCH (*Chanting*):
Rapunzel, sweet lettuce,
So tender and rare,
Spread out your green leaves,
And perfume the air.
(*She begins to pull weeds and dig with trowel.* BOY *and*

GIRL *are heard laughing off right, and* FRANZ *looks up from his work, smiling.* GIRL *and* BOY *enter down right and approach* FRANZ.)

GIRL: Hello, Franz! We've come to watch you make dolls. Is that doll finished?

BOY (*In a superior tone*): Of course it's not finished! Can't you see? It hasn't any hair yet.

FRANZ (*To* BOY): Well, well! And who is this fine fellow?

GIRL: He's my cousin from Hamburg.

BOY: I didn't want to come. She made me. (*Snorts in derision*) Dolls! They're for girls. Don't you make anything for boys, like tin soldiers or tigers?

FRANZ: No, I'm afraid not. Only dolls. (BOY *turns away to explore yard.*)

GIRL (*Indicating doll*): Franz, what color is her hair going to be?

FRANZ: Brown, to match her eyes. I have a nice brown wig here. (*Picks up wig, fits it on doll's head*) What do you think?

GIRL: I think she wants yellow hair.

FRANZ: All right, let's try this wig of long golden braids. (*He sets blonde wig on doll's head.* GIRL *nods and* FRANZ *begins gluing wig into place.* BOY *looks through gate into* WITCH's *garden.*)

BOY: What a funny garden!

GIRL (*Alarmed*): Come away from there!

BOY: What for?

GIRL: That garden belongs to a witch!

BOY (*Lightly*): Huh! I'm not afraid of witches! (*Points to* WITCH, *who is watering lettuce*) Is that the Witch? (GIRL *peers through gate fearfully and nods.*) My word! Did you ever see such big lettuce!

GIRL (*In hushed tone*): She's singing to herself. Listen!

WITCH (*Chanting*):
Rapunzel, sweet lettuce,
So tender and rare,
Spread out your green leaves
And perfume the air.

BOY: What a frightful old hag!

GIRL: Shh-h! She'll hear you. She might put some kind of spell
on us!

BOY (*Swaggering*): I'd like to see her do it! What's her name?

GIRL: Dame Gothel.

BOY (*Shouting through gate*): Hey! Old Woman! Witch Gothel!
You don't scare me!

GIRL (*Upset*): Stop it! (WITCH *turns to them, shaking trowel
menacingly.*) Now see what you've done! You've made her
angry. *Run!* (GIRL *screams and runs off right.* BOY *makes a
face at* WITCH, *then laughs and dashes off after* GIRL.
WITCH *comes to gate.*)

FRANZ (*Nervously, to* WITCH): Don't mind them, Dame Gothel.
You know children, they don't mean anything.

WITCH (*Sarcastically*): Oh, don't they! (*Points to doll he is holding*) That's a pretty doll you have there. I like golden hair.
There's magic in golden hair.

FRANZ: Is that so? Well, well! (WITCH *walks away abruptly
and exits left.* EMMA *enters up right, carrying a sewing basket, from which she takes a doll's pinafore.*)

EMMA: Franz, here is the doll's apron. May I put it on her now?

FRANZ (*Handing her doll*): Yes, Emma, I'm finished with her.

EMMA (*At table, tying on pinafore*): She's beautiful. How I wish
we could have a real little girl like her.

FRANZ (*Gently patting her shoulder*): Maybe someday we
will, Emma.

EMMA: There, she's all dressed. She *is* a darling! I shall hate
to part with her. Franz, couldn't we keep her for our own little
girl when she comes?

FRANZ: Of course, my dear. To tell the truth, I've become quite
fond of her myself.

EMMA (*Sniffing air*): Mmm-m, what's that perfume I smell?

FRANZ: It's rapunzel—a kind of sweet lettuce that grows in
Dame Gothel's garden.

EMMA (*Eagerly*): Let me see! (*She peeks through gate.*) Oh, how
good it looks! I must have some for dinner.

FRANZ: But that's impossible! You know Dame Gothel wouldn't
give us a single leaf.

EMMA: Then we'll buy it from her. She might be willing to sell

it. (WITCH *reenters left and goes to bed of rapunzel.*) There
she is now. (*Calls*) Dame Gothel!

WITCH: Yes, what is it?

EMMA: Would you sell us some of that fine lettuce?

WITCH: Sell this lettuce? Indeed I won't.

FRANZ: We'll be happy to pay you.

WITCH (*Holding up a head of lettuce she has picked and waving
it toward* EMMA *tantalizingly*): You haven't enough money to
buy this. It's priceless. From this lettuce I make my magic
potions. Now go about your business and don't bother me
again. (*She exits left with head of lettuce.*)

EMMA (*Sitting at table*): Oh, the mean old thing! (*She bursts
into tears.*)

FRANZ (*Surprised*): Now, now, Emma, don't cry. It's not that
important.

EMMA: Well, maybe it isn't to you, but it is to me. Oh, Franz,
I've never wanted anything so much in my life as that lettuce.
If I don't get it, I'll die.

FRANZ (*Trying to calm her*): Nonsense, my dear.

EMMA: You don't care!

FRANZ: Of course I care, but what can I do?

EMMA: *Get me some of that lettuce!*

FRANZ: Very well, you shall have the lettuce. I'll get it for
you tonight.

EMMA (*Stamping her foot*): No! I want it now—*now*, do you
hear? (*She runs off up right, sobbing.*)

FRANZ (*Looking after her, shaking his head*): I've never seen
her in such a state—and all over a bit of lettuce. Well, I'd
better get it or she'll never forgive me. (*He tries gate.*) It's
locked. I'll just have to take my chances and climb over the
wall. I hope Dame Gothel doesn't see me. Then I *would* be in
a pickle. (*He disappears behind back wall of garden and a
few moments later reappears over top of wall. He looks about
cautiously.*) So far, so good. (*He jumps down into garden and
goes to bed of rapunzel.*) Two heads of lettuce should be enough
to satisfy Emma. (*As he kneels to pull up lettuce, he doesn't
see* WITCH, *who enters stealthily from left.*)

WITCH: Not so fast, my friend! (FRANZ *cries out and jumps to his feet*.) Stealing my lettuce, are you?

FRANZ: But you wouldn't sell it to me, and if my wife doesn't have some of it to eat, I don't know what she'll do.

WITCH: Very well. I will make a bargain with you. You may have all the lettuce you want—on one condition.

FRANZ: Name it.

WITCH: When your first child is born, you must give it to me.

FRANZ (*Horrified*): *What*! Oh, no!

WITCH: Oh, *yes*!

FRANZ: No, I couldn't agree to that. And neither would Emma. You can keep your lettuce. (*He throws it down and turns to leave*.)

WITCH: Stop! You're not going to get out of it as easily as that. You came into my garden uninvited. You tried to steal my precious rapunzel and you have refused to bargain with me. Do you know what it means to defy a witch? It means you shall be put under a spell!

FRANZ (*Trembling*): What kind of spell?

WITCH: Do you see these stones here in my garden? Once they were real people. But they came into my garden to steal my rapunzel and I changed them into stones. And that is what you will be—a stone!

FRANZ: No!

WITCH: And I shall put a curse on your wife. She will hunger for my lettuce until she dies!

FRANZ: Don't hurt Emma, please!

WITCH: Do you promise to give me your first-born child?

FRANZ: I'd promise anything to save Emma.

WITCH: Good! I have your word and I'll hold you to it. Now, take the lettuce to your wife. I hope she enjoys it! (WITCH *laughs and goes to unlock gate.* FRANZ *slowly picks up heads of lettuce and exits into his own yard. As* WITCH *locks gate, she jeers at him*.) Don't forget to tell your wife the good news! (*She cackles as she exits left*.)

FRANZ (*To himself*): I won't tell Emma. I can't. It would break her heart. (EMMA *enters up right*.)

EMMA: Oh, Franz, you have the lettuce! Give it to me! (*She

grabs it from him and sits at table, eating it hungrily.) How delicious it is! Did you have to steal it?

FRANZ (*Quietly*): No.

EMMA: Don't tell me Dame Gothel *gave* it to you, after all the fuss?

FRANZ: No, I paid for it—dearly.

EMMA: Don't look so glum, Franz. Whatever you paid, it's worth it. (*She smacks her lips with relish.*)

FRANZ: Is it, my dear? I wonder. (*He gazes fearfully at garden. EMMA is too busy devouring lettuce to notice. Curtain*)

* * * * *

SCENE 2

TIME: *A year later.*

SETTING: *Same as Scene 1. Doll is on bench.*

AT RISE: FRANZ *enters from up right, carrying a bassinet, followed by* EMMA, *who carries doll.*

FRANZ (*Singing boisterously as he waltzes about yard*): Rock-a-bye, baby, on the treetop. When the wind blows, the cradle will rock—

EMMA: Be careful! Don't drop her.

FRANZ (*Indignantly*): What! Drop my little girl? What do you take me for? (*Sings*) When the bough breaks, the cradle will fall—

EMMA (*Clearing space on work table*): Here, set her down. (*FRANZ swings bassinet in a wide arc as he lowers it to table.*) Gently, gently!

FRANZ (*Singing*): Down will come baby, cradle and all! (*He sets bassinet down on table with a slight bump.*)

EMMA: You are so rambunctious!

FRANZ (*Strutting about*): And why shouldn't I be rambunctious? I'm a happy father.

EMMA (*Gazing adoringly into bassinet*): Just look at her! If she isn't the image of an angel, I don't know what is.

FRANZ: I've never seen a more beautiful baby. Her hair is like spun gold.

EMMA (*Placing doll in bassinet*): What shall we call her, Franz? It should be something that goes with her hair, don't you think? Like Glorianna, or Oribel—that means "golden beauty."

FRANZ: A flower-name would be nice. There's Marigold and Mignonette and Primrose—(*While they talk,* WITCH *enters garden from left and swiftly crosses to gate, where she stands listening.*)

EMMA: Arelia? Dorlisa? What shall it be?

WITCH (*Speaking suddenly*): Why not name her Rapunzel?

FRANZ (*Whirling to face her and crying out in alarm*): Dame Gothel!

EMMA: Why, how do you do, Dame Gothel? Have you been away? I haven't seen you since my husband bought the lettuce from you last summer.

WITCH: That's right dearie. Would you like some more?

EMMA: Oh, no, thank you. I haven't been hungry for it since that day.

WITCH: Is that your baby? I want to see her. (*She unlocks gate and comes out of garden.*)

FRANZ (*Quickly stepping in front of bassinet*): No!

EMMA: Why, Franz, where are your manners? Let Dame Gothel see the baby.

FRANZ (*Vehemently*): No, no!

EMMA: What's the matter with you, Franz?

WITCH: I'll tell you what's the matter. He made a bargain with me and he hasn't kept it.

EMMA: What bargain?

WITCH: In exchange for the rapunzel you wanted, he promised me your first-born child.

EMMA (*Horrified*): Franz, is this true?

FRANZ: Yes, Emma. It was the only way I could get the rapunzel for you. And she threatened to harm you if I refused.

EMMA: Oh, Franz, how could you do such a thing?

WITCH: Come now, give me the child.

EMMA: Please, Dame Gothel, don't take my baby!

WITCH: Why shouldn't I take what belongs to me? You had

your lettuce—now I will have the child. A bargain is a bargain.

EMMA: *I* made no bargain with you. You shall not have her.

WITCH: Very well. If you won't give her to me, then I shall have to get her in another way.

EMMA: Never! I will die first.

WITCH: No, not die, but be changed into stone—both of you! (*She raises her arms and chants.* EMMA *and* FRANZ *freeze.*)
Change to stone, change to stone!
Flesh and hair, skin and bone.
Statues be and statues stay,
Do not move when I'm away.
(*She picks up bassinet and goes to gate, where she turns to face rigid forms of* EMMA *and* FRANZ.)
My curse forever on you lies
Unless for love Rapunzel cries.
And she will never cry for love, I'll see to that! I will shut her up in a tower and teach her how to become a witch. She will learn the fun of mixing potions and making spells. And then she will laugh! She will laugh for *hate*! But never cry for love—never, never, never! (*Cackling,* WITCH *passes into garden, closes and locks gate and runs off left. Curtain*)

* * * * *

SCENE 3

TIME: *Fifteen years later.*

SETTING: *A tower room. A casement window is right, and near it are a table and a stool. Bassinet and doll are on cot at left.*

AT RISE: RAPUNZEL *is seated on stool, gazing out window. Her golden hair is plaited in one long braid, which is wound about her waist like a sash, the end hanging down to the floor. As she looks out window, she sings an appropriate folk song such as "Greensleeves." At end of song, she sighs, then leans forward out window to look at something below.*

RAPUNZEL: Here comes Dame Gothel with my food for today. I hope she's brought something special.

WITCH (*Calling from offstage*): Rapunzel! Rapunzel! Let down your hair! (RAPUNZEL *unwinds braid from around her waist and lowers it out window.*)

RAPUNZEL (*Calling down*): Here you are, godmother. (*She grips braid with both hands and braces herself.*) Ow! Please don't yank so hard! It hurts!

WITCH (*Louder, from offstage*): Stand still, will you! (*She appears outside window with a knapsack strapped to her back. RAPUNZEL helps her over sill.*) How do you expect me to get a good foothold if you jerk the braid like that?

RAPUNZEL: I'm sorry, godmother, but it does pull, you know. I shall never get used to it.

WITCH (*Swinging knapsack onto table*): Here is your food—and a surprise.

RAPUNZEL (*Happily*): Oh, what is it? Indian pudding? Gingerbread?

WITCH: It's a book. (*Takes book from knapsack*)

RAPUNZEL (*Disappointed*): A book! It's awfully big. (WITCH *hands it to her and she reads title.*) *The Black Arts.* What does that mean?

WITCH: Enchantment! Sorcery! Witchcraft! This is my book of spells, Rapunzel.

RAPUNZEL: But what has it to do with me?

WITCH: It has everything to do with you, my little salad. (*Taps book with her finger*) This book will teach you how to become—*a witch!*

RAPUNZEL (*Dropping book on table*): But I don't want to become a witch!

WITCH: Bah! You are fifteen years old now, and it's time you made something of yourself.

RAPUNZEL: Then let me go out into the world and live like a human being.

WITCH: When you go out into the world, it will not be as a human being but as a witch, a powerful witch! Now, open that book and start studying. Learn the first lesson by heart. I shall test you when I return. (*She goes to window.*) Goodbye, my little lettuce leaf. Mind you, study your lesson well. (*She steps over windowsill and disappears, as if climbing down* RA-

PUNZEL's *braid.* RAPUNZEL *draws up her hair, goes to table, opens book, and reads.*)

RAPUNZEL: "Lesson I. Make a brew of the following ingredients: the eyes of a lizard; the tail of a mouse; the legs of a spider; the wings of a bat; the skin of a toad." Ugh! (*She shivers.*) "Let stand for three days, then drink a thimbleful by the light of the waning moon." Oh, it's horrible! I won't do it, I won't, I won't! (*Sound of birds twittering is heard.* RAPUNZEL *turns to window.*) Hello, little birds! You sound very happy. How I envy your freedom! You can go wherever you like, but I'm locked in a cage.

PRINCE (*Calling from offstage*): Rapunzel! Rapunzel! Let down your hair!

RAPUNZEL (*Starting up in dismay*): Oh, good heavens, it's Dame Gothel! She's back already, and I haven't studied the lesson. She will be furious with me! (RAPUNZEL *hastily places book open on stool by window and starts memorizing text, at the same time lowering her braid out window. She keeps her eyes on page, mumbling to herself as she studies.* PRINCE FREDERICK *appears outside window and jumps into room.* RAPUNZEL *looks up from book in alarm.*) Oh! Where is Dame Gothel!

PRINCE: You mean that old woman who just left? Far away, I hope. Don't be afraid. I won't harm you.

RAPUNZEL: Who are you?

PRINCE: My name is Prince Frederick. I was riding through the forest and heard you singing. Your song was so sad, it touched my heart, and I stopped to listen. As I stood at the foot of this tower, I saw the old woman come, so I hid in the trees, and heard her call to you—"Rapunzel! Rapunzel! Let down your hair!" Then, when she left, I called to you myself, and here I am.

RAPUNZEL: You must go away at once. If Dame Gothel finds you here, I don't know what she'll do.

PRINCE: I'm not afraid of her. But why are you shut up in this tower—a beautiful girl like you?

RAPUNZEL: Dame Gothel keeps me here. She's a witch—and she's going to make me a witch, too!

PRINCE (*Horrified*): Then you must come away with me at once!

RAPUNZEL: How can I? There is no way of getting down from this tower except by my hair.

PRINCE: I have a strong rope in my saddlebag. I'm sure it is long enough to reach down to the ground. I'll get it. (*He climbs out window and disappears.*)

RAPUNZEL (*Calling after him*): Hurry! Dame Gothel may be back any minute. (*Looks off into distance*) Oh, here she comes! Slide down quickly! There, he's safe. (*Calls to* WITCH) Godmother! I saw you coming and let down my hair. (WITCH *appears outside the window.*)

WITCH: Help me up, will you?

RAPUNZEL (*Helping her into room*): Oh, you're so much heavier than the Prince! (*She exclaims in horror as she realizes what she has said.*)

WITCH: Prince? What Prince?

RAPUNZEL: N-n-nobody, godmother.

WITCH: So! A prince has been here, has he? And is coming back, no doubt! Well, he'll get a warm welcome from me. Come here! I'll teach you to deceive me. (*She picks up a pair of huge scissors from table.*)

RAPUNZEL (*Backing away*): What are you going to do?

WITCH: This won't hurt. (*She grabs* RAPUNZEL's *braid and cuts it off.*) Snip! Snap!

RAPUNZEL: Oh! You've cut off my hair! How can the Prince climb up to me now? (*She starts to weep.*)

WITCH: I'll show you how. (*She fastens the braid to a hook by window.*) Wait until he comes, my pretty. Wait until he sees who is holding this golden braid. (*A whistle is heard.*)

RAPUNZEL: There he is! (*She rushes to window but* WITCH *seizes her and pushes her back.*)

WITCH: Keep still! Now, stand over there out of the way. (*She points to other side of room.*)

PRINCE (*Calling from offstage*): Rapunzel! Rapunzel! Let down your hair! (WITCH *lowers her braid out window, then crouches at one side so* PRINCE *does not see her until he has jumped into room. A length of rope is coiled over his shoulder.*) Rapunzel, here is the rope.

WITCH: Aha! You have come to fetch your lady love, have you? Well, look on her for the last time, because you will never see her again. When your sight returns, she and I will be far, far away. (WITCH *raises her arms and chants*.)
Demons of darkness,
Black cats of night!
Scratch out his eyes,
Take away his sight!
(PRINCE *cries out and falls to his knees, covering his eyes with his hands*.)

RAPUNZEL (*Running to him*): Frederick! What has she done?

PRINCE: She has cast a spell over my eyes! I cannot see!

RAPUNZEL (*Turning on* WITCH *in a fury*): You wicked old hag!

WITCH (*Picking up book*): Come with me! I'm taking you far away from here. (*She grips* RAPUNZEL *by the arm*.)

RAPUNZEL (*Pulling back*): I won't go!

WITCH: Oh yes, you will. (*She drags* RAPUNZEL *to window and climbs onto sill*.)

RAPUNZEL: Let go of me! Let *go*! (*With a mighty effort, she jerks her arm free.* WITCH *loses her balance and falls from sight*.)

PRINCE (*Anxiously*): Rapunzel! What happened? Are you all right?

RAPUNZEL (*Leading him to a chair*): Yes, I am all right. But the witch has fallen from the tower and is gone forever.

PRINCE (*Smiling*): Thank heaven, you are saved.

RAPUNZEL (*Pityingly*): But you, my prince, you are not saved. The witch is not here to remove the spell. (*She weeps*.) Oh, whatever will we do?

PRINCE (*Putting his hands to her eyes*): What do I feel? Tears?

RAPUNZEL: Yes, dear Frederick, tears of love. I shall never leave you. I will take care of you always.

PRINCE (*Looking at her in amazement*): Why, what is this? I can *see* you, Rapunzel!

RAPUNZEL: You can *see*?

PRINCE: Oh, Rapunzel, your tears of love have broken the witch's spell! (*Suddenly there is a loud thunderclap and lights flicker.*) Quickly, we must leave this tower! Is there anything you want to take with you?

RAPUNZEL (*Getting doll from cot*): Yes, this doll. My true parents gave it to me when I was a baby. (PRINCE *helps her out window, then climbs down after her as the stage is in darkness, and thunder is heard. Curtains close. After a moment, lights come up, and* RAPUNZEL *and* PRINCE *hurry in right, in front of curtain.*)

PRINCE: We escaped just in time.

RAPUNZEL (*Pointing off right*): Look, Frederick! The tower has disappeared. Was it a spell that did it?

PRINCE: Yes, Rapunzel, the spell of love, the greatest magic of all. (*Voices are heard off left, and* EMMA *and* FRANZ *enter, looking about, dazed.*)

EMMA: Where are we, Franz? How did we get here?

FRANZ: I haven't the slightest idea, Emma. (*He crosses to* PRINCE.) Your pardon, sir. Could you tell us, please, where we are?

PRINCE: You are at the edge of the enchanted forest.

FRANZ: The enchanted forest! Well, well! That probably accounts for it.

PRINCE: Accounts for what, my man?

FRANZ: Why, the way it happened. It was very strange. There was a loud thunderclap and suddenly we were here. (EMMA *takes* FRANZ *aside.*)

EMMA (*Speaking excitedly*): Franz, that doll—in the girl's arms. Isn't that the doll you made for our baby?

FRANZ (*Peering at doll*): Why, I believe it is!

EMMA (*Hopefully*): Do you think—? Could it possibly be—?

FRANZ (*Going to* RAPUNZEL): Young lady, may I ask where you got that doll?

RAPUNZEL: Why, I've had it ever since I was a baby. My parents gave it to me.

EMMA: Who were your parents, my dear?

RAPUNZEL: I don't know. I was brought up by a witch called Dame Gothel.

FRANZ *and* EMMA: Dame Gothel!

EMMA: Oh, Franz, it *is* our child! Rapunzel!

RAPUNZEL: Mother! Father! (*They rush into each other's arms.*)

EMMA: My little girl!

FRANZ: My dearest daughter!

RAPUNZEL (*Introducing* PRINCE): Father, Mother—this is Prince Frederick, who rescued me from the witch. Oh, I have so much to tell you!

PRINCE: But not here, Rapunzel. Come, let us go to my kingdom where we can talk to our hearts' content, happily ever after. (*He leads the way off left as curtain falls.*)

THE END

Production Notes

RAPUNZEL

Characters: 3 male; 4 female.

Playing Time: 25 minutes.

Costumes: Witch wears black robe; and Prince has appropriate royal costume. Others wear peasant dress. Rapunzel has blonde hair, with a long braid.

Properties: Watering can, trowel, glue, paint, pots and brushes, doll, dark and blonde doll's wigs, doll's pinafore, bassinet, book, scissors, knapsack, rope, sewing basket.

Setting: Scenes 1 and 2: Witch's garden and front yard of Franz's cottage. The garden is at left, separated from the yard by a stone wall extending part way down center and ending in a high iron gate. The wall continues along the back of the garden. In the center of the garden is a bed of lettuce, and oddly-shaped rocks and flowers are scattered about. In Franz's yard are a bench and a work table, which is strewn with material and tools for making dolls. Down right is sign: FRANZ—DOLLMAKER. Exits are left, up right and down right. Scene 3: A tower room. A casement window, through which characters enter and exit, is on the right wall. There is a hook beside the window. Nearby are a table and stool, and at left is cot.

Lighting: Lights dim and come up at the end of Scene 3.

Sound: Birds singing, thunder as indicated.

The Big Stone

by Eleanore Leuser

Characters

THE KING
THE KING'S FOOL
FARMER JOHN
FARMER JOHN'S WIFE
THREE TOWNSPEOPLE
PRIME MINISTER
TWO COURT LADIES
VILLAGE LAD
LAD'S SMALL BROTHER

SETTING: *A road near the castle of the King. Bushes and trees border road upstage, and low stone wall is beside it downstage.*

AT RISE: KING *is talking to his* FOOL. *He looks rather worried, much more so than* FOOL, *who is cavorting about even when talking to him.*

KING: Fool, stop your gambolings. Cannot you see that I am sore perplexed? Else I would not have left my bed so early in the morning to think upon my problems.

FOOL (*Stopping his tricks and coming up to* KING): But why worry and grow gray hairs, O King, over a matter so easy to settle?

KING (*Fretfully*): So easy to settle, you say. Here I must leave all the affairs of my kingdom to go on a long and difficult journey. What will happen while I am gone?

FOOL (*Cavorting around*): You can always read the papers, sire.

KING: Be still, Fool. Tell me where I can find someone good enough and wise enough to take my place while I am gone.

FOOL (*Putting finger on nose and striking an attitude*): Someone can be found to take your place, sire, but who can fill it?

KING (*Paying no attention to him*): There must be some way of choosing the right one. There are many who would like it, but how can I possibly be sure?

FOOL (*Capering about*): How about a test, sire? Testing may be a little overdone, but it is still better than choosing a person who may be a little underdone.

KING (*Musing*): Testing? Hmm! Maybe you have an idea. But we must have someone who will think of others before himself; who will not be afraid to work hard; and above all, will have a sense of honor. Where will we find a test for all those things?

FOOL (*Pretending to look through spectacles and turn the pages of a book*): Your Majesty has Wise Men whose job is to give you information . . . from a book.

KING: Pah! All my Wise Men would like to be kings themselves.

FOOL (*Capering about and coming to a sudden stop*): Would your Majesty be willing to accept an idea straight from a mind and not a book?

KING (*Testily*): Stop capering around so. Whose mind?

FOOL (*With a low bow and hand on heart*): Mine!

KING (*Surprised*): I didn't suppose you had one. Well, let me hear it.

FOOL: This road that we are on, your Majesty, is usually a very travelled one, is it not?

KING: Usually, when it is not early in the morning like this. Come to the point.

FOOL: Many of the people in your kingdom pass up and down upon it—strong ones, weak ones—fat ones, lean ones—

KING (*Irritably*): I'm not interested in their shapes. What next?

FOOL: Among them you may find the one best suited to leave in charge of affairs while you are gone.

KING: And I suppose you would stand here and pick out the best-looking one. No, Fool, it is not so easy as that. You have no mind after all.

FOOL: Pardon me, sire, you will see it at work if you will but listen a little longer. We will block the road with those huge stones you see over there (*Points off*), and under the stones we will place a purse of gold.

KING (*Startled*): You are indeed crazy! I have no wish to push
stones around, nor yet to provide a treasure for someone to
find like a game of hide and seek. I am looking for a leader
for my people.

FOOL (*Urgently*): You will find one, sire, if you will do what I
say. Listen. (*He whispers to* KING *and* KING *finally nods his
head in approval.*)

KING: Good, my Fool! We will try what you suggest. Let us get
the stones from over there. We must hurry before the people
start to come this way. (*They start moving the stones as the
curtain goes down and stays down long enough for the stones
to be moved into place, blocking the road from the small stone
wall across to the bushes. When the curtain rises,* KING *is
very much out of breath, pushing the last stone in place.* FOOL
is helping him. KING *settles crown on head and dusts his
hands.*) There, that's done! I confess I never thought to work
so hard in all my life.

FOOL (*Also adjusting his cap and dusting his hands*): Nor I.

KING: Someone is coming. Hurry, Fool. (*They hide behind a
bush as* FARMER JOHN *and his* WIFE *enter. They are
carrying laden market baskets. They stop as they see the stones
in the road.*)

FARMER'S WIFE: Lackaday! Now how did those monstrous big
stones get into the road?

FARMER JOHN (*Angrily*): It's a crying shame, that's what it
is! Stones in the middle of the road! How do they expect us to
get over them? It's a plot, that's what it is, to keep the farmers
from getting to market. I wish I had the fellows who did it.
I'd feed them to the crows, that I would.

FARMER'S WIFE: But whatever shall we do, John?

FARMER JOHN: We'll fool them, that's what we'll do. We'll go
the long way round and get to market anyway. (*He starts to
go back the way he came.*)

FARMER'S WIFE (*Following after him*): But, John, it's a good
five miles farther. What will become of our butter in the hot
sun?

FARMER JOHN (*Going right along*): Come on, woman, come
on. We'll show those miserable plotters that we won't be done

out of our rights. We'll get to market if the butter runs out of our baskets. Come. (*The two hurry off, the* WIFE *lagging in the rear.*)

FOOL (*Coming out from behind bush and prancing around*): Hmm! How would your Majesty like to be fed to the crows? I confess it has no appeal for me.

KING (*Coming out*): Be still, Fool! Our purpose is beyond those blockheads. Crow-bait, indeed! (*He is furiously pacing up and down when the* FOOL *hastily pulls him behind the bush.* THREE TOWNSPEOPLE *enter, talking and laughing gaily. They stop short when they see the barrier.*)

1ST TOWNSPERSON: Well, well, the road has erupted in the night and spit forth stones.

2ND TOWNSPERSON: A young mountain in the making!

3RD TOWNSPERSON: Well, mountains can be climbed, and for my part I see no reason why we should be kept from the merrymaking at the next village.

1ST TOWNSPERSON: Nor I, for I have a great appetite for Mistress Mary's cakes and a great thirst for a cooling drink from her spring. Let us climb your mountain.

2ND TOWNSPERSON: See, the narrowest part is there. I can make it easily. But how about you others? I hate to mention it, but there is so much more of you to get over. (*The others laugh.*)

3RD TOWNSPERSON (*Good-naturedly*): Hold your peace, friend, the bigger the man, the larger the heart. See, I climb as well as you. (*The three climb over the stones at the narrowest part, making hard work of it but with much fun and laughter.*)

1ST TOWNSPERSON (*Who has fallen sprawled on the ground— rising, dusts himself off*): Well, we are full-fledged mountain climbers now. Hail to the Alps! (*He makes a low bow in the direction of the stones. The others laugh.*)

2ND TOWNSPERSON: Come—on to the next village. My mouth waters for that pastry.

3RD TOWNSPERSON: Forward the mountain climbers—heroes all! (*They put hands on each other's shoulders and march off gaily.* KING *and* FOOL *come out and look after them.*)

KING (*Exasperated*): Such fools!

FOOL (*Sighing*): And not even hired by your Majesty for the post.

KING: If they only realized what they have missed.

FOOL: How can anyone be so stupid who is not paid for it?

KING: Ah, here comes my Prime Minister. I have a feeling he is the man we need.

FOOL: I have a feeling he thinks so too. Ouch! (KING *takes him by the collar and pulls him behind the bush.* PRIME MINISTER *enters with* TWO COURT LADIES.)

IST LADY: It is so good of your Highness to take an interest in us who have so newly come to court, and show us around the countryside.

2ND LADY: Everything is so wonderful!

PRIME MINISTER: Yes, his Majesty has a nice little kingdom. But if you'll promise not to breathe a word, Ladies, I'll tell you a secret.

BOTH (*Breathlessly*): We won't!

PRIME MINISTER (*Behind his hand*): The Kingdom will be even better when I get hold of it. (*They all laugh.*)

IST LADY (*As they come up to stones*): But why do you have such big stones in your road? It makes it very hard for people to pass by.

2ND LADY: It's quite unsightly, too.

PRIME MINISTER (*Looking over the situation*): What idiot did this? If I catch him I vow he shall feel my anger. Your Ladyships, I ask your pardon for such a happening. We will not even try to pass but leave the barricade to the fool who built it. Come, I have other sights to show you nearer home. (*They walk back the way they came.* KING *and* FOOL *come out from behind the bush.*)

FOOL: Well, your Majesty, the Prime Minister was almost right as usual. He just didn't know that two fools built the barricade instead of one.

KING (*Incensed*): When he gets hold of my kingdom, indeed! I'll see that he waits a long time for that to happen. Yet I would have sworn that he was a man after my own heart.

FOOL: That's the trouble, sire, that is what he's after—you and a kingdom to boot.

KING: Perhaps you are right. I am a fool, not much better than you.

FOOL: Oh, don't say so, your Majesty. Let us at least be equal.

KING (*Impatiently*): Peace, stupid one. So far, this brilliant idea has been woefully lacking in results. I am still no nearer finding the leader I desire. Perhaps it would be better to give the whole thing up.

FOOL (*Coaxingly*): Just one more passerby, your Majesty, just one. The very next person may be the right one.

KING (*Frowning*): Well, this shall be the last. If it is not he, then, Fool, you may put all the stones back from where they came, by yourself. Moreover you shall be banished from my sight.

FOOL (*Fearfully*): I had best pray that the next traveller on the road be the right one . . . for both the King's sake and mine. Ah, here he comes. May fortune favor us. (*As a* VILLAGE LAD *comes whistling along with his* SMALL BROTHER *at his side,* KING *and* FOOL *hurriedly go into hiding.*)

VILLAGE LAD (*As he comes up to the stones*): Hello, what have we here?

SMALL BROTHER: It seems like a goodly pile of stones to keep us from going on our way.

VILLAGE LAD: That it will not do. We are going ahead somehow. (*He looks at the stones from every angle.*)

SMALL BROTHER: Are you looking for a place to climb over, brother?

VILLAGE LAD: Then what would those do who come after us? Suppose they were too old to climb or had a cart and horse. No, my small brother, that would not be sensible.

SMALL BROTHER: Are you going to move all those stones?

VILLAGE LAD: Do you think you are big enough to help me?

SMALL BROTHER: Oh, yes, the two of us can do anything, can't we?

VILLAGE LAD: We can try. At least we are not afraid of a little work. (*The two start moving the stones. They move them carefully to the side of the road with a great appearance of*

effort. The big stone is left till last. The two brace themselves
and start to push. They move it only a little when SMALL
BROTHER *discovers the bag of gold hidden underneath.*)
SMALL BROTHER (*Excitedly*): Brother, see what I have found!
VILLAGE LAD (*Going to see*): What is it?
SMALL BROTHER: A bag full of shiny yellow pieces.
VILLAGE LAD (*Looking in awe*): A bag of gold!
SMALL BROTHER: Real gold? Then we can take it home and
never be cold or hungry any more.
VILLAGE LAD (*Taking bag and holding up a piece of gold*):
Yes, we could, couldn't we? (*He seems to think a moment—*
then slowly puts the gold back in the bag and shuts it tightly.)
But we won't, my little brother, because we'll take it to the
King.
SMALL BROTHER (*Astonished*): Take it to the King? But he
has plenty of gold!
VILLAGE LAD: It is not his gold either. It belongs to whoever
left it here. The King is a fair and just man, so he will see
that it is returned to the owner. Come, let us move this last
stone. Then the road will be clear for all to pass. (KING *and*
FOOL *step out from behind the bush.* KING *halts them with*
upraised hand.)
KING: Stop! Don't bother to move that stone, my lad. Someone
else will do it for you. You are the person we have been looking for.
VILLAGE LAD (*Dazed*): *You* have been looking for me, your
Majesty?
FOOL: Yes, I was almost afraid you weren't coming.
KING: You are the one we have been waiting for—the one who
will take care of my kingdom while I am gone.
VILLAGE LAD (*Overwhelmed*): But I am only a village lad,
sire. How can this be?
KING: A village lad can be better than the highest nobleman
if he so chooses. These stones were set as a test. Whoever
removed them would not be afraid of the hard work to do it.
Moreover he would think of the countless others besides him-
self who needed the road cleared for travelling.
FOOL (*Nudging the* KING): Don't forget the bag of gold, sire.

KING: Yes, and when he found the bag of gold, he would be too honorable to keep it, for he knew it would belong to someone else. You did all of these things, my lad, and of these things are leaders made.

SMALL BROTHER (*Joyfully*): My brother is always like that.

VILLAGE LAD (*Still dazed*): Sire, words fail me. I can only thank you.

KING (*Jovially*): No need of thanks. We have found the one person whom we sorely need. Fool, your idea was a good one after all.

FOOL (*Bowing*): Your Majesty, I have a still better one.

KING: And what is that?

FOOL (*Touching the big stone*): Let the Prime Minister push this big stone back where it belongs. It is far better for him to do it than for a Fool like me. (*Curtain*)

THE END

Production Notes

THE BIG STONE

Characters: 9 male, 3 female.

Playing Time: 20 minutes.

Costumes: The King wears a long dark robe with an ermine collar and a crown. The Fool wears the traditional jester costume with a pointed cap. The Prime Minister wears a dark suit. The Court Ladies are dressed in long full skirts and flowered blouses. The rest of the characters wear suitable peasant costumes.

Properties: Market baskets, bag of gold, gold pieces, several large cardboard stones.

Setting: A road near the King's castle. Bushes and trees border road upstage, and low stone wall is beside it downstage.

Lighting: No special effects.

The Snow Witch

by Dorothy Dixon

Characters

MARINA, *peasant grandmother*
KATYA, *little girl*
SNOW WITCH
PRINCESS VALESKA
DRIVER
IVAN, *young soldier*
VERA, *dancer*
DANCERS

SCENE 1

TIME: *A cold winter evening in old Russia.*
SETTING: *Simple peasant kitchen, with fireplace down right, table and two stools up right with shelf for cups behind table. Window with "snow" is in rear wall. Door to outside is center left; rocker is between window and door.*
AT RISE: MARINA *is looking out window;* KATYA *is setting table.*
MARINA: It is a fine night, Katya, but cold. My, how the stars are shining! They are as white as the snow that covers the steppes. And the snow—how it whirls wherever the wind passes. Now it looks like a shawl streaming in the wind—now like a woman with a crown of frost leaves. (*Looks off left*) There are the lights in the village. Down there the boys and girls are dancing. (*Wistfully*) Dancing ... (*Tries a few steps*) No, no, Marina, your feet are too old for that. (*Looks out window again*) Ah, there is something moving out there.
KATYA (*Crossing to window*): Where, Babushka?

242

MARINA: Why, it's the Snow Witch who goes abroad before the flakes come flying. I wonder why she was at my window? (*There is a knock at door.*)

SNOW WITCH (*Calling; offstage*): Marina, Marina, let me come in.

KATYA (*Frightened*): Oooh!

MARINA: The Snow Witch is calling me!

KATYA: I'm afraid, Baba. Don't open the door.

MARINA: Don't worry, child. All the Snow Witch does is wander about before a storm. I'll let her in. (*Opens door.* SNOW WITCH *whirls in and around stage, then stops right of* MARINA.)

SNOW WITCH (*Kindly*): There is no need to be frightened. I am a good witch. I use my powers to shelter the animals of the forest and to help honest villagers. I warn people when a storm is coming. Sometimes I follow the roads; sometimes I stop at the doors of people's houses. Tonight I saw the friendly gleam from your window, and I said to myself, "Marina will make me welcome." (*Whirls around stage.* KATYA *huddles in rocker, listening.*)

MARINA: Will there be a storm tonight?

SNOW WITCH: No, the night is sharp and clear, but tomorrow clouds will gather and the flakes will fly.

MARINA: You must see strange sights on your travels.

SNOW WITCH (*Moving about as she speaks*): I see great white wastelands where never a person stirs. I see forests black against the stars. I see fields where the drifts lie deep and the lone wolf is swift as a moving shadow. (*Looks around*) You must be very happy in this little house of yours, Marina.

MARINA: Happy? All my years behind me and no joy to come. If only I were young now like the girls dancing in the village, or rich like the Princess Valeska—then not a soul hereabouts would be happier than I!

SNOW WITCH: Would you like to change, Marina?

MARINA: Change? (*Excitedly*) Have you the magic power to let me change, Snow Witch?

SNOW WITCH: Just lay your hand in the hand of the person you would like to be, and you will change places. (MARINA *looks at* SNOW WITCH *in disbelief.*) I see you do not believe me, Marina. Look into my eyes and do not doubt me.

MARINA (*Looking into* SNOW WITCH's *eyes*): There *is* magic in your eyes, Snow Witch.

SNOW WITCH: Now you can change your lot, if you will. That is my magic gift to you.

MARINA (*Joyfully*): Is it really true? Oh, to think I don't have to be old Marina any longer! It is a great gift. (*Curtsies in front of* SNOW WITCH) Thank you, thank you.

SNOW WITCH: I must go now, but when I return I will see what you have done with your gift. Choose wisely, Marina. (*Glides out.* KATYA *shuts door.*)

MARINA: Choose! I have the whole village to choose from. Young or old. I can be whatever I like. (*During following speech,* MARINA *stands center, acting out parts as she speaks.* KATYA *mimics her behind her back.*) Why, I can change places with a handsome soldier with a sword, or a driver on a painted sleigh with three beautiful horses—and when we have changed, how the soldier will rage to find himself in petticoats, knitting, instead of marching along to music!

KATYA (*Laughing*): Oh, Babushka, you are so funny!

MARINA: No, after all, it is better to stay a woman. Let me see, shall I be Maria Toplova? No, her nose is too long. Anna Paloska? No, she is too poor. To be happy one must be rich and noble. (*Sound of sleigh bells is heard.*) Hark! Sleigh bells. I wonder who can be passing.

KATYA (*At window*): Baba, it is a beautiful sleigh with three white horses! (*Knocking at door is heard.*)

DRIVER (*Stepping in*): Do you have a fire here and shelter for the Princess Valeska?

MARINA: Oh, my, the Princess! Yes, yes. Come in, your Excellency. (PRINCESS *enters.*) All I have is at your service. (*Curtsies*)

PRINCESS (*To* DRIVER): Wait for me outside. (DRIVER *bows, exits.* PRINCESS *sweeps over to fireplace; to* KATYA) Here, child, warm my cloak. (*Tosses cloak to* KATYA, *who holds it close and nuzzles the fur*)

MARINA: How may I serve your Excellency?

PRINCESS: The warmth of your fire is what I need. Soon I must go on, but I am so cold.

MARINA: Will your Excellency taste my tea? It is all I have to offer.

PRINCESS: No, no. I want only the heat and light. I am afraid of the night. I shiver even through my furs.

MARINA: You fear the night, Excellency?

PRINCESS: Yes, the night and the robbers.

MARINA and KATYA: Robbers!

PRINCESS: It comes of having gold and jewels. Always the robbers follow me. Sometimes they move like shadows from the edge of the forest and gallop after my sleigh to the very doors.

MARINA: Heaven have mercy! I should die of terror.

PRINCESS: Even in my dreams I see them, their greedy cruel eyes. Have you never shaken yourself to sleep, good mother?

MARINA: Oh, no. Never, never.

PRINCESS: I see peace dwells beneath your roof. A princess must travel about, but a peasant is at home, safe from danger. It is a free and happy moment I spend with you, Marina. You may kiss my hand. (*Holds out hand*)

MARINA (*Drawing back*): No, no! I mean—I shall not touch your snowy white hand with one such as mine.

PRINCESS (*To* KATYA): Call my driver, please, child. (MARINA *takes cloak from* KATYA, *wraps it around* PRINCESS.)

KATYA (*Opening door and calling*): Driver, the Princess is ready to leave.

MARINA: May your Excellency speed well and safely. (*Curtsies*)

DRIVER (*At door*): Your Excellency, the sleigh is ready. (PRINCESS *and* DRIVER *exit.* MARINA *and* KATYA *watch at window as bells fade, then cross center.*)

MARINA: I shiver to think of what would have happened had I put my hand in hers! Darkness and robbers! (*Firmly*) I would not be the Princess for a thousand rubles.

KATYA: Nor I, Babushka. To have robbers chasing me . . . oh, no!

MARINA (*Thoughtfully*): It is bad luck to be a woman. If I were a lad, now, with the world before me—like Ivan, the soldier, so strong and handsome. He'd be a match for a dozen robbers.

IVAN (*Entering quickly*): Why, so he would, Marina, unless they were a match for him.

MARINA: Ivan, how you startled me! (KATYA *goes to* IVAN, *smiling.*)

IVAN: The world is full of surprises, Marina. (*Twirls* KATYA *around*)

MARINA: It is, indeed. What would you say if you suddenly found yourself turned into an old woman knitting by the fire?

IVAN (*Laughing and going to fireplace to warm his hands*): And what would you say if you found yourself a soldier? You think it would be wonderful with a cloak and clanking sword, but you should see us on the road with our shoes frozen to our feet, and nothing to eat but crusts and snow, no roof over our heads at night, marching, marching, marching. (*Shakes his head*) You would not envy us then, I give you my hand on it. (*Extends his hand to* MARINA)

MARINA (*Stepping back*): No, no, don't give me your hand. I'll take your word for it. I didn't know what it was like to be a soldier. (*Dance music fades in.*) Listen, there's music, Ivan. The dancers must be coming from the village. (*Voices and humming are heard offstage.* VERA *and* DANCERS *pass by window.*)

KATYA: Yes, here they are!

MARINA (*Opening door*): Welcome, pretty ones. Come in, come in. (VERA *and* DANCERS *enter.*) Will you dance for us here? (*Moves rocker up left, sits, and watches*)

VERA: Good evening, Marina and Katya, and to you, Ivan. (*All ad lib greetings.*) Yes, we will dance for you. (*Folk music is heard.* DANCERS *take positions and dance. At the end of dance,* MARINA, KATYA, *and* IVAN *applaud.*)

MARINA (*Approaching* VERA): Ah, to dance like that once more! Vera, there's no one as beautiful and light of foot as you. Will you take a step or two with an old woman? (*Holds out hand. Suddenly, sound of wolf howl is heard in the distance.*)

VERA: Hush, what was that?

IVAN (*Joking*): The werewolf is calling you, Vera.

MARINA (*Pulling hand back*): Heavens, you can't mean that, Ivan. Have the evil powers cast a spell over her?

VERA: He is only joking. Come, Marina, take my hand, the music is calling.

MARINA (*Nervously*): No, no. I was joking, too. My feet are too old for dancing now. Dance and be happy while you can.

VERA: Well, then, goodbye to you. We'll be going. Come, folks. (*VERA and DANCERS dance out.*)

MARINA: Ivan, you were joking, weren't you? It's not true that there's a spell on Vera.

IVAN: You can't tell about another's life, good neighbor. There are dark spells woven in the sun, and bright ones in the shadow. No life is all shadow or all sun. Good night to you both. (*Twirls KATYA again and exits. KATYA shuts door and watches from window.*)

MARINA: I don't know whether he jokes or not, but I'm sure of one thing now. I shan't try to change places with anyone. The princess is always in terror, Ivan suffers when he marches, and Vera—was it true about the werewolf, I wonder?

KATYA: I hope not, Baba. She is so beautiful.

MARINA: Anyway, I am glad I didn't take her hand. No, it's better just to be myself, with my own troubles.

SNOW WITCH (*Entering swiftly and quietly*): Well spoken, Marina. I see you have learned wisdom. Look, the fire has burned low and the charm has ended. You may lay your hand in mine without fear. (*Takes MARINA's hand, leaving gold ring in it*) Look again into my eyes. (MARINA *does so.*) May you keep your peace, Marina. Goodbye. (*Floats softly out door and shuts it*)

MARINA: Look, Katya, she gave me a ring! It's beautiful! And there's writing on it.

KATYA: What does it say, Babushka?

MARINA (*Reading slowly*):
"Choose not another's life or pelf.
Happiness lies within thyself."
Yes, yes. I'm thinking the Snow Witch speaks truly. (*Curtain*)
THE END

Production Notes

THE SNOW WITCH

Characters: 5 female; 1 male; 1 male or female for Driver; male and female
dancers.

Playing Time: 15 minutes.

Costumes: Peasant dresses for Marina and Katya. Flowing white gown for
Snow Witch. Royal robes and fur for Princess. Uniforms for Ivan and Driver.
Peasant costumes for Dancers.

Properties: Whip for Driver; gold ring for Snow Witch.

Setting: Simple peasant kitchen: fireplace down right with large tea kettle on
hearth; behind table and two stools up right is wall shelf with three or four
cups and plates. Window in rear wall; outside door center left; rocking chair
between window and door.

Sound: Wind; sleigh bells; suitable folk music for dance; wolf howl.

Lighting: No special effects.

The Shoemaker and the Elves

by Rowena Bennett

Characters

SHOEMAKER
SHOEMAKER'S WIFE
GENTLEMAN
TWO ELVES

TIME: *A winter evening, long ago.*
SETTING: *The Shoemaker's shop.*
AT RISE: SHOEMAKER *is sitting at his bench, working on leather for a shoe.* SHOEMAKER'S WIFE *enters, bringing two crusts of bread on a plate.*

WIFE (*Passing bread to* SHOEMAKER):
Shoemaker, Shoemaker, what shall we do?
We've nothing to eat but a bread crust or two.
The pantry is empty, and so is our purse.
We soon will be starving, and what could be worse?

SHOEMAKER (*Sighing heavily as he slowly takes one of the crusts*):
Yes, most folks are feasting. It's hard to believe
We have only bread crusts on Christmas Eve.
We've nothing at all we can market or use,
But just enough leather for one pair of shoes.

WIFE:
We're poorer than church mice who live in a pew.
Oh, Shoemaker, Shoemaker, what shall we do?

SHOEMAKER (*Rising*):
I've done what I can. I've cut out the leather;

249

And early tomorrow we'll get up together.
We'll pound with a hammer; we'll sew with the thread.
We'll have the shoes done when folks get out of bed.
Then maybe some neighbor will come in to try them.

WIFE:
What good will that do us if no one will *buy* them?
And who will come shopping on St. Nicholas Day?
At Christmastime people think only of play.

SHOEMAKER (*Moving toward door right, his* WIFE *following*):
We'll pray for some help as we go now to rest.

WIFE:
But what of tomorrow?

SHOEMAKER:
We'll hope for the best.
(*They exit right, eating their crusts. The room gets darker and there is a sound of light, "elfin" music. ELVES enter left, skipping and running. They prance over and under everything. At last, they leap on* SHOEMAKER's *bench and begin to sew and pound the pieces of cut-out leather into a pair of shoes.*)

ELVES (*As they work*):
Fly, magic thimblekin;
    Fly, magic thread.
Work while the Shoemaker
    Sleeps in his bed.
Work for an honest man;
    Be spry and nimble,
Little white needlekin,
    Little gold thimble.
Fly, fly, fly!

Pound little hammer head,
    Start on your pounding.
Make the toe pointing and
    Make the heel rounding.
Tap while the Shoemaker's
    Shutting his eyes.
Tap till the old man
    Starts to arise.

How he will smile when he
  Sees the surprise!
Tap, tap, tap!
1ST ELF (*Setting the shoe he has finished on the bench*):
There! That is done.
My, it was fun!
2ND ELF (*Putting his shoe down*):
We finished fast. It's not too late
To do a dance to celebrate.
A good deed done on Christmas Eve
Should call for dancing, I believe.
1ST ELF (*Sadly, coming forward to address audience*):
Yes, dancing's just what I would choose.
But we can't dance in ragged shoes.
For, though the floor is clean and neat,
It would put splinters in our feet.
And though we make shoes for the shelf
Of honest shoemakers, an elf
Must never sew things for himself.
On Christmas Eve that would be selfish,
And, anyway, it is not elfish.
2ND ELF (*To audience*):
In summertime we use oak leaves
For little coats with flapping sleeves.
We put the acorns on for caps,
And find some moccasins, perhaps,
Among the yellow orchid flowers;
But in the winter, snow and showers
Soon wear to rags these clothes of ours.
(*They both turn away from the audience.*)
ELVES (*Together as they exit*):
We hate to go in the cold
In clothes that are so thin and old.
(*The music changes from lively, happy music to slower, sad music at the end of the elf scene. After the* ELVES *exit, it changes to "Silent Night." Bells chime in the distance. The stage gradually gets lighter.* SHOEMAKER *and* WIFE *enter. They carry a burnt-out candle, and are shivering with cold.*

They go over to the table and start to sit down by it. Suddenly they see the finished shoes. They look at each other in amazement.)

WIFE (*Taking up one shoe*):

What's this? A shoe already made?

Is this some sort of joke you've played?

SHOEMAKER (*Taking up the other shoe and looking at it closely*):

No, no. I'm as surprised as you.

I never made so fine a shoe.

WIFE:

Someone worked here in the night.

SHOEMAKER (*Puzzled*):

There was not even candlelight.

WIFE:

Elves work by moonlight when they choose—

These must be magic fairy shoes!

(*She looks around room.*)

If fairies have been in this place,

They surely must have left some trace.

(*When she comes to the shelves, she lets out a little cry of surprise.*)

Come here and look upon this shelf.

Here is the footprint of an . . .

(*There is a sudden loud knocking at the door.*)

SHOEMAKER (*Going to door and opening it*):

Come in, come in, good gentleman.

We're glad to help you if we can.

(*A very richly dressed GENTLEMAN enters.*)

WIFE (*Curtsying*):

Good morning, sir. Why do you choose

To come in here?

GENTLEMAN (*Bowing*):

I want some shoes.

For on my way to church alone,

I cut my boot upon a stone;

And so I want a brand-new pair.

SHOEMAKER (*Holding out the shoes the* ELVES *made*):
Are these the kind you like to wear?
GENTLEMAN (*Taking them and looking them over*):
Upon my word! What a surprise!
They are my style. They are my size.
I'm in a hurry. But before
I go, I want to order more.
(*He gets out his purse.*)
Here, take this gold and make another
Pair; and for my wife and brother
I will order some tomorrow.
WIFE (*Aside, to* SHOEMAKER, *while* GENTLEMAN *counts his money*):
This is the end of all our sorrow.
SHOEMAKER (*Wrapping up shoes and handing them to* GEN-TLEMAN *in exchange for the gold*):
Oh, thank you, sir! I'll gladly do
Those other cobbling jobs for you.
GENTLEMAN (*As he exits with his package*):
Good. By tomorrow I'll be ready.
WIFE (*Sinking into a chair*):
Dear me! I'm feeling rather heady!
SHOEMAKER:
We shall be rich. Oh, I must know
Who came last night and helped us so!
WIFE:
It was a pair of little elves.
I found their footprints on those shelves.
SHOEMAKER:
If we could only thank them—bless them.
WIFE:
The best thing we can do is *dress* them.
Those footprints showed a ragged shoe,
And little toes all sticking through.
(*She leads* SHOEMAKER *over to empty shelves and points out footprints.*)
See! Aren't they tiny things, and cute?
I'm going to make each elf a suit.

SHOEMAKER (*Going over to the table and picking up scraps
  of leather*):
And from these little scraps of leather
I'll make them shoes for any weather.
(*He takes his tape measure and measures one of the footprints.*)
WIFE (*Suddenly fearful*):
But what if they should not come back?
SHOEMAKER:
All we can do is sew and tack,
And hope and pray they will come back.
(SHOEMAKER *and* WIFE, *carrying materials for dressmak-
ing and shoemaking, exit. There is a short pause, then the
ELVES tiptoe in. They are covered with snow. They look cold
and unhappy.*)
1ST ELF (*Blowing on his hands*):
My fingers are all blue with cold.
2ND ELF (*Drawing tattered coat about him*):
My rags have grown so thin and old
I cannot make them keep me warm.
1ST ELF:
Mine almost blew off in the storm.
2ND ELF:
I'm sure the Shoemaker won't care
If we come in out of the air,
To wait until the wind stops blowing.
1ST ELF:
To wait until the snow stops snowing.
(*They sit down back to back on the floor near the workbench.
They hug their knees and rock back and forth, saying a lullaby
in singsong.*)
Snuggle down, my little brother,
Slumber where you are.
Out of doors the rocking treetops
Cradle every star.
Out of doors the snow's white blanket
Covers up the moon.
Go to sleep, my little brother
To the night wind's tune.

ELVES (*Together*):
  Snuggle down, for you must know
  Wool is warmer, far, than snow.
2ND ELF:
  Hush you, now, my little brother,
  All things go to sleep:
  Both the oxen in the stable
  And the folded sheep.
  And the tired horses neither
  Stamp their feet nor neigh,
  For the bells no longer jingle
  On their master's sleigh.
ELVES (*Together*):
  Snuggle down, for houses all
  Are warmer than a barn and stall.
  (*They grow sleepier and sleepier as they sing. Their voices
  fade, and they fall asleep at end of the song. Soft music is
  heard offstage. It continues for a few moments, then fades
  away. SHOEMAKER and WIFE, carrying finished clothes
  and shoes, enter.*)
WIFE:
  My fingers never were so nimble.
SHOEMAKER:
  I seemed to have a magic thimble.
  (*They hold up their work for each other to see. Then they move
  toward the workbench, but start back in surprise as they see
  ELVES.*)
  We've made something they can use.
WIFE:
  Come quick! We have no time to lose.
  We'll tiptoe softly up behind them
  And put these clothes where they can find them.
  (*They lay the clothes on workbench. Just as they are about to
  tiptoe offstage, SHOEMAKER sneezes loudly. ELVES jump
  and open their eyes. SHOEMAKER and WIFE hide quickly
  behind a screen or curtain. They peek out now and then.*)
1ST ELF (*Waking up*):
  What *was* that noise? What *was* that sound?

2ND ELF (*Looking about*):
  I don't see anyone around.
1ST ELF:
  But what are those things over there?
  (*He points to clothes on workbench.*)
2ND ELF:
  They look like clothes for elves to wear.
  (*They jump up, clapping their hands in delight. They rush to the bench and begin to put on the little coats, hats, and shoes.*)
1ST ELF:
  These must be for us. They're very
  Small and only fit a fairy.
2ND ELF:
  I'd almost wager with my life
  They're from the old man and his wife.
1ST ELF (*Waving his arms as though weaving a magic spell*):
  Good luck to them! I'll make some magic
  To keep their lives from being tragic.
2ND ELF (*Waving his arms*):
  Good luck to them! I'll wave a charm:
  "May kindness keep this cottage warm."
  (*They look at each other, admiring the new clothes.*)
ELVES (*Together, proudly*):
  A hand for a sleeve and a foot for a shoe,
  And two little elves are as good as new.
  (*They hold hands and dance about the room. SHOEMAKER and his WIFE look out from behind screen. They smile happily and wave after the ELVES as they dance off into the night. Curtain falls.*)

THE END

Production Notes

THE SHOEMAKER AND THE ELVES

Characters: 2 male; 1 female; 2 male or female for Elves.

Playing Time: 15 minutes.

Costumes: Shoemaker wears apron over old clothes. His wife wears long, patched skirt, blouse, white cap. Gentleman is richly dressed in cape, top hat, and boots, one of which is torn. Elves wear ragged brown clothes with little green caps and long stockings. Later they put on new clothes—coats, hats, and shoes.

Properties: Shoes, scraps of leather or brown cloth, large needle, thimble, plate, crusts of bread, hammer, candle, purse, gold coins, paper to wrap shoes in, tape measure, colored cloth, artificial snow.

Setting: Shoemaker's shop, a poor, bare room. At center are bench and stool. There are some empty shelves along back wall, and nearby two three-legged stools. At left is a screen, and near it a window. Doors right and left lead to the rest of the house and to the street.

Lighting: Lights dim, then rise, to indicate evening and passage of time.

Sound: Light, elfin music; sad music; chiming bells; lullaby.

The King and the Miller

by Ruth Vickery Holmes

Characters

KING
FOUR COURTIERS
MILLER
JOAN, *his wife*
RICHARD, *his son*

SCENE 1

SETTING: *A glade in Sherwood Forest at noon. Trees are painted on backdrop.*

AT RISE: FOUR COURTIERS *enter left, assemble at center.*

4TH COURTIER (*Calling off left, bowing low*): This way, your Majesty. (KING *enters and stands center, looking all about.*)

KING: As fine a glade is this as any in Sherwood Forest. Let's rest awhile after the morning's hunt.

1ST COURTIER: Ah, your Majesty, perhaps the morning's hunt was too long for your Majesty's strength.

KING (*Quickly*): Not at all. On the contrary. I never felt better.

2ND COURTIER (*Bowing*): Quite right, your Majesty. Who else in all your Majesty's kingdom can equal your Majesty in endurance?

3RD COURTIER (*Bowing*): Who else has such tireless vigor as your Majesty?

4TH COURTIER (*Bowing*): Indeed, it is hard for your Majesty's court to keep up with your Majesty.

KING (*Impatiently*): How I wish to high heaven that my court would not keep up with me! (COURTIERS *draw back anx-*

iously.) Is there never to be any end to this bowing and scraping?

4TH COURTIER (*Bowing*): Your Majesty's person is one always to revere.

2ND COURTIER (*Bowing*): Indeed, no homage is too much to offer your Majesty.

KING (*Raising his hand, exasperated*): Enough. Enough. Your loyalty is *quite* apparent to me. But this afternoon I'll have solitude. (*Slowly, with emphasis*) I—will—have—solitude. (COURTIERS *bow low.*)

4TH COURTIER (*Smoothly*): Yes, your Majesty. Solitude.

2ND COURTIER (*Agreeing*): If solitude is what your Majesty desires, then we will follow you closely, and see that your Majesty has solitude.

KING (*Grimly*): Solitude with all of you close on my heels? No. *Privacy* is what I long for. I'll hunt *alone*.

1ST COURTIER (*Dismayed*): *Alone*, your Majesty?

3RD COURTIER (*Pleading*): Surely, your Majesty, you do not mean *alone*?

4TH COURTIER (*Anxiously*): In case of danger, who would protect your Majesty?

KING (*Laughing*): Danger? Here in Sherwood Forest? My own preserve, where death's the penalty for poaching? Ah, what danger could there be?

2ND COURTIER (*Seriously*): But your Majesty—have you not heard? Sometimes ruffians hide here in Sherwood. Or your Majesty might even meet a highwayman.

1ST COURTIER (*Gloomily*): And the paths are not so clearly marked. Your Majesty might lose his way.

KING (*Interrupting*): Ridiculous. These fears are nonsense. I'll hunt alone. (*Pointing right*) These woods are yours. (*Pointing left*) And those are mine. Off with you, every one, till sunset, when we'll meet here in this glade.

4TH COURTIER (*Bowing*): As your Majesty wishes.

3RD COURTIER (*Bowing*): Since your Majesty insists.

2ND COURTIER (*Bowing*): Yes, your Majesty.

1ST COURTIER (*Bowing*): As your Majesty commands.

KING (*As he exits left, turning back*): Adieu, my loyal friends. Till sunset. (*Curtain*)

* * * * *

SCENE 2

TIME: *That night.*
SETTING: *The same, but with dim blue lighting.*
AT RISE: KING *enters left, goes center, where he turns around, looking about carefully.*

KING: Yes, this is the glade. At last I've found it. (*Looks up*) Dark as it is, I recall those two great trees with interlocking branches. I'll wager there was a pretty to-do when sunset came, but not me. (*Goes right, looks out*) Still not even one in all my train stayed here to wait for me. (*Sighs*) And I have great need of rest and food. (*Off right is heard sound of underbrush crackling, then* MILLER *singing or whistling.*) Ah, someone is coming. (*Puts hand to his ear, listening*) No courtier, I warrant. The strain is too lusty. I'll hide till I see who it is. (*Steps close to tree left as* MILLER *enters right, holding staff and carrying sack on his shoulders. He pauses near center, mops his brow, and blows out his breath.*)

MILLER: Whew! This sack weighs a pound more every mile. 'Twill be a full ton by the time I reach Mansfield. A miller's not meant to be a pack-horse.

KING (*Stepping away from tree*): So, a miller you are. A good evening to you.

MILLER (*Startled*): And good evening to you. (*Holds up staff, threateningly*) But don't come any nearer.

KING (*Smiling*): What? Have you fear of me?

MILLER: I have fear of no one. Not with my staff in hand.

KING (*Drawing himself up*): But surely, you do not take me for an evil-doer?

MILLER (*Gruffly*): 'Tis not my business to take you for anything. I'm just a miller. Honest John Cockle I am, who owns the Mill of Mansfield. But if my business were to guard Sherwood Forest, that would be different.

KING (*Smiling*): Ah, it seems you do not altogether trust me.

MILLER (*Kindly*): Now don't you worry about that. In spite of myself I can't help liking you. I promise that I'll not give your hiding place away.

KING (*Protesting*): But, sir, I am *not* hiding.

MILLER: Let the King and the King's men guard Sherwood as they can. When it comes to poaching, live and let live, say I.

KING (*Taken aback*): But men are hanged for poaching.

MILLER (*Nodding*): Ay, if they're caught. And more's the pity. For what's a deer or two where there are so many? I am not one to blame you, rest assured.

KING (*With emphasis*): But I am *not* stealing deer. On my word, I'm no poacher.

MILLER (*Sternly*): Then yours is another case. And though I had begun to like you, I'll tell you plain: I do not hold with what goes on in your profession.

KING (*Astonished*): Why, good sir, what do you take me for?

MILLER (*Gently*): Ah, you're not common. Nor mean. To the devil I'll give his due. But, not to mince words, I doubt not that you are (*With emphasis*) a gentleman thief.

KING (*Laughing*): By the rood, sir, you abuse me too much. A thief I am not. But a gentleman, yes. A gentleman who means no harm to anyone, but who is in great need of lodging and food.

MILLER (*Grimly*): And has not, so I'll wager, so much as a farthing to pay for them.

KING (*Quickly*): There you're wrong. (*Takes leather pouch from his belt and holds it up*) I'd gladly pay you anything you ask. See, here is gold.

MILLER (*Dubiously*): Gold, do you say? Oh, I see. (*Nods*) You are joking. But even if you really had some money in that pouch, I'd take not a farthing of it. You'd be welcome in my home as my guest. That is, if only I felt sure you're speaking the truth when you say you are up to no mischief.

KING (*Gravely*): As to that, I give you my oath. (*Stretches out his hand to* MILLER) Here's my hand on it.

MILLER (*Hastily*): Not so fast, my good man. Come first to my

house, where I can see you in full light. Then, so be it you
have an honest look, *then* I'll shake hands.

KING (*Laughing heartily*): That's right, John Cockle. Take care
whom you call friend. 'Tis wise to take no chances. But lead
on now. I'll follow.

MILLER (*Starting left*): Ay, follow. (*Turns and holds up staff*)
But follow at twenty paces. If you close in on me, you'll feel
my staff's full weight.

KING (*Chuckling, then calling out*): Ay, I'll follow at twenty
paces, John Cockle. Just lead the way. (*Curtain*)

* * * * *

SCENE 3

TIME: *Later in the evening.*

SETTING: *The Miller's house. Table is right of center and
benches are at rear and right of table. There is large bowl on
table. Down right is door that leads to bedroom; down left, a
door to larder. Bucket is next to door. There is a wide double
door at rear center, on each side of which are hung lanterns.
Candles are on table, and there is a fire in the hearth at left.*

AT RISE: JOAN *is setting table and humming.*

JOAN (*Calling off right*): Richard!

RICHARD (*Entering right*): Ay, Mother.

JOAN (*Pointing to bowl on table*): Fill the bowl with cider, son.

RICHARD (*Picking up bowl*): Ay, Mother. Is the larder locked?

JOAN (*As she takes key from pocket*): Ay, safely locked. In spite
of all I've used of the last deer you brought home, two fine fat
flanks are hanging there.

RICHARD (*Taking key*): Ay, 'twas a well-fleshed deer. (*Starts
out left*)

JOAN (*Anxiously*): Richard, are you sure that no one saw you?
Such dire punishment there'd be if you got caught.

RICHARD (*Turning*): Now, Mother, have no fear. I met no one
going to Sherwood, nor on my way home again. The keepers
can't count every deer in Sherwood. How could one deer be
missed?

JOAN (*Uneasily*): Still, sometimes there are searching parties. (RICHARD *shrugs his shoulders and exits.*) Yes, how could one deer be missed? (*Goes on setting table. After a few moments,* RICHARD *reenters with bowl, which he places carefully on table.* JOAN *stands back, observes table.*) There, now everything is ready. (*Crosses and stoops over hearth, lifting cover from pot*) Ah, 'tis done just to a turn.

MILLER (*Calling from off left*): Hello!

JOAN (*Pleased*): Ah! Your father's home. (RICHARD *goes rear, unbars door, and swings it open to* MILLER.)

RICHARD: Hello, Father. Welcome home. (MILLER *enters through doorway.*) Let me take your sack.

MILLER: Thank you, Richard. (RICHARD *removes sack from* MILLER'*s shoulders and places it at right of doorway, where he turns and holds out his hand to take the staff.*) No, my staff I'll keep, Richard. There is a stranger with me.

JOAN (*Puzzled*): A staff in hand is not the way to give a welcome, husband.

MILLER (*Slowly*): Well, I'm not sure yet whether a welcome's safe. (*Peering out left, calls*) Now, sir, come closer. (*After a moment,* KING *stands in doorway, bows to* JOAN *and nods to* RICHARD.) Come here where the light will show me who you are. (MILLER *and* KING *come center.*) Look carefully, Joan. (*To* RICHARD) And, Richard, you too. (JOAN *draws nearer, looks at* KING *carefully, then nods to* MILLER.)

JOAN: By my troth, husband, he is a handsome youth.

MILLER (*Slowly*): Ay, I like your face well, sir. It has a good honest look.

RICHARD (*Critically*): Yes, honest, I'd say. (*Turns to* JOAN) But Mother, did you say *handsome*? (JOAN *looks closely at* KING *again, then turns to* RICHARD.)

JOAN: Well, anyway, he's honest. (*With emphasis*) I do feel sure he's honest.

KING (*Smiling as he bows*): I thank you for your kind opinion.

JOAN (*Quickly*): But, husband, 'tis best to act with caution. (*To* KING) Are you sure you are no runaway? Show me your passport, then all will be well.

KING (*Shrugging his shoulders*): I have no passport, for I've

never been a servant. I am simply a courtier who got lost in
the forest. For any kindness and welcome I shall be grateful.
And someday, if fortune favors me, I hope to offer you hospitality in return, under my own roof.

JOAN (*Nodding*): Now that shows that he's no homeless good-
for-nothing. It would certainly be a shame to turn him away
from our door.

MILLER (*Nodding*): Ay, very true. I like the way he speaks
up to us without any bowing and scraping. (KING *chokes,
suppressing laughter. MILLER turns to KING inquiringly,
then shrugs shoulders, turns back to JOAN.*) Though he must
know full well that we're no hangers-on about the court the
way he is. (*Thumps chest*) We're free owners of our mill and
land.

KING (*Exploding with laughter*): I am glad that you consider
me guiltless of bowing and scraping. Indeed, though I do hang
about the court a good deal, I never did hold with subser-
vience.

RICHARD (*Approvingly*): Ay, Mother, he'll do. Let him say.
(JOAN *nods.*)

MILLER (*With outstretched hand*): Well, young man, we've decided you're welcome. And here's my hand now.

KING (*Shaking hands*): I feel honored.

MILLER: You shall share Richard's room.

KING (*Nodding to RICHARD*): And well lodged I'll be.

JOAN: There'll be fresh straw and good brown hempen sheets
on your bed.

KING (*Delighted*): Ah, fresh straw, good brown hempen sheets.
It's not every day I have those.

MILLER (*Putting his hand on KING's shoulder, and pointing to
table*): Come, sit down.

JOAN (*Smiling cordially*): We're glad to have you with us.
(KING *and* MILLER *sit on bench at rear of table;* RICHARD
sits at right; JOAN *turns toward hearth.*)

KING (*Smiling*): My heartiest thanks. Your welcome was given
with no reckless haste. (*Laughs, and others join in*) But it
means the more for that.

MILLER (*Nodding*): Ay, I take great care whom I call friend. But now, feel sure of this —you can count on us all as friends.

KING: And you can count on me.

MILLER (*Reaching for bowl*): Now, first of all, we'll drink, sir, to your good health. (*Drinks, then gives bowl to* RICHARD)

RICHARD (*Heartily*): In faith, I feel as does my father. The more I see you, the better do I like you. Here's to you. (*Drinks and hands bowl to* KING)

KING (*Holding up bowl*): Now I will drink to you. (*In earnest*) In all my life I've never been judged before just for myself alone. You are the first, the *only* friends I've made who weighed me as a man. How glad I am you felt that you could trust me. (*Nods to others, in turn, then drinks*)

JOAN (*Crossing from hearth, with pasty held aloft*): And now we must eat. Here's a fine pasty—well-cooked and tender. (*Places it in front of* KING, *who helps himself to it.* JOAN *sits next to* RICHARD.)

MILLER (*Cordially*): You must take all you wish, good sir . . . but mind you, make no waste.

KING (*Handing pasty to* JOAN, *who helps herself and the others*): Yes, I'll be careful. (*Takes a bite; surprised*) Ah, is it venison?

RICHARD (*Smiling*): Ay, venison.

KING: What a surprise! I'll wager it costs a pretty penny.

RICHARD (*Thumping table with emphasis*): There you're wrong. Not a penny do we pay. From merry Sherwood we are well supplied. Every now and then we make bold with the King's deer.

MILLER (*Uneasily*): But say nothing about this wherever you go. We wouldn't for anything have this matter known to the King.

KING (*Solemnly*): I promise you. Never, from any word of mine, shall the King learn more of this matter than he knows this moment.

RICHARD (*Serenely*): Yes, I pick out the best and the fattest deer in all Sherwood.

KING (*Impressed*): Indeed, sir, you are lucky. You live better than the King.

MILLER (*Nodding*): So long as the King knows nothing about it.

RICHARD (*Laughing*): Ay, if the King knew, we'd not live at all.

JOAN (*Troubled*): I like not the way that Sherwood Forest is governed. The laws are cruel. I wish the King would change the ruling.

MILLER (*Firmly*): That he will, when once he puts his mind to it.

KING (*Quickly*): Ah, why are you so sure?

MILLER (*Confidently*): Oh, the King is a good fellow. That is known to all.

KING (*Delighted*): So then, you like the King?

MILLER (*Considering*): Of course, I haven't *seen* him. Still, I feel sure. (*Takes up bowl*) Let's drink to the King. (*Drinks, then hands bowl to* KING)

KING (*Holding up bowl*): To the King! (*Passes bowl to* RICHARD)

RICHARD: To the health of the King! (*Curtain*)

* * * * *

SCENE 4

TIME: *Next morning.*

SETTING: *Same.*

AT RISE: JOAN *is brushing hearth.* MILLER *stands down left with armful of twigs.*

JOAN (*Briskly*): Now, John, the hearth is brushed and clean. Lay down the twigs here.

MILLER (*Piling twigs neatly*): Ay, then I'll go grind the corn while you get breakfast. (RICHARD *enters right.*)

RICHARD: The stranger's still asleep. I did not wake him.

JOAN (*Nodding*): Ay, tired he was. Let him lie longer. . . . Richard, would you fetch some water for me? (*Suddenly, hunting horns are heard offstage.*) What is that? (*Turns, listening.* RICHARD *opens door, looks off left.*)

RICHARD (*Excited*): Horses and men. (*Turns and points right as horns sound again*) And over there, too. The men are dismounting and coming up the path. (MILLER *goes to look out, followed by* JOAN.)

MILLER (*Anxiously*): I wonder what's going on? Richard, you'd best come in the house. (RICHARD *enters and stands in front of table.*) And, Joan, stand here with me beside the hearth. (*Goes down left; JOAN stands in front of him. 1ST and 2ND COURTIERS enter left. 3RD and 4TH COURTIERS enter right and stand crowding doorway and rear. MILLER bows to them.*) Good morning, good sirs. 'Tis early you must have left your beds. (JOAN *curtseys. RICHARD bows.*)

1ST COURTIER (*Gruffly*): Left our beds! Ha, we never slept in them!

2ND COURTIER: We've been scouring the countryside the whole night through.

MILLER (*Troubled*): Why? Has something gone amiss?

3RD COURTIER (*Interrupting*): Amiss? Amiss? It is much worse than that. We're asking every householder for help.

MILLER (*Firmly*): If you would have my help, you'll have to tell me more.

4TH COURTIER (*Coming forward*): We're searching every house for venison. (MILLER, JOAN, *and* RICHARD *exchange anxious looks.*) If we find but a trace of venison, then, no doubt we'll learn who brought the King to harm.

MILLER (*Quickly*): What do you mean, sir? What's happened to the King?

1ST COURTIER: Why, yesterday, in Sherwood Forest, the King was lost! (MILLER *turns to* JOAN *and then to* RICHARD, *all three filled with consternation.*) And 'tis clear: The miscreants who killed the deer have done away with his Majesty himself.

4TH COURTIER (*Impatiently*): So show us your larder, at once.

1ST COURTIER (*Pointing right*): Is that the larder door?

MILLER (*Shaking head*): No, it's not.

1ST COURTIER (*Pointing to door left*): Ah, then this.

JOAN (*Taking step center with outstretched arms*): But, sir, the larder door is locked.

1ST COURTIER (*Angrily*): Quick, woman, the key. Or else we'll break the door.

JOAN (*Faltering*): The key—I must think now. Where did I put the key?

4TH COURTIER (*Raising clenched fist*): By my faith, all this delay is much the same as out-and-out confession.

2ND COURTIER (*Drawing nearer*): Ah, dire punishment you'll get, as you deserve. (*Suddenly, KING enters and stands down right.*)

KING: What's going on here? (COURTIERS, *astonished, kneel.*)

1ST COURTIER: Your Majesty is safe!

4TH COURTIER: Ah, your Majesty.

2ND COURTIER: Has your Majesty suffered no harm?

3RD COURTIER: At last, we've found your Majesty. (*Stunned, MILLER, JOAN, and RICHARD drop to their knees.*)

KING (*Nodding*): Ah, yes, I'm safe and sound. I never spent a better night. But tell me (*With emphasis*) what's going on? (*Motions everyone to rise*)

1ST COURTIER (*Indignantly*): We're certain these people have stolen your Majesty's deer.

KING (*Calmly*): I spent the night as guest under this roof and kinder hospitality I never had.

4TH COURTIER (*Protesting*): But your Majesty, we're sure they've poached from Sherwood Forest.

KING (*Gravely*): That is a serious accusation. On what, sir, is it based?

1ST COURTIER (*Pointing to MILLER and JOAN scornfully*): They are loath to let us see their larder. They make pretense that they've mislaid the key. They must be hiding venison beyond that door. Their guilt is plain, your Majesty.

MILLER (*In extreme distress*): Oh, your Majesty, I beg you—

KING (*Interrupting quickly*): To see the larder for myself? (*Nods*) Yes, I will grant that favor. I will investigate the larder myself. (MILLER, JOAN, *and* RICHARD *exchange nervous glances.* KING *goes left;* COURTIERS *start after him, but* KING *stops, turns.*) No, you stay here—two of you stand guard beside each man. (COURTIERS *turn back.*) Now (*To* JOAN), if I may have the larder key.

JOAN (*Taking key from pocket and handing it to* KING): Here is the key, your Majesty.

KING (*Nodding*): Now, we shall see. (*Exits left*)

1ST COURTIER (*Angrily*): So, now you can remember where you put the key?

4TH COURTIER (*Sneering*): 'Twas not forgetfulness, but consciousness of guilt.

2ND COURTIER (*To* MILLER): You'll die for this.

3RD COURTIER (*To* RICHARD): And you as well. Think not you can escape.

KING (*Reentering left*): My lords, I have searched the larder through and through. On every shelf I looked, and behind each cupboard door. (*Emphatically*) No further search is needed.

1ST COURTIER (*Astonished*): But, your Majesty, was there no venison hidden there?

4TH COURTIER (*Incredulously*): Why, I could have sworn—the way they acted, your Majesty. Are you sure?

KING (*Decisively*): When I shared this family's supper and found lodging here, I called them friends. And friends I call them still.

MILLER, RICHARD, *and* JOAN (*Bowing; ad lib*): I thank your Majesty. Thank you, your Majesty. (*Etc.*)

KING: To them I give my warmest thanks for their kind welcome. Never before had I an evening like it. Not one dull moment! And now, before we hurry back to court, there's this. (*Draws forth sword and holds it aloft*)

MILLER (*Kneeling; fearfully*): Ah, your Majesty, it was too much to hope. But, I beg you, Richard's so young.

KING (*Ignoring* MILLER's *words; tapping his shoulders with blade of sword*): Rise, Sir John Cockle.

MILLER (*Dumbfounded, as he rises*): What? Me—a knight?

KING (*Nodding*): Ay, Sir John Cockle, a knight, indeed. (*To* JOAN) And you are Lady Cockle. And Richard is a squire.

RICHARD (*Amazed*): A squire! (JOAN *curtseys to* KING.)

JOAN (*To* MILLER, *in amazement*): Did you hear that, John? I am now *Lady* Cockle!

KING (*Smiling*): Someday I shall summon you to court to return your hospitality. (*Motions to* COURTIERS *to exit. As they turn toward door to take positions at right and left,* KING *puts his hand on* MILLER's *shoulder.*) When you come, be sure of this:

I'll not hold you on the threshold while I make up my mind to bid you enter.

MILLER (*Shaking his head ruefully*): So much there is for your Majesty to pardon, and forget.

KING (*Smiling*): All has been pardoned, but never will I forget. (*Goes to doorway. To* COURTIERS) Come, let's be off. (*Turns back, bows low*) My thanks again. Adieu. (*Curtain*)

THE END

Production Notes

THE KING AND THE MILLER

Characters: 3 male; 1 female; 4 male or female for Courtiers.

Playing Time: 25 minutes.

Costumes: The characters are dressed, each according to rank, in costumes of the Robin Hood period. The King carries a sword.

Properties: A sack of corn, a stout staff for the Miller, rough dishes and cutlery, a brown bowl for cider, a pot of venison pasty, a hearth brush, twigs, water buckets.

Setting: Scenes 1 and 2 are played against a forest backdrop. Scenes 3 and 4: A table is right of center and benches are at rear and right of the table. Down right is a door that leads to Richard's room; down left, a door to the larder. There is a wide double door at rear center, on each side of which are hung lanterns. Candles are on the table, and there is a fire in the hearth at left.

Lighting: Bright daylight overheads and footlights in Scene 1 with spots from wings for sunlight effect. Dim blue in Scene 2. For Scene 3 the light from the fireplace, candles and lanterns should be sufficient. In Scene 4 use early morning lighting with sunlight from windows.

Sound: Hunting horns.

Puss-In-Boots

by Josef A. Elfenbein

Characters

PRINCE PHILLIP
PUSS-IN-BOOTS
OLD WOMAN
KING
PRINCESS ANITA
VOICE OF THE OGRE

SETTING: *Courtyard of a medieval castle. Large wooden door with brass knocker is right. Bench is center and downstage left is well.*

AT RISE: PHILLIP, *in tattered clothes, stands knocking at the castle door.* PUSS-IN-BOOTS *sits watching.*

PHILLIP: Oh, Puss, I do hope someone answers the door. I am so hungry.

PUSS (*Sadly*): Meow.

PHILLIP: You're hungry, too, poor friend. All day we've walked and walked. Not a drop of milk for you. Not a crust of bread for me.

PUSS (*Agreeing*): Meow.

PHILLIP: A rich *prince* must live in *this* castle. Never in all my travels have I seen such a one. Surely, here we will be given some milk and cheese to help us on our way.

PUSS (*Comforting*): Meow.

PHILLIP: We may even be able to sleep here tonight. But, listen, I hear someone coming to the door. We must be polite, Puss.

OLD WOMAN (*Offstage*): Who is it? What do you want?

PHILLIP: Open the door, good woman. I will not harm you.

OLD WOMAN (*Opens door*): Quickly, lad, what do you want here?

PHILLIP: We are hungry and tired. We wonder whether your master would give us a bit of food and let us sleep in your stable tonight.

OLD WOMAN (*Horrified*): Eat *here*? *Sleep* here? Boy, do you know to whom this castle belongs?

PHILLIP: Nay.

OLD WOMAN: This is the castle of a very wicked ogre. He will eat you if he finds you here. He is taller than the trees, stronger than twenty horses and he can turn himself into anything he wishes by his great magic powers. So, you had better be gone.

PHILLIP: Hasn't anyone ever tried to kill him?

OLD WOMAN: Many brave knights have tried, but they were all slain. You see, nothing can hurt the ogre. *Nothing can kill him.*

PHILLIP: Nothing at *all*?

OLD WOMAN: Nothing except water. If he were ever to be thrown into water so that it covered him completely, then he would die. But he is so big, there is not enough water here ever to cover him. So, you see, you had best be on your way. You have a musical pipe there in your belt. Take it down to the village and play for the people. They will pay you and give you all the food you need.

PHILLIP: I cannot. This is a magic pipe and whenever it plays, it forces people to laugh and laugh so hard their sides ache. Then the people throw sticks at us and chase us.

OLD WOMAN: Then, you ought to go home to your family, for you are indeed in trouble.

PHILLIP: I have no home. My friend Puss-in-Boots, there, and I are all alone in the world. Please help us.

OLD WOMAN: There is not time to fetch food for you. But, here, take this bowl of milk and this bit of bread. It was for the kitchen boy. Take it and hurry down the road.

PHILLIP: Thank you, kind lady.

PUSS (*Thankfully*): Meow.

PHILLIP: Puss-in-Boots thanks you, too.

OLD WOMAN: You're welcome, both of you. Now hasten away.

I must close the door. The ogre sleeps in the next room and I dare not wake him. Farewell. (*Exits, closing door*)

PHILLIP (*As he walks to bench with milk and bread.*): Here, Puss, you take the milk and I'll take the bread. (*Sits*) It isn't much, but I'll share everything I have with you.

PUSS (*Comforting*): Meow.

PHILLIP: I feel so all alone, Puss. If only you could speak to me. I *wish* you could speak.

PUSS: I *can* speak, Master Phillip.

PHILLIP (*Jumping up and looking around*): Who's there? Who spoke?

PUSS: I did. Puss-in-Boots.

PHILLIP: You? You, Puss? I never knew you could speak.

PUSS: You never asked me.

PHILLIP: Oh, Puss, I need your help so much. Ever since Father had to go away and leave us alone, I haven't been able to take care of you. The magic pipe he gave me is no help. And no one wants us. What will I do? Tell me, Puss.

PUSS: Do not worry, master. I will help you.

PHILLIP: How can *you* help me?

PUSS: A pussy cat learns many things that would surprise you. Now, if you promise to do as I say and ask no questions, your worries will be over before the sun has set. Do you promise?

PHILLIP: I do, Puss. I promise with all my heart.

PUSS: Then we must act quickly, for I see the King's coach coming over yonder hill. If luck is with us, his Majesty may help us with our adventure.

PHILLIP: What do we do?

PUSS: First, give me your magic pipe.

PHILLIP (*Giving* PUSS *the pipe*): That's easy enough.

PUSS: Now climb into that well and hide on the ledge just out of sight. Be careful that you do not fall into the water and drown.

PHILLIP: I don't understand.

PUSS: Remember your promise? No questions, master.

PHILLIP: I'm sorry. I shall do as you say. (*Goes to well*)

PUSS: When you hear me call out, "By my bootstraps," you cry out, "Help, help, I'm drowning."

PHILLIP: When you say, "By my bootstraps," I will call for help. I understand.

PUSS: Good. Now, quickly, into the well. The royal carriage has stopped and the King is coming down the road.

PHILLIP (*Disappearing into the well*): Good luck, Puss. Good luck! (PUSS-IN-BOOTS *steps behind well, out of sight.*)

KING (*Hurriedly entering from off left, mopping brow furiously*): Anita! Anita, where are you? Where *are* you? Oh, my poor head. (*Sits on bench*) I must rest again. That daughter of mine will drive me to my grave.

PUSS (*Coming from behind well, bowing low*): Good day, your Majesty.

KING (*Gasping in great surprise*): By my royal crown! A talking cat! A cat who speaks!

PUSS: How may I serve your Royal Highness?

KING: Serve me? Why, a talking cat *might* help at that. Cat, you may best serve me by finding the Princess. (*Sadly*) She has run away again.

PUSS: Run away?

KING: She is a very disobedient girl. I try to please her. I do my best. I really do.

PUSS: I believe your Majesty.

KING: But she is so stubborn. She won't listen to my troubles.

PUSS: What troubles, sire?

KING: I am growing old and it is time I sat back and let someone else rule this kingdom. I have no other children. Just Princess Anita. I want her to be married so that she and her husband may take my place.

PUSS: Doesn't she want to be married?

KING: Nay, she won't even speak to the fine princes that come to see her. She runs away and hides. Like today. Since noon, I have been searching. If only I could find her and make her obey me.

PUSS: That's a simple task.

KING: It *is*?

PUSS: I'll use one of Prince Phillip's magic instruments. Prince Phillip is my master and this is his pipe.

KING: It looks like an ordinary musical pipe.

PUSS: Nay, 'tis *truly* magic. If you play on this pipe, your daughter will surely hear it. When she does, the music will make her laugh so hard that she will come running to you, begging you to stop.

KING: I could make her promise to be good before I stopped playing.

PUSS: And if she didn't keep her promise, you could play again.

KING: Excellent! Amazing! Wonderful, *if* true.

PUSS: Listen and I will prove it to you. (*Begins to play*)

KING (*Laughs almost to exhaustion, holds sides in pain*): Ho! Ho! Ho! Ha! Ha! Ha! Stop! Enough, I say! Stop, I believe you. Pray stop, my sides *ache* with laughter!

PUSS (*Stops playing*): Now do you believe in the magic of the pipe?

KING (*Holding sides. Still panting*): I do. I do. It is magnificent. It will solve my problem.

PUSS: Then, take it. It is yours. Prince Phillip gives it to you, with his compliments.

KING: What shall I give him in return?

PUSS: Nothing, your Majesty. Prince Phillip is so rich he has everything he desires.

KING: Really? He is *that* rich?

PUSS: Even richer.

KING: I should like to meet him.

PUSS (*Pointing*): Why, there he comes now.

KING (*Peering about*): Where? Where?

PUSS (*Whirling* KING *around*): That way. No, that way. Here. There. Oh, *no!* He fell into the well. *By my bootstraps,* he fell into the well!

PHILLIP (*Within well*): Help, help, I'm drowning. Help!

KING: Hurry, Cat, we must save him. I'll help. Come along.

PUSS (*Holding* KING *back*): Nay, *I'll* save him. He would not wish you to see him with his fine clothes all soiled and wet, his velvet cape all muddy and torn.

KING: I'll go to my carriage and bring some of my own clothes for him. But, save him quickly. (*Exits left*)

PUSS (*Runs to the well and looks far down*): Master, the King is bringing some fine clothes for you. Put them on quickly and come out when I give my signal.

PHILLIP (*Only his head showing*): I'm confused, Puss-in-Boots. But, I'll do as you say. Only, I hope we won't offend the King. He might throw both of us into *prison* if we did.

PUSS: No more talking. Hide yourself once more. The King will return shortly. (PHILLIP *disappears into well again.* PUSS *runs to the castle door and knocks rapidly, looking back toward* KING.) Good woman, good woman. Hurry to the door.

OLD WOMAN (*Opening door*): Who's there?

PUSS: It is I who command you.

OLD WOMAN: You? A cat? You command *me*?

PUSS: I have come to make you free of the horrible ogre.

OLD WOMAN: You will make me free of the ogre?

PUSS: Aye, if you do as I command.

OLD WOMAN: I'll do *anything* to be free of him.

PUSS: Then there are two things you must do. When next I knock on this door, tell anyone who asks you that the owner of all these lands and of this great castle is Prince Phillip.

OLD WOMAN: I will do that.

PUSS: Then invite the people to dine. Tell them to take their carriage to the other entrance so that the coachmen may be fed and the horses may be watered.

OLD WOMAN: I'll do that as well.

PUSS: Then wake the wicked ogre and tell him I wish to see him.

OLD WOMAN: He will surely eat you.

PUSS: Then he will eat me and it will be my fault. Now close the door quickly and await my knocking.

OLD WOMAN: Farewell, for now, Cat, and bless you. (*Closes door*)

KING (*Rushing on*): Here. Here are some rich clothes for Prince Phillip. Is he safe? (*Gives wrapped bundle to* PUSS)

PUSS: Quite safe. He is standing just inside the well. (*Takes bundle to well*) Here, Prince Phillip. The King gives you these clothes. He will speak with you when you are ready to come out. (*Gives bundle to* PHILLIP *in well*)

PHILLIP (*In well*): I shall be out in but a moment.

KING: While the prince is dressing, I shall try this magical pipe. Tell me how to work it.

PUSS: Put this end of the pipe into your mouth.

KING (*Does so*): Like this?

PUSS: Just right. Now as you blow, move your fingers up and down over these holes.

KING (*Removing pipe from mouth*): I see. I shall try it. Better clasp your paws tightly over your ears, for I am about to begin. (*Plays pipe for a few seconds and stops*) Nothing happened, Talking Cat. (*Aside*) Oh, his paws are over his ears and he cannot hear me. I must shout. (*Shouts*) Nothing happened. The Princess did not come laughing.

PUSS (*Shouting back. Paws still over ears*): Keep trying. Give her time.

KING: Very well. I shall try once more. (*Blows loudly*)

ANITA (*Enters laughing with great force holding sides*): Ho Ho Ho! Ha Ha Ha! Stop! Father, please stop! My sides ache from so much laughing. Stop! I'll do anything you wish, only please stop playing that pipe.

KING (*Stops playing*): I shall stop, Anita, if you promise never to run away and never to disobey me.

ANITA (*On bench gasping for breath*): I promise. Only, don't play that pipe any more. It makes me laugh so much. Wherever did you get it?

KING: Talking Cat gave it to me from his master, Prince Phillip.

ANITA: Prince Phillip? I have never heard of him! What did you give the prince in return?

KING: Nothing.

ANITA: *Nothing?*

KING: He would take nothing. He is so rich that he has everything.

ANITA: Indeed? And, what does the Prince look like?

PUSS (*Bowing low*): He is most handsome, fair Princess. Young and handsome. And *by my bootstraps,* here he comes! (PHILLIP *comes out of the well finely clothed.*)

KING: Good day to you, Prince Phillip.

PHILLIP: Greetings to you, your Majesty, and to you, Princess.

ANITA: Thank you, Prince Phillip. I am pleased to meet you. Why have you never visited us at our palace?

PHILLIP: I—I—that is—

PUSS: The Prince has been away on a long journey, your Highness.

ANITA: I see. And where are your lands and your castle, great prince?

PHILLIP: They are—they—they—

PUSS: They are right here. These lands are all his and this castle is his.

ANITA: Indeed? I have always believed that this belonged to a horrible ogre.

KING: As a matter of fact, that is what I heard. How do you explain that, Prince Phillip?

PHILLIP: Well, your Majesty, I—I—that is—

PUSS: It is nonsense made up by the superstitious villagers.

ANITA: I don't know about that. This whole thing seems quite strange.

KING: And the Prince seems so slow of speech.

PUSS: Perhaps you ought to knock on the door and inquire there.

PHILLIP: But—but—

ANITA: A good idea. Do it, Father.

KING: Very well, I shall. (*Knocks at door*)

OLD WOMAN (*Behind door*): Who is it?

KING: It is I, the King of the land. (*Door opens*) Now, tell me, good woman, who owns all these lands?

OLD WOMAN: They belong to the good Prince Phillip.

ANITA: And who owns this fine castle?

OLD WOMAN: It, too, belongs to the good Prince Phillip.

KING: Thank you.

OLD WOMAN: We should be honored if you would join us at dinner.

KING: I accept your invitation.

OLD WOMAN: But first, please tell your coachmen to drive the royal carriage to the other entrance that they may be fed and the horses watered.

KING: I shall do as you suggest. (*Door closes*)

PUSS: Prince Phillip, go along with the King and Princess Anita. See how fine the workmanship is on the royal carriage.

ANITA: Please do.

PHILLIP: I shall.

KING: Won't you join us, Talking Cat?

PUSS: Nay, I have further important business here.

KING: We shall see you later, then. Come along, Anita, Prince Phillip. (*They exit.* PUSS *runs to castle door and knocks heavily upon it. There is a roll of thunder and a blinking of lights. The door opens slowly. Whenever* OGRE *speaks, the building shakes but* OGRE *is never seen.*)

OGRE: WHO DARES TO DISTURB THE GREAT OGRE?

PUSS: It is I, one who has heard of your marvelous magic.

OGRE: WELL, WHAT DO YOU WANT?

PUSS: The villagers say that you can change yourself into anything you wish.

OGRE: THAT'S TRUE.

PUSS: I cannot believe it. Why, they tell me that you can change yourself into a wind that blots out the sunlight and makes the world dark and cold.

OGRE: I CAN DO THAT EASILY ENOUGH. WATCH THIS. (*The lights black out and a great wind is heard. When the wind stops, the lights go on.* PUSS, *who has been hiding under the bench, crawls out and walks back to the castle door.*)

PUSS: That was excellent, Ogre. But I have also been told that you, who are taller than these trees, can make yourself a tiny animal, like a mouse.

OGRE: I CAN MAKE MYSELF A MOUSE OR EVEN SMALLER—AN ANT—OR A FLY—OR A BEE—ANYTHING . . . IF I WISHED.

PUSS: A mouse would satisfy me. But you must admit that is impossible.

OGRE: IMPOSSIBLE! IMPOSSIBLE! I SHALL TURN MYSELF INTO A MOUSE AND THEN WHEN I AM AN OGRE AGAIN I SHALL EAT YOU.

PUSS: Very well, but let me see you turn into a mouse.

OGRE: THEN SEE THIS! (*There is a roll of thunder and a little rubber mouse is pulled across stage by a string from the castle towards the well.* PUSS *pounces on it and throws it into the well and looks down after it.*)

PUSS: There, wicked Ogre, you are completely covered with water. And that means you live no more. No longer will you eat or harm anyone. No one shall be afraid any more. (KING, PHILLIP *and* ANITA *rush on.*)

PHILLIP: Puss, Puss-in-Boots, are you all right?

ANITA: We heard a deafening thunder.

KING: A cold wind swept over us and blotted out the sunlight.

PUSS: It was nothing at all, good friends. Now, if you are ready, we shall enter Prince Phillip's castle and dine. It has been a most difficult day.

PHILLIP: Is everything *truly* all right?

PUSS: Truly, indeed, and your future is secure.

PHILLIP: Then, Princess, take my arm and let us enter my castle.

ANITA (*Taking his arm*): I shall be proud to. Come along, Father.

KING: After a moment. First, come hither, Talking Cat, and kneel before me.

PUSS (*Does so*): As you wish, your Majesty.

KING (*Drawing sword and placing it, in knighting fashion, over* PUSS-IN-BOOT's *head*): I, King of all this country, do knight thee for thy services done today. Henceforth you will be known as Knight of the Magic Pipe, called evermore Sir Puss-in-Boots. (*Curtain*)

THE END

Production Notes

PUSS-IN-BOOTS

Characters: 4 male; 2 female.

Playing Time: 20 minutes.

Costumes: Phillip should have his fine clothes on under his tattered ones. He removes the tattered ones while in the well. All the costumes may be as elaborate or as simple as desired. Puss could wear a mask and should have a tail and bright red boots.

Properties: Magic pipe, bowl, slice of bread, bundle of clothes, rubber mouse on long string, sword.

Setting: The courtyard of a castle. At right is large wooden door with brass knocker, the entrance to the castle. At center is a wooden bench, and at downstage left the castle well, which must be large enough to accommodate Phillip. Backdrop may portray a castle garden.

Lighting: The lights blink when the Ogre speaks, and blackout completely as he changes into the wind.

Sound: Thunder (drums, or large sheet of metal which is shaken or hit). Wind (blow into microphone, use wind machine or omit).

Cinderella

by Alice D'Arcy

Characters

CINDERELLA
PRUNELLA ⎫ *her stepsisters*
GRISELDA ⎭
FAIRY GODMOTHER
BALL GUESTS, *extras*
TWO TRUMPETERS
FOUR ATTENDANTS
PRINCE

SCENE 1

SETTING: *Kitchen in Cinderella's house. Fireplace with stool in front of it is in center upstage wall. Small cage is next to fireplace. Table and two chairs stand center. Two capes are hung over back of chair.*

AT RISE: CINDERELLA, *ragged and with a smudge of soot on her face, is sweeping in front of fireplace. She puts broom in corner and sits on stool gazing into fire.*

CINDERELLA (*Dreamily*): Tonight is the night of the ball. (*Sighs and cups head in her hands*) If only *I* were going. (PRUNELLA *and* GRISELDA *enter wearing ball gowns.* PRUNELLA *carries large piece of lace,* GRISELDA, *a ribbon and ruffle.*)

PRUNELLA: Will you look at this lazy goose! (*Snickers*) Ella-sit-by-the-cinders! Have you nothing else to do?

GRISELDA: Of *course* she has nothing else to do! (*Clips words*) She is too stupid!

CINDERELLA (*Rising*): How *lovely* your gowns are!

GRISELDA: Come here and help us dress. (*Hands her ribbon*) Tie this ribbon around my neck. (CINDERELLA *begins to tie ribbon, but* GRISELDA *pushes her hand away.*) Not like that, you simpleton! I'll tie it myself! Go help Prunella pin that ruffle to her sleeve.

CINDERELLA (*Perplexed*): A ruffle to her sleeve? Why, I didn't know—

PRUNELLA (*Haughtily*): Of *course* you didn't know. How would you know anything about fashion? (CINDERELLA *hastily adjusts ruffle, while* GRISELDA *ties ribbon into bow.*)

CINDERELLA: My, how beautiful you look! (*Sisters parade back and forth smoothing folds, admiring selves, etc.*)

PRUNELLA: I think we might as well be off, Griselda.

GRISELDA: Yes, we must not be late. Who knows—the Prince may choose one of us to be his dancing partner for the evening. (*Claps hands*) Cinderella! Get our capes. (CINDERELLA *takes capes from chair and places them on sisters' shoulders.*)

PRUNELLA (*Excitedly*): Imagine! Everyone will be there! (*She and* GRISELDA *flounce off.*)

CINDERELLA: Oh, dear—oh, dear. (*Begins to weep*) Why am I so plain? (*Walks to stool, sits, and sobs*) If only I could go to the ball! (FAIRY GODMOTHER *enters quietly.*)

FAIRY GODMOTHER (*With cracking voice*): Why, you poor child!

CINDERELLA (*Looks up, startled*): You frightened me. (*Confused*) Do I know you?

GODMOTHER (*Kindly*): I've seen you many times, but we have never met. I am your Fairy Godmother.

CINDERELLA (*Unsure*): Fairy Godmother?

GODMOTHER: I am here tonight because you need me.

CINDERELLA (*Delighted*): How wonderful! You mean you will stay here with me so I won't be so lonely?

GODMOTHER: You sweet child, I will do more than that for you. (*Pause*) I will see that you get to the ball.

CINDERELLA (*Excited*): But how did you know that I longed—

GODMOTHER: Fairies know everything. Now you must hurry. We have no time to lose.

CINDERELLA (*Eagerly*): Just tell me what you want me to do.

GODMOTHER: Do you have a pumpkin?

CINDERELLA: Why, yes, there's one right in the cupboard. (*Goes to cupboard; hesitating*) But my sisters told me to make a pumpkin pie for their dinner tomorrow.

GODMOTHER: Bring the pumpkin. I shall return it. (CINDERELLA *gives pumpkin to* GODMOTHER.) Thank you. Now, I need four white mice. (CINDERELLA *walks to side of fireplace and picks up cage with mice in it.*) I shall change the pumpkin into a splendid carriage to take you to the ball; the mice into handsome horsemen. No one shall arrive at the ball in greater splendor!

CINDERELLA: Oh, how kind you are, dear Fairy Godmother. (*Suddenly upset*) But—I cannot go to the ball after all.

GODMOTHER: And why not, pray tell me?

CINDERELLA: I have nothing to wear. Nothing that could be worn in such a beautiful carriage.

GODMOTHER: You shall wear a lovely gown—all shimmering white and silver, and a silver tiara for your hair.

CINDERELLA: But how?

GODMOTHER: With my magic spell you will have the loveliest gown on earth. *But you must promise me one thing.*

CINDERELLA (*Excitedly*): Anything, Fairy Godmother—*anything*.

GODMOTHER: You must leave the ball before the stroke of twelve—or you will become Cinderella again, right there, and your coach will become a pumpkin, and your horses nothing more than these mice.

CINDERELLA (*Seriously*): Before the stroke of twelve. I'll remember, I'll surely remember!

GODMOTHER: Very well, then. Now hold this pumpkin so that I may have one hand free. (CINDERELLA *takes pumpkin.*) My spell I cast over you—(*Curtain falls slowly.*)
Kala wala woo,
My spell over you
One is for the carriage
With horses so fine—

* * * * *

SCENE 2

SETTING: *Ballroom of the palace. At center stage is a splendid royal throne.*

AT RISE: *Music is heard and dance is just ending. When music stops,* GUESTS *move about in groups.* PRUNELLA *and* GRISELDA *stand downstage center gazing at other guests.*

PRUNELLA (*In stage whisper*): No one is in finer fashion than we are!

GRISELDA: I am *sure* that one of us will be chosen as the Prince's dancing partner!

1ST GUEST (*Heard above the others*): Where can his Royal Highness be? I do hope he doesn't disappoint us.

2ND GUEST: Have no fear. The Prince is always thoughtful. (*Trumpet sound is heard off.*)

PRUNELLA (*Eagerly*): The Prince must be on his way here now! (TRUMPETERS *enter, cross to center stage and take places on either side of throne.* TWO ATTENDANTS *enter before* PRINCE, *two others follow.* PRINCE *ascends throne, and* AT-TENDANTS *take places on either side.*)

GRISELDA: Isn't he *handsome!* (*As* PRINCE *reaches throne, he turns and faces court in a regal manner.* GUESTS *curtsy and bow as* PRINCE *is seated.*)

PRINCE (*With dignified wave of hand*): Let the dancing continue. As is the custom of the realm, I shall select a dancing partner from among the fairest of this fair land. (*Music starts, and dancing begins. Only a few bars are played, when* PRINCE *arises quickly.*) Stop! Stop, I say. (*Music ceases.*) Page! (*Points offstage*) Who is that lovely maiden I behold standing in the outer court?

1ST ATTENDANT (*Looking off*): I do not know her, Your Highness.

PRINCE: I want to meet her! Go and ask her to come in. (*Urgently*) Be quick, be quick, I say, else she may slip away! (AT-TENDANT *rushes off.* PRINCE *sits, impatiently drums fingers on arm of throne.* BALL GUESTS *murmur excitedly.* ATTENDANT *returns.*)

ATTENDANT (*Bowing*): The beautiful lady begs Your Highness

to continue with the ball. She desires no more than to stand
on the threshold and watch.

PRINCE: A humble maiden, I would say! I did not know that
such existed in my land—and as beautiful as she is modest!
(*Rises from throne*)

2ND ATTENDANT: Do you wish me to fetch her, Your Majesty?

PRINCE: Thank you, but I shall escort her to the ballroom myself. (PRINCE *exits.* GUESTS *murmur among themselves
curiously, then gasp as* PRINCE *and* CINDERELLA, *in ball
gown, enter.*)

GUESTS (*Ad lib*): What a gorgeous gown! She's the loveliest
lady here! What a striking couple they make! (*Etc.*)

PRUNELLA (*Vexed*): Where do you suppose *she* came from? A
stranger to spoil our chances!

GRISELDA: Bad luck! She's probably from a neighboring
kingdom.

PRINCE (*Waves hands*): Please, be merry and return to your
dancing! (*Music starts and all begin dancing.* PRINCE *and*
CINDERELLA *dance together and mime conversing and
laughing. After a couple minutes a gong strikes twelve.* CIN-
DERELLA *looks suddenly upset and hastily runs off. Music
stops.* PRINCE *calls after her; confused*) Wait! Wait! (*To his*
ATTENDANTS) After her—do not let her get away! (AT-
TENDANTS *rush off.*) Why, I do not even know that lovely
creature's name. (ATTENDANTS *return quickly.*)

2ND ATTENDANT: She is nowhere in sight, Your Majesty.

3RD ATTENDANT: She is as swift as a deer.

4TH ATTENDANT (*Holding out glass slipper*): Your Highness,
as she fled she lost this glass slipper.

PRINCE (*Taking slipper*): A glass slipper! What a dainty foot
she must have! Tomorrow I will search the entire realm for
the maiden who can wear this slipper. To her I shall offer
my heart, hand, and kingdom! (GUESTS *and* ATTENDANTS
murmur excitedly as curtain closes.)

* * * * *

SCENE 3

SETTING: *Same as Scene 1.*

AT RISE: CINDERELLA *is busily sweeping in front of the fire-*

place. PRUNELLA *is hobbling about in shoes that are too small;* GRISELDA *is seated in chair with feet wrapped in cloth.*

PRUNELLA: Oh, I can't bear it! (*Kicks shoes off and sits down in chair, stretching feet and wiggling toes*)

GRISELDA (*Crossly*): Anyone would know that you cannot make your feet small by forcing them into shoes two sizes too small!

PRUNELLA (*Snapping*): Oh, and what makes you think that wrapping your feet in hot towels will shrink them?

GRISELDA (*Removing cloth from feet and sighing*): I suppose we have both been rather foolish. I don't think anything will do much good now.

CINDERELLA (*Stops sweeping*): Dear sisters, why should you wish to make your feet smaller? Have they not served you well all these years?

GRISELDA (*Throwing up her arms impatiently*): Don't you ever know what's going on in this world?

PRUNELLA (*Wearily, with a wave of her hand*): Tell her, tell her what happened.

GRISELDA: Well, last night at the ball—(*Stops suddenly and looks perplexed*) That's strange! Cinderella, now that I think of it, you have asked no questions about the ball. Aren't you curious? (CINDERELLA *begins to sweep again.*)

CINDERELLA (*Guardedly*): I—I—was waiting for you to mention it.

PRUNELLA: If that isn't just like a stupid goose! (*Rises, still in stocking feet, and goes to doorway as if in search of someone*)

GRISELDA: Anyway, the Prince, after keeping everyone in suspense for hours, chose a beautiful lady as his partner.

PRUNELLA (*Glancing back from doorway and interrupting*): From a neighboring kingdom—

CINDERELLA: What makes you say she was from a neighboring kingdom?

GRISELDA: I will *not* finish my story if you two are going to persist in your interruptions.

CINDERELLA: Oh, please—please go on—

GRISELDA: Well, his dancing partner left the ball unexpectedly, and as she was running—heaven knows why!—she lost one of her glass slippers. It was a very small one—

CINDERELLA (*Murmuring to herself; excitedly*): Then the *Prince* must have found the slipper!

PRUNELLA (*Hurriedly returning from window*): He's here! His Royal Highness just turned into our road.

CINDERELLA (*Flustered*): You mean the Prince is coming *here* to our humble dwelling?

GRISELDA: He is visiting every house in the land to find the owner of the glass slipper.

PRUNELLA: And to offer her his hand in marriage!

CINDERELLA (*Bewildered*): Oh-h-h! (*A loud knock is heard.*)

PRUNELLA: Well, don't just stand there acting like the simpleton you are, Cinderella. Answer the door!

GRISELDA: Yes, and then leave the room. The Prince wouldn't want anything of you.

PRUNELLA: No, allow her to stay—the contrast will be all in our favor! (CINDERELLA *opens door, and* PRINCE *and* ATTENDANTS *enter.*)

1ST ATTENDANT: His Majesty begs that you forgive his intrusion, but he is most desirous of finding the owner of this glass slipper. (2ND ATTENDANT *holds slipper in front of him.*)

PRUNELLA: It is a great pleasure to receive His Royal Highness. (*Both sisters curtsy before* PRINCE. CINDERELLA *goes to corner by the fireplace.*)

2ND ATTENDANT (*To* GRISELDA): May I fit your foot?

GRISELDA: By all means! (*Giggles as she tries to force foot into slipper*) I'm sure it will go on!

PRINCE: You are mistaken. It will not fit. (PRUNELLA *brushes past* GRISELDA *and holds out her foot.* 2ND ATTENDANT *grimaces as he tries slipper on her. He shakes his head to let* PRINCE *know slipper doesn't fit.* PRINCE *sighs, wearily.*) I have searched everywhere, but in vain. (*Looks about and sees* CINDERELLA) Who is this young lady who sits by the fire?

CINDERELLA (*Rises and curtsies to* PRINCE): Please, Your Royal Highness, I am only Cinderella.

PRINCE (*Smiles*): You are humble and gentle, as is the lady I am searching for. Would you try on the slipper?

CINDERELLA: If it pleases Your Royal Highness. (2ND AT-
TENDANT *steps forward, but* PRINCE *takes slipper from
him.*)

PRINCE: It will be my pleasure this time. (PRUNELLA *nudges*
GRISELDA. *When* CINDERELLA *easily slips foot into slipper,
sisters look at each other, amazed.* PRINCE *beams.*)

PRINCE: At last, I have come to the end of my quest! I knew
from your eyes you were the one.

GODMOTHER (*From offstage*): Cinderella! Cinderella!

CINDERELLA (*Distressed*): Forgive me, Prince, but someone to
whom I owe a great deal is calling me. (*Runs off*)

PRUNELLA: Can you imagine! Such rudeness!

GRISELDA: What can you expect?

PRINCE: I am certain Cinderella had a very good reason for
her actions. Let us not judge her before she returns. (*To* AT-
TENDANTS) Today is the day I shall take a bride home with
me—one who will be the sweetest princess ever known.

PRUNELLA (*Flabbergasted*): But surely Your Highness is
joking!

PRINCE (*Irritated*): And why should I be joking?

PRUNELLA: You cannot mean Cinderella!

PRINCE (*Striding across stage*): Most certainly I do mean Cinderella—and who are you to question my judgment?

GRISELDA (*Alarmed*): Please forgive my sister for her
thoughts. You cannot really blame her, though. After all,
Cinderella is nothing but a little drudge. Why, you have but
to look at her clothes—

PRINCE (*Angrily*): Enough! Enough, I say. What care I for her
appearance? She is kind and thoughtful. (PRINCE *stops
speaking abruptly, as if suddenly realizing something, and
then seizes* 3RD ATTENDANT *by the arm.*) You think Cinderella will accept *me*? It is true I have everything to offer her,
but maybe she will prefer the simple life.

PRUNELLA (*Snorting*): If she does she would be a bigger fool
than I thought—

PRINCE (*Sharply*): Hush! I will have no more of such talk!

GRISELDA (*Quickly*): She didn't mean anything against dear

Cinderella. (*Elbows* PRUNELLA) We love her, do we not, Prunella?

PRUNELLA: Most certainly we do!

GRISELDA: We just—well, Your Highness, we thought you were searching for the lady who wore that slipper to the ball. And since Cinderella was not at the ball last night—

PRINCE: You are sure she was not at the ball?

PRUNELLA: Most gracious Prince, Cinderella refused to go to the ball with us. She said she was *ashamed* of us—her very own sisters.

GRISELDA: Indeed she did!

PRINCE (*Disturbed, walks up and down stage for a few minutes*): That's strange—most incredibly strange! The slipper fits her as if it were made for her. (*Shakes his head*) I cannot believe that Cinderella is anything but the sweet, lovely maiden I picture her.

PRUNELLA: That is only because you do not know her as we do.

GRISELDA: Why, if you only knew—

4TH ATTENDANT (*Looking off, gasps as he sees* CINDERELLA, *who enters, wearing same gown she wore to ball*): Your Highness, look!

PRINCE (*Turns, sees* CINDERELLA; *joyfully*): How right I was! (*He drops to one knee at her feet.*) Cinderella, will you return to my castle to take your place at my side on the royal throne? Everything I have is yours, and I offer you my heart forever.

CINDERELLA (*Clasping hands*): Oh, my Prince Charming! Gladly will I go with you. Even my loveliest dreams were never as beautiful as this. (PRINCE *rises and takes* CINDERELLA's *hand. Sisters look at each other.*)

PRUNELLA (*Eagerly*): It won't take us a minute to get ready!

PRINCE: Ready for what?

GRISELDA: Why, to go with dear Cinderella, of course!

PRINCE: Oh, no, you're not going anywhere. I know that Cinderella is so kind and forgiving that she will want you to visit at the palace occasionally. That you may do.

CINDERELLA (*To* PRINCE): You are so kind!

PRINCE (*To* ATTENDANTS): Lead the way. I cannot wait to

spread the good news over the land! My Cinderella! (PRINCE *and* CINDERELLA *start to exit as curtain falls.*)
THE END

Production Notes

CINDERELLA

Characters: 4 female; 1 male; at least 12 male or female for ball guests, trumpeters, and attendants.

Playing Time: 20 minutes.

Costumes: Ragged dress for Cinderella; fussy ball gowns for Prunella and Griselda; sparkling, fanciful attire for Fairy Godmother. Cinderella changes into sliver and white ball gown with silver tiara. Prince wears regal outfit and crown. Appropriate courtly costumes for guests, trumpeters, and attendants.

Properties: Broom; ribbon; lace and ruffles with Velcro on them so they can be attached to stepsisters' dresses; 2 capes; pumpkin; glass slipper; small shoes for Prunella; cloth for Griselda to wrap around feet in Scene 3.

Setting: Scenes 1 and 3: Kitchen in Cinderella's house. Fireplace with stool in front of it is in center upstage wall. Small cage is next to fireplace. Table and two chairs stand center. Scene 2: Palace ballroom. At center stage is royal throne.

Lighting: No special effects.

Sound: Clock striking 12.